Praise for *The Business of Healthcare*

"The editors and writers of *The Business of Healthcare* have created a compelling and highly informative set of books that merge various disciplines and perspectives to create a comprehensive look at the challenges facing the healthcare industry. These books should prompt valuable discussion and, hopefully, action that will strengthen and advance the U.S. health system."

Craig E. Holm, FACHE, CHE
Health Strategies & Solutions Inc. Philadelphia

"Thoughtful and provocative, *The Business of Healthcare* is a clearly articulated exploration of critical issues facing healthcare leaders today."

C. Duane Dauner
President, California Hospital Association

"Just when the pressures and challenges on healthcare practitioners and organizations seem unbearable, Cohn and Hough have skillfully assembled this work which offers advice and comfort, not only on how to cope with today's climate, but how also to take advantage of the opportunities that abound while not abandoning the call to serve humanity."

Robert A. Reid, M.D.
Director of Medical Affairs, Cottage Health System,
Santa Barbara, California
Past President, California Medical Association

"Now, more than ever, this three-volume set is necessary and important. The format and breadth of content is impressive; rather than a prescriptive set of how-tos, I come away with an expanded vision of 'want to' and 'able to.'"

Leonard H. Friedman, Ph.D., MPH
Professor and Coordinator Department of Public Health,
Oregon State University

The Business
of Healthcare

Volume 1: Practice Management

EDITED BY
KENNETH H. COHN, MD
DOUGLAS E. HOUGH, PHD

PRAEGER PERSPECTIVES

Westport, Connecticut
London

Library of Congress Cataloging-in-Publication Data

The business of healthcare / edited by Kenneth H. Cohn, Douglas E. Hough.
    p. cm. — (Praeger perspectives)
    Includes bibliographical references and index.
    ISBN 978–0–275–99235–4 (set : alk. paper)
    ISBN 978–0–275–99236–1 (v. 1 : alk. paper)
    ISBN 978–0–275–99237–8 (v. 2 : alk. paper)
    ISBN 978–0–275–99238–5 (v. 3 : alk. paper)
    1. Medical care—United States. 2. Medical offices—
United States—Management. 3. Medical care—United States—Quality
control. 4. Health services administration—United States. 5. Health care re-
form—United States. I. Cohn, Kenneth H. II. Hough, Douglas E. III. Series.
    [DNLM: 1. Delivery of Health Care—organization & administration—
United States. 2. Leadership—United States. 3. Practice Management,
Medical—United States. 4. Quality of Health Care—United States.
W 84 AA1 B969 2007]
RA395.A3B875 2008
362.1068—dc22   2007031135

British Library Cataloguing in Publication Data is available.

Library of Congress Catalog Card Number: 2007031135
ISBN: 978–0–275–99235–4 (Set)
      978–0–275–99236–1 (Vol. 1)
      978–0–275–99237–8 (Vol. 2)
      978–0–275–99238–5 (Vol. 3)

First published in 2008

Praeger Publishers, 88 Post Road West, Westport, CT 06881
An imprint of Greenwood Publishing Group, Inc.
www.praeger.com

Printed in the United States of America

The paper used in this book complies with the
Permanent Paper Standard issued by the National
Information Standards Organization (Z39.48–1984).

10 9 8 7 6 5 4 3 2 1

Contents

Preface

The healthcare system in the United States is a mass of paradoxes. We lead the world in the creation and application of technology for the clinical practice of medicine; yet the United States lags behind the rest of the developed world in basic health indicators (e.g., infant mortality rate, life expectancy). We provide some of the highest quality care in some of the premier health institutions that are the envy of the world; yet 45 million Americans cannot take advantage of these benefits because they lack health insurance. We outspend every other country on healthcare; yet almost no one is satisfied with the results: patients may get unparalleled quality care, but they pay a lot for that care and access can be erratic; payers are frustrated that they (and their customers) are not receiving good value for their growing outlays; and providers are feeling harassed by payers and regulators and unappreciated by patients.

Some claim that healthcare is being ruined by the intrusion of business interests, which put the bottom line ahead of the appropriate care of patients and denigrate the professionalism of those sworn to care for the sick. They worry that these interests are making healthcare no different than any other "industry" in this country. Others argue that the problems of inconsistent quality, sporadic access, and high and rising costs can only be solved by imposing the discipline of the market. To these observers it is business thinking and processes that can transform the current system.

The editors of *The Business of Healthcare* believe that the issue is not professionalism *or* business in healthcare, but professionalism *and* business. We believe that the healthcare system in the United States needs the perspectives and expertise of physicians and economists, nurses and accountants, technicians and strategists. We have organized this three-volume set for Praeger Perspectives to demonstrate how these mutual viewpoints can yield innovative solutions to our healthcare conundrum.

In designing *The Business of Healthcare,* the editors recognized that the solutions to the challenges facing the U.S. healthcare system will not come from one source. Rather, the solutions must address both the micro and the macro aspects of the system. Individual medical practices, as the foundation of healthcare delivery, must be operated as efficiently as possible. Healthcare organizations of all types must be led in ways to maximize the effectiveness of both human and financial resources. Finally, attention must be paid to the systems currently in place that affect all aspects of the healthcare sector.

To that end, we have organized *The Business of Healthcare* into three volumes that address each of these levels of the healthcare system in the United States. Volume 1 *(Practice Management)* focuses on those areas critical to the successful operation of physician practices: the process of joining and leaving a practice; promoting a practice; and managing the human and financial resources of a practice. It addresses the current structure of physician practices (including the continuing viability of solo practice) as well as the very future of the physician practice itself.

Volume 2 *(Leading Healthcare Organizations)* shifts the focus to the complex tasks of leading in healthcare. The chapters in this volume illustrate that leadership involves the integration of relationship management (such as the appropriate involvement of physicians in healthcare organizations), new modes of care (including such disparate areas as biotechnology, complementary and alternative medicine, and pastoral care), and operations (informatics, clinical supplies, liability risk management).

Volume 3 *(Improving Systems of Care)* widens the lens to consider how systems in healthcare can be transformed to resolve the paradoxes that we noted above. The chapters in this volume address systems to improve clinical quality and safety, development systems (e.g., for moving scientific ideas from the lab to the market, for developing medical technologies), operational systems (e.g., disaster response, information technology, and end-of-life care), and financial systems (such as the new "Massachusetts Plan" to cover all members of society). The volume also includes the voice of the patient in improving systems of care.

We are grateful to all of our chapter authors who volunteered scarce time to write about aspects of healthcare about which they are passionate. Our goal has been to provide works by experts that will engage stakeholders in discussions of issues important to our nation's health and economy. We hope that we have succeeded.

VOLUME 1: PRACTICE MANAGEMENT

It used to be that physicians could graduate from medical school, complete a residency, and be confident that they could start a practice that was financially and professionally successful almost from the first day. Those halcyon days are long gone, with the advent of constrained reimbursements, increased regulation, and real competition for patients. Today, physicians must run their practice as if it was a business—because it is. Although many physicians may be accidental business people, they must pay attention to the most critical operational aspects of their practice if they are to achieve their professional goals.

To that end, we asked our authors to bring forward the issues that they see from their experience as those most critical to the operational success of the medical practice. They responded with eight focused and insightful chapters on how to:

- Manage the continuing opportunities and challenges of solo practice
- Join and leave a practice
- Measure performance in a medical practice
- Build a culture of accountability in a practice
- Manage difficult physicians
- Promote a practice
- Create a practice marketing plan
- Manage the revenue cycle

In addition, two authors took a broader look at the environment of medicine, one exploring the potential and realities of the new pay-for-performance and the other considering the future of the medical practice.

In all, these chapters should provide physicians and practice administrators with the most up-to-date practical thinking on the effective management of physician practices.

VOLUME 2: LEADING HEALTHCARE ORGANIZATIONS

Leadership is the art of instilling in people the desire to strive together to create a better future. Leaders listen, observe, provide direction and meaning, generate and sustain trust, convey hope, and obtain results through their influence on other employees. The challenge is to energize people to push themselves beyond what they thought they could do (Cohn, Cannon, and Boswell 2006).

Nowhere are these principles more evident than in the chapters in Volume 2, where nationally known authors discuss the need for and evidence of leadership in healthcare. Diane Dixon begins this volume with an analysis of six healthcare leaders who embraced a positive, can-do mindset that enabled them to transform their institutions. Drs. Waldman and Cohn describe ways to transcend the adversarial relations that traditionally accompany physician-hospital relations and the dividends to patient care of engaging physicians in clinical priority setting, which Jayne Oliva and Mary Totten build on by describing the dual opportunity and responsibility of physicians serving on hospital boards.

The final six chapters highlight the need for and benefits of leadership in specific sectors of healthcare, including biotechnology, informatics, complementary and alternative medicine, supply costs, risk management, and pastoral care.

In healthcare, as in other fields that serve the public welfare, dedicated professionals prefer being inspired to being supervised. Through their influence on business strategy and especially on organizational culture, effective leaders:

- Create a safe environment for reflection and learning
- Improve the practice environment and hence practice outcomes
- Help people reconnect with the values that attracted them to healthcare in the first place

The purpose of this series and of Volume 2 in particular is to create a nurturing environment that stimulates further reflection, discussion, and action, resulting in improved healthcare for our communities. Only then can we consider our efforts successful.

VOLUME 3: IMPROVING SYSTEMS OF CARE

The imperative for improvement is clear for everyone who works in healthcare. Through breakthrough studies championed by the Institute of Medicine, we have learned that inadequate systems of care jeopardize the health and recovery of hundreds of thousands of patients annually, adding billions of dollars of expense to an unsustainable healthcare budget.

For people inside and outside the nonsystem of fragmented U.S. healthcare, the complexity can be overwhelming. A framework that treats a patient or healthcare processes as a number of mechanical parts, without paying attention to interactions of human beings with other human beings, is likely to fail.

We are fortunate in Volume 3 to have chapters written by experts who have created a platform for learning and discussion that can inform the healthcare debate, point out the choices we need to make, and help us maintain optimism about our future. Carl Taylor provides practical and organizational insights that can guide us in meeting the needs of patients, families, and healthcare workers during the next man-made or natural disaster. Michael Doonan and Stuart Altman use the recently enacted Massachusetts health plan to discuss a way forward for dealing with the needs of the uninsured and underinsured. Philip Buttell, Robert Hendler, and Jennifer Daley define quality and safety in operational metrics that permit tracking, improvement, and cultural change. Jack Barker and Greg Madonna analyze the similarities and differences between aviation and healthcare and offer promise that simple practical steps like briefing, debriefing, coaching, and team training can enhance skill sets in communication and improve safety outcomes, as they did in aviation nearly three decades ago.

Hospitals' success increasingly relies on sharing information to prevent adverse outcomes in medication administration and proactive disease management, as seen in the next three chapters on informational technology solutions, medical technology, and improving outcomes and reimbursement. In the final four chapters, Donald McDaniel, Anirban Basu, David Kovel, and Ian Batstone argue that despite the expense of our poorly coordinated (non)system of care, healthcare creates high-wage, high-tech, and high-touch jobs that form the backbone of the American economy. Rudy Wilson Galdonik, who has been a caretaker and a patient, offers practical suggestions for improvement of systems of care from a humanistic perspective. Lynn Johnson Langer notes the rapid uptake that accrues when scientists translate the results of their research to the business community to serve the interests and needs of society. Finally, Kenneth Fisher and Lindsay Rockwell point out the tremendous cost of care in the last year of life and the billions of dollars that could be freed to support systems improvement if we instituted practical changes in the way that we provided terminal care.

Although change may feel like failure when we are in the middle of it, we have reached a critical time when we can move from individual "blame-storming" to ways to ameliorate systems of care. This volume and indeed the entire three-volume series will only be successful if the insights contributed by our authors inspire us to create an environment conducive to questioning our past assumptions and learning new ways to study and improve patient care.

Kenneth H. Cohn, MD, MBA
Douglas E. Hough, PhD

REFERENCE

Cohn, Kenneth H., S. Cannon, and C. Boswell. 2006. "Let's Do Something: A Cutting-Edge Collaboration Strategy." In *Collaborate for Success! Breakthrough Strategies for Engaging Physicians, Nurses, and Hospital Executives*, ed. Kenneth H. Cohn, 76–77. Chicago: Health Administration Press.

CHAPTER 1

The Solo Practitioner: Opportunities and Challenges

William L. Doss

GROUP DYNAMICS: THE SEED FOR THE SOLO PRACTITIONER

What might lead you as a physician to strike out on your own? Is it ego? Is it rebellion against authority? Is it the challenge of sailing into unchartered territory? Is it the need to achieve financial freedom? For the emerging solo practitioner, it may be all of these factors as well as a few others.

The group model has its attractions. As you emerge from residency, you may feel a need for comfort and security, both professionally as well as financially. Why this need? Perhaps the simplest answer is that as a premedical student, medical student, intern, and resident, you have competed within, sweated through, and survived the gauntlet of a medical education, and quite honestly, you are fatigued. You need a break. You need the nurturing of a practice that has already fought the battles and that can give you a refuge to lick the wounds that all physicians encounter in this journey. You also need the cash. You have denied your financial needs for at least 12 years, and the need to make a salary as well as to pay off your student loans makes the prospect of going into solo practice immediately out of residency foolhardy at best.

Ironically, it is the very qualities that propelled you through and allowed you to succeed in medical school that provide the impetus to pursue a career as a solo practitioner.

Let's first look at the group model. The process of joining a group starts during your last year in residency. You attend a specialty meeting (whether the meeting is the Digestive Disease Workshop for gastroenterologists or the American

Academy of Pediatrics for pediatricians) and come in contact with either physician headhunters or actual representatives of the practice. As in many other professions, there is an exchange of curriculum vitae, followed by a meeting with the headhunter or partners in the practice. Afterwards, there is dinner sponsored by the partner, and if all goes well, a flight out to the practice location for you to meet the other partners and practice personnel. This is followed by a tour of the hospital with which this practice is affiliated.

Throughout this process, you hear little mention of the negative aspects of the practice for which you are interviewing, or of the different personalities within the practice. To mention these negative, but honest, aspects might kill any desire for a graduating resident to join. Any practice, whether law or medicine, wants to represent itself favorably. While the positive attributes of the practice are being extolled to you, the significant aspect of the contract makes its appearance. Depending on the numbers written into the contract, and the favorability of the on-call schedule, you may sign the contract regardless of any uneasiness you may have experienced during the recruiting process.

It is the naïve journey by the young physician into the jungle of private practice that sows the seeds of the desire for solo practice.

While the prospect of group practice is seductive for obvious reasons, that is, a favorable on-call schedule, shared overhead, and inroads into referral sources, the individual personalities of each physician in the group still have to mesh. Communication is the key and all the members of the group must be in continual accord as to goals and procedures. Maintaining this accord is easier said than done. An example of a potentially disagreeable issue is the on-call schedule. Typically a favorable schedule would be at the very least 1 in 4, meaning that each physician would be on call for one out of every four weeks to handle phone calls, answering service, and hospital coverage. This is fine as long as everyone agrees to it. However, let's say the senior partner who may have started the group decides he does not want to retire, but he wants to have less call because he feels that he has paid his dues and wants to be on call 1 in 8. This one request can lead to total upheaval within the practice, because now the other three physicians will now be on call 1 in 3. Depending on the time of the month, one of them may be on call twice within the month. This is much different than the previous 1 in 4 call schedule.

As physicians, we all have been on call as residents, so this concept is not new, and you know that call is necessary for emergency patient care; however, this is one issue that can lead to discord because most physicians want to do less call, not more.

The issue of call is compounded when the physician is married and compounded further when there are children are involved. Rightfully, every physician feels that his or her family is of greater importance than all other issues that may arise in life, and that includes on-call dynamics within a practice. Any infringement by a practice on the time that a physician spends with family will eventually lead to bitterness on the part of that physician toward that practice.

We have examined how such a simple thing as an on-call schedule can cause disharmony with a group. Now, let's look at another aspect of a group practice, that is, its direction.

When you join a practice, you are only seeing a snapshot of what that practice is about. You have little idea of what direction the practice wants to go and little knowledge of the group's standing within the local medical community. This knowledge will only become apparent after you have joined the group. Unfortunately, this limited knowledge can become a huge problem, and again put fertilizer on the seed of desire to go into solo practice.

Let's say, for example, that you are an internal medicine specialist who has a strong interest in geriatric medicine. You enjoy the patient interaction, and you are fascinated with how an elderly person presents differently with infection by not mounting a febrile response. You may also be intrigued by how certain over-the-counter medications like Benadryl can have a significant effect on the cognitive status of an 80-year-old patient. These and other nuances of elderly patients pique your specialist's interest. Of course, most of the elderly have Medicare as their primary insurance with Blue Cross/Blue Shield or other private carrier as their secondary insurance.

Now let's add the wrinkle. The group you joined has decided that because of declining Medicare reimbursement, they will no longer accept Medicare patients. Although you may have dissented with this vote, you have been outvoted by other members of the practice, and this directly impacts your preference for geriatric patients.

You, the new physician, now have a dilemma with which you must come to terms: Accept the group's decision and thus change focus to younger internal medicine patients? Or strike out solo, and begin a practice where you can focus on seeing the geriatric population? Again, this is only one example of potential difficulties with group practice. However, it illustrates how a change in direction of the group can significantly negatively impact the physician within the group even when a particular decision may fiscally be the right move for the practice.

Now, the seed has been planted, and fertilizer has been added. The next aspect in growing the solo practice fruit is making the soil stronger by adding limestone. This comes as a direct result of you having been outvoted by other members of the group. You now have the feeling that the other members of the group do not appreciate your unique quality of serving the geriatric population. This feeling may be in direct opposition to the group's actual opinion of either you or of the elderly; nevertheless, the perception has been created by the group's decision to not accept Medicare patients and the collateral damage of this decision is that you now are questioning your role within the group.

To this wonderful budding fruit of solo practice, let's add water. You have performed well within the group despite the group's decision to not accept Medicare patients, and the issue of contract extension and partnership has come to the forefront.

Despite your great performance, the other members of the group are hesitant to increase your salary because of some other financial obligations; also because of your continued desire to see elderly patients, and your reluctance to see younger patients. But you have had good billings and collections, and you feel that a salary increase is in order regardless of the group's feelings. You feel that three years is sufficient payment of dues.

Again, the issue of money and who shares and who doesn't is always very delicate, and what is said or implied can go a long way to determine whether an individual stays within the group or leaves. In our example, you see the hesitancy of the group as a lack of confidence in you and you start considering options.

Now, let's see the fruit of solo practice ripen and be ready for harvest by adding sunlight.

You, the individual physician, are considering other options and one of these options is going solo. You talks with other colleagues who are solo reveal that although they work hard, they are generally content with their practice. They are able to see the type of patients they want to see. They do not have to worry about being outvoted; they do accept Medicare patients and enjoy working with them. This is the impetus that motivates you, the individual physician within the internal medicine practice, to strike out in solo practice. You like the adrenaline charge of charting your own course for success or failure.

The fruit of the solo practice has been harvested, not owing to major flaws with the group or you the individual, but to circumstances that have compounded and led the individual and the group to part ways. Although this is only one scenario, it demonstrates how little subtleties can lead an individual to the challenging opportunity of becoming a solo practitioner.

DESIGNING THE GARDEN OF SOLO PRACTICE

The fruit of the solo practice concept has been picked. Now comes the moment of truth: deciding what kind of practitioner you want to become. Do you want a mixture of outpatient and inpatient practice? Or do you want to be solely outpatient, and designate a hospitalist to care for your patients in the hospital? Obviously, there are advantages and disadvantages to each pathway of practice.

Let's look at a mixture of inpatient/outpatient practice. As practitioner, you will have your own set of well patients, and those who are less healthy will need to be admitted and followed in the hospital. This requires rounding on these patients, and also being on call for these patients if, for example, medication orders need to be clarified or an emergency arises.

The downside is that rounding on these patients takes time away from your outpatients, and being on call requires you to be available every night unless you share call with another practitioner. The upside to this mixture is that you maintain continuity of care with your patient; you do not lose the patient to another practitioner; and the reimbursement is higher for inpatients than for outpatients.

Conversely, the strict outpatient model allows you to see more patients in the office without the hassle of being on call, as the hospitalist will take care of on-call responsibilities as well as emergencies. This is especially appealing for those who do not enjoy doing inpatient medicine.

The negative side of this scenario is that you lose contact with your patient and thus are out of the loop with any change in her medical status. Also, once that patient is discharged, there is no guarantee that patient will be referred back to your office. Unfortunately, the hospitalist is now the gatekeeper, and depending on the mandates set forth by his or her employer, the hospital, he or she may have to refer the patient to another physician.

This is where you, the budding solo practitioner, need to make an honest self-evaluation of your practice preference in order to set up the practice accordingly. In the first example, your office staff will need to allow breaks in the office schedule for rounding. In the second model, you have to maintain constant communication with the hospitalist and the inpatient nursing staff regarding your patient's progress.

The next order of business is location. The physical setup of your practice is most important because patients need access to your office. Richard Tanner, a member of the American College of Osteopathic Family Physicians' Practice Committee, advises that proximity to the hospital provides a distinct advantage, because it provides the patient with a reference point for your office location (Tanner 2003). If you cannot be near a hospital, proximity to a pharmacy is good because your patients frequently access it not only for medicines, but also non-medical items. The helpfulness of proximity to a pharmacy cannot be overstated, as it allows you the practitioner to provide referrals to the pharmacist, and also allows you to articulate your prescription writing patterns to the pharmacist and create a harmonious relationship. The proximity to the pharmacist also allows you to enlist the pharmacist's assistance in patient education.

Also, parking access is very important. A patient will frequently use inadequate parking as an excuse for not seeing you, the particular physician. When this happens, you not only may have lost that patient to a competitor, but also to any type of care. The latter loss can be particularly devastating, because that patient may have presented to you initially healthy, but later may re-present in far worse health, and would have come to you if your troublesome parking had not led that patient to seek out another physician.

BUILDING THE FRAME OF THE GARDEN

Next, let's look at setting up the financial foundation of the practice. In male-female relationships, there is an old saying, "Romance, without finance, has no chance." The same is true in the field of solo practice. The romance is your solo practice and the relationship is the one you develop with the patients. Strong financial building blocks are required to make this relationship possible. Significant missteps here will prevent you from setting up a viable practice that you can enjoy both professionally and fiscally.

When setting up the financial structure of the practice, look at the church model as a good way to set up the practice. When new churches begin, they do not have large arenas or assembly halls. The pastor may have the first sermons in his house with two or three members. Expansion to bigger facilities only takes place when membership exceeds the capacity of the initial location. As a physician, you want to provide the best care; however, you equate best care with the best facilities. As a beginning solo practitioner, you are not in an adequate fiscal position to provide the finest facilities, but you still can provide excellent care.

Your first step in laying the foundation of the practice is to develop a relationship with a commercial or community-based bank. This relationship has usually been established when you were part of a group practice. Another option is to enlist an accountant. Most other practices or other solo practitioners have developed a long-term relationship with accountants in the area, and the accountants in turn usually know bank professionals with whom to begin a business partnership.

Next is to establish an organizational structure. At the very least, you have to obtain an employer identification number (EIN) (also called the tax identification number), which will allow you to bill for your services and receive payments. My personal preference is to form an S-corporation. As an S-corporation, owners must be U.S. citizens, and the ownership is based on one class of stock. Unlike a sole proprietorship, there is only limited liability to the assets of the practice (which exclude the physician's personal property). Also, the solo practitioner is treated as an employee, and is paid like one. The sole proprietor takes draws from the practice, and is subject to estimated taxes. Table 1.1 points out the major differences between a sole proprietorship and a solo practice set up as an S-corporation.

Either a bank or an attorney can set up the corporation for you. Financial institutions usually charge a fee of $150 to $300. An attorney will charge in excess of $500. Once the incorporation has been established, your accountant can set up the S-corporation.

Now, the corporation and the accountant have been established. What's next in building the financial foundation is obtaining a line of credit. This seems much harder than it is. Physicians are good financial risks because of their earning potential and the fact that they will be a fixture in the community. Thus, banks are eager to lend to physicians. However, one must provide a track record of earnings. Your accountant can prepare a personal financial statement, which will include your earnings through your previous practice. This statement will also disclose debts

Table 1.1
Sole Proprietorship vs. S Corporation

	Sole Proprietorship	*S Corporation*
Liability	Unlimited	Limited
Federal level of taxation	Single	Same
Number of owners	One	Up to 75
Necessary documentation	Minimal	Articles of incorporation must comply with subchapter S requirements
Permitted class of owners	Individual	One class of stock
Centralized management	N/A	Board of directors

including school loans and credit cards. (This is one reason why having little credit card debt is important.)

The next order of business is setting up the office space via a rental agreement or via the purchase office space with the intent of a mortgage. My preference is to purchase space if at all possible. One will usually come out with lower costs by doing this, as interest rates for mortgages and the corresponding monthly note are usually less than entering a lease agreement.

In my initial setup of my practice, my financial institution was willing to provide 100 percent financing for my office space. This insured that I would be in relationship with that institution for at least 10 years and possibly for the duration of the mortgage (15 to 30 years). Leasing does not cement that relationship, as most practitioners will not sign longer than a three-year agreement.

Office equipment will also need to be obtained. Furniture should be purchased outright. This will be a one-time purchase and will cut down on your monthly bills. For equipment that is in use every day, and is subject to wear and tear such as fax machines, copiers, and printers, a lease agreement is best. Why? Leasing equipment usually involves a corresponding service agreement, so these items can be repaired on an ongoing basis. Also, loaner equipment can be provided under a lease with a service agreement. However, if you purchase office equipment, there is no corresponding service agreement, and obtaining service for these items can be problematic.

CARETAKERS FOR THE GARDEN

Let us shift gears and talk about the execution of the solo model. You have all of the logistical items in place: incorporation, office space, and equipment. Now, it is time for hiring your personnel. The hiring of the right personnel is paramount for the smooth running of the practice. Mistakes here can be devastating, and more importantly, adversely affect your reputation in the community. Fairly or unfairly, a lot of your reputation as a physician is connected to how your staff treats patients or other practitioners.

Now, my personal preference for office personnel is to hire older employees. There are basically three reasons for this preference:

1. Older personnel have an established work ethic. They work either because they want to and enjoy it or because they have to in order to support their households. This makes them either less stressed because they enjoy working or more receptive to instruction because they cannot afford to lose a steady job. Either way works in your favor.
2. Older office staff are usually empty nesters and don't have the childcare-related problems that may create issues in the office.
3. Older office staff often have established health insurance coverage through their spouses.

Two particular qualities that are vital in your office staff are the ability to multitask, and attention to detail. A solo practice rarely has more than five employees. You do not have several different physicians to get used to; however, you, the one physician, will have plenty of work volume that needs to be divided among the employees. Also, every staff person should be well versed in the duties of everyone else. This is of particular importance if one staff person is on vacation or sick.

In a large group, there are many employees with one specific job. If one employee is absent this does not significantly impact the practitioners. However, in your solo practice, if a nurse is absent and there is no other person who can obtain vital signs, then you are giving suboptimal care to your patients. So everyone in the office needs to be able to answer phones, take vital signs, do daily deposits, and so forth, because of the enormous impact that one staff person's absence has on the day-to-day operation of the practice.

Whereas multitasking for the employees is important, attention to detail on the part of the employees cannot be overemphasized. Even though you, the solo practitioner, have your own practice, the medical record has to be accessible to other parties, such as other practitioners, attorneys, patients, case managers, and even auditors. A medical record that is not current with progress notes, lab reports, or patient correspondences will put you as solo practitioner at risk for tort claims, auditing, or worse—damage to your reputation.

I will illustrate how important this is with an example. If a patient, say Ms. Jones, was seen for an office visit in 2003, and was not seen again for four years, the physician is still responsible for that record. Now, let us add a wrinkle: a progress note from the initial encounter with Ms. Jones was not placed on the chart. Let us add another wrinkle and state that the transcription service only keeps old transcriptions for 90 days, and has purged its system and thus Ms. Jones's progress note. Now, suppose Medicare conducts an audit of the practice. Medicare wants this particular chart. Its progress note cannot be accounted for. You know you have dictated the note; your staff have seen the note; however, the note never made the chart and you have billed for the services. Medicare now decides that you have been billing for services that you have never provided. Next, Medicare not only requests Ms. Jones's chart, but also requests all the charts of the new patients you saw in 2003, which is over 150 new encounters. Therefore, what started out as a misfiling has now led to a Medicare audit, and may result in money being paid back to Medicare with penalties and interest.

This is not the kind of working knowledge of Medicare one wants to acquire. This lesson is best learned through other practitioners' experience and not your own. It is for this reason that you as solo practitioner should have checklists on what the chart should have; should do a monthly or quarterly internal audit of the charts to make sure that the medical record is complete; and should employ staff who can pay attention to the details that keep you out of trouble.

Your management style is also paramount to your relationships with your employees. In *The One Minute Manager,* Kenneth Blanchard and Spencer Johnson (1993) discuss the autocratic manager who is hard-nosed, bottom-lined, profit-minded; and conversely, the democratic manager who is participative, nice, and humanistic. They then write about the effective manager who says, "How can I get results if not through people? I care about people *and* results. They go hand in hand." This latter approach is probably the best management style for a physician's office. It falls in the realm of benevolent dictatorship. You are willing to listen to other opinions and suggestions, but your word is final. As a solo practitioner, you want to trust your staff to work independently, but also give them the direction that you want for the practice. Also, if your management style is more hands-off with few rules, you have to be willing to strongly enforce these rules or you will lose control of your staff.

Everything is now in place with your office: financing, location, equipment, and staff. Now you are ready to open your practice for patients. One of the things that you may want to consider when starting out is alternative office hours.

Remember you are starting your practice with zero patients and you are in competition with other colleagues with similar ability, age, and ambition. You have to market yourself in a way that differentiates you from your colleagues, and this differentiation is an attraction for patients to seek you out. One of the ways to do this is to provide alternative office hours.

Physician office hours are typically from 9 A.M. to 5 P.M. This corresponds to most people's work schedules and unless they request sick or vacation time for their physician visits, they will not be able to see you. Most patients do not want to take this time for physician visits. One way to avoid this potential conflict with patients is to extend your office hours. Instead of providing only 9 A.M. until 5 P.M. as your office hours, you can extend the end of your office day until 6 or 6:30 P.M. This extra 90 minutes will allow patients to see you after work, and avoid their having to take any vacation time to see you. This may not be feasible for your staff, as you have changed the workday from 8 hours to 9.5 hours. However, this change can be handled by opening the office at 10 A.M. instead of 9 A.M. or by staggering the hour when staff members arrive. One staff person can arrive at 9 A.M. and leave at 5 P.M., and the other can come in at 10 A.M. and leave at 6 P.M.

Another option is to provide Saturday office hours. For example, you can provide office hours from 9 A.M. until 12 noon. This will allow patients who cannot see you Monday through Friday to have access to you on Saturday. Furthermore, you can allow a staff person to have Friday off with the stipulation that he or she will come in on Saturday morning with you.

These alternative hours do not need to be long-term, but the hours allow you to attract patients, thereby building up your clientele quickly and establishing a firm patient base. Referring physicians will know that they can send their patients to you on off hours, which will endear you to them.

PRUNING AND WATERING THE GARDEN OF SUCCESS

The elements necessary for success are in place. Now, it is time to see patients, bill their insurance, and wait for payment. This sounds good, but a few common-sense strategies should guide you in this next area.

Understanding the next point is crucial in maintaining the well-oiled machine of private practice. Cash flow as defined by www.investorwords.com (2007) is "a measure of a company's financial health. Equals cash receipts minus cash payments over a given period of time."

This is key to the operation of the practice. This does not mean how much your practice is collecting or whether all of your expenses are paid in full. It simply means how much cash does one have in one's operating account at any given time.

Remember, as a solo practitioner, you do not have the luxury of having other members of the practice generating revenue. You are it. Anything that prevents you from generating revenue directly impacts cash flow. This is one area where vigilance is desirable.

Another factor that impacts a physician's cash flow is the lag time between when a physician bills the insurance company and when he receives payment. Unfortunately, this is the albatross of medicine. Medicine is the only profession where the practitioner does not directly contract with the consumer (patient). By contrast, in law, one directly pays a lawyer a retainer fee. In accounting, the accountant is billed for services rendered and the customer, not an insurance company, is expected to pay. Even a plumber or electrician expects and receives payment once services are rendered.

Patients pay a copayment at the time of service, but this is minuscule compared to the rest of the service we have billed to the insurance company, and you may wait anywhere from two weeks to two months for payment—assuming that there are no denials!

In order to manage cash flow properly, one must understand the golden rule of investment: "Pay yourself first!" Remember, your practice is you and if you do not take care of yourself first, then you cannot take care of anything else. What does this mean? The easiest example is to assume that you have $1,000 in the operating account. Your payroll is $500, and you have outstanding expenses for transcription of $500. You have the decision either to make payroll and keep your employees happy, or to pay your outstanding transcription cost in full and keep your creditors happy. Given this choice, it is probably wise to keep your employees happy and keep your creditors partially happy. That is, take care of your payroll completely, and afterward pay your creditors.

This may not seem fair to your creditors, but you have an obligation to your practice first, and everyone else is secondary. This does not mean that you don't pay anything on your transcription costs. You pay half of the costs, that is, $250, and not the full $500. Obviously, your creditors would be happy with full payment, but they will not refuse half of the amount.

It is this method that I recommend in bill paying. Pay half of the amount of the outstanding balance so that service can continue, that is, medical supplies, and pharmaceuticals.

This method does not apply to all creditors. There are some essential bills that must be met or the practice cannot operate, namely:

1. rent/mortgage
2. medical billing service

3. utilities
4. taxes (payroll and property)
5. licenses
6. insurances (malpractice, health, property)
7. payroll

These are the essential expenses that must be met in order to keep the practice running smoothly.

Let us look at the aforementioned model of paying half of the bills, thus maintaining positive cash flow, and how this can be useful.

In Table 1.2, by paying all of the expenses in full, the practitioner's cash flow is zero; and if any emergency expenses arise, such as a plumbing problem in the bathroom that costs $200, one has to wait until the next business day for more cash to come in before this problem can be addressed. In Table 1.3, this practitioner has chosen to pay half of the expenses, has maintained a positive cash flow of $500, and now can pay an emergency plumbing expense the same day. This seems very logical, but most people are fearful of debt, want to maintain a zero balance at all costs, and frequently run into cash flow problems.

Another effective method for maintaining cash flow is to take advantage of the float system of the banks and mail. Remember, when you personally deposit

Table 1.2
Neutral Cash Flow

Creditors	Expenses	Payment	Cash in Operating Account
			$1,000.00
Transcription	$150	$150	$850
Pharmaceuticals	$400	$400	$450
Copying paper	$100	$100	$350
Advertisement	$350	$350	$0

Table 1.3
Positive Cash Flow

Creditors	Expenses	Payment	Cash in Operating Account
			$1,000.00
Transcription	$150	$75	$925
Pharmaceuticals	$400	$200	$725
Copying paper	$100	$50	$675
Advertisement	$350	$175	**$500**

money into your checking account, it takes a couple of days for that cash to be available for use. When you have an expense that has to be paid immediately, this works against you, but in solo practice this works for you.

One has to know the business day of the bank in order to use the float system to one's advantage in maintaining positive cash flow. For example, listed below are some financial institutions and their banking days.

Financial Institution	Lobby Hours	Banking Day Begins	Banking Day Ends
Wachovia	0900–1600	0900 hours	1400 hours
SunTrust	0900–1700	0900 hours	1700 hours
Virginia Company Bank	0900–1700	0900 hours	1400 hours

What does this mean? Even though the lobby hours for these institutions end at 4:00 and 5:00 P.M., the banking day for Wachovia and Virginia Company Bank ends at 2:00 P.M. and at SunTrust, it ends at 5:00 P.M. This means that any deposits into the account or checks written against the account that appear by 2:00 P.M. will be reflected on that day's statement. Any deposits or checks that appear after 2:00 P.M. will be reflected on the next day's statement.

Why is this nuance so important and how does this impact cash flow? Well, the significance of this banking feature is that it allows you to maintain your liquidity on any given business day. Take the payroll for example. Let's assume that your total payroll for September 15 is $1,500. In your operating account, your balance is only $1,000.00, and you have one check in the amount of $350.00 that has yet to post to your account. The morning mail run reveals that you have a

Table 1.4
Float (optimal)

Balance in Operating Account 9/15 @ 0900 hrs.	Deposits Before 1400 Hours	Outstanding Checks Posted by 1400 hrs.	Payroll Done After 1400 hrs.	Balance in Operating Account 9/15 @ 1700 hrs
$1,000.00	$750.00	$350.00	$1,500.00	**$1,400.00**

Table 1.5
Float (not optimal)

Balance in Operating Account 9/15 @ 0900 hrs.	Payroll Done Before 1400 Hours	Outstanding Checks Posted by 1400 hrs.	Deposits After 1400 hrs.	Balance in Operating Account 9/15 @ 1700 hrs
$1,000.00	$1,500.00	$350.00	$1,500.00	($850.00)

total of $750.00 to deposit. Now, by doing the math you will have a total of $1,750 in the account, but your expenses (payroll of $1,500.00 plus the outstanding check of $350.00 totaling $1,850.00) will put your operating account in the red by $100.

However, let us put the bank's float system to work. If our financial institution is Wachovia and we can post the $750.00 in checks *before* 1400 hours (2:00 P.M.) we have an operating balance of $1,750.00 for that day, say September 15. At the same time, we conduct our payroll for *after* 1400 hours. Even if all of the employees deposit their checks at the same time, because it is after 1400 hours, these checks will not count against our operating balance until the next business day, September 16. So in fact, we still have an operating balance of $1,750.00 for September 15, and if our outstanding check is posted, we still have a positive balance of $1,400.00 for September 15.

As long as the deposits for September 16 are $100.00 or greater, we maintain a positive cash flow position in our operating account. Had the opposite situation occurred and we did our payroll before 1400 hours and our deposits after 1400 hours, this would have put the operating account in the red by $500.00, and we would still have had the worry of the outstanding check posting by 1400 hours, which would have put us further in the red by another $350.00 for a total of $850.

This one nuance can make the difference between keeping your creditors and employees happy, and having the creditors knocking at your door and your employees walking out. This is one of the main reasons why employers do not give employees their checks before 1400 hours on payday.

Another practical tip for employee relations is to maximize your bill paying after payday, and to minimize it before payday. One sure way to lose employees is to bounce a payroll check or tell them that they will not receive a paycheck. Remember, a lot of the workforce does not have the luxury of significant cash reserves and lives check to check. So, a missed or bounced check can be particularly devastating. If you are having cash flow difficulties, it is better to tell your employees that their checks may be a day late than to give them their paycheck on time knowing that it will not clear.

Minimizing bill paying on the week of payday and implementing the "pay half" strategy on bill paying can reduce this stressor and assure your employees that you will have enough in the operating account to meet payroll. It is imperative that your office manager understands this detail, to save you unpleasant embarrassment.

ALTERNATIVE SOLO PRACTICE MODEL

There are many ways to prepare an omelet. Developing a solo practice is no different. There are numerous workable solo practice models. Ken Zonies in the September 2006 issue of the *Physician Executive* illustrates such a model, which contains inherent aspects of group practice. One of the features is the economic principle of *economies of scale*. Simply put, economies of scale as a principle states that the costs of a business operation decline as the size of the operation (or in this case, the number of physicians) increases. With multiple practitioners, the cost of the running each practice is cheaper because the costs are spread across each of the practitioners. Also, it becomes easier to do large-volume tasks, such as copying documents for all members of the group rather than doing copying for each individual separately.

In his model, Zonies and the other solo practitioners have collaborated to form a "management services organization" that operates all the nonclinical aspects of each practice. These services include staff hiring, purchasing of supplies, and leasing of office space. Each solo practitioner still maintains autonomy as each one has a separate EIN number, and separate billing.

Another helpful aspect of this setup is that the group of solo practitioners has developed a cost-sharing system that does not penalize each individual's practice style or productivity. They have determined that certain fixed expenses are divided equally among all the physicians. Also, they have determined that each member of the group is responsible his or her portion of the variable expenses based on the amount of usage.

This particular method of cost sharing does not punish the physician who does not have a lot of variable costs. It also gives comfort to the physician who does have a lot of variable costs because other members of the group will share some at least of his or her overall expenses. Table 1.6 illustrates the fixed expenses that are shared by all practitioners, and the variable expenses that are allocated according to the usage of each practitioner.

Table 1.6
Expense Chart

Fixed Expenses (Unrelated to Patient Encounters)	Variable Expenses (Related to Patient Encounters)
Accounting	Insurance, health, dental
Computer	Office supplies
Employment services	Payroll
Furnishings	Postage
Insurance, business	Records
Legal	Temp help
Maintenance-building	Waste removal
Equipment	Management fee
Manager-salary/benefits/payroll taxes	
Payroll administration	
Property insurance	
Rent	
Subscriptions	
Telephone	

NO MEDICARE: SHOULD I OR SHOULDN'T I?

Many physicians are considering opting out of Medicare because of the decrease in Medicare reimbursement. In the November 5, 2006, edition of the *Daily Press,* Cyndi Cho reported on several practices in the Hampton Roads, Virginia, area that have shut down because they could no longer afford to provide care. These practices consisted of 80 percent Medicare patients. This shutdown is not surprising because the costs of caring for Medicare patients have increased significantly over the last five years, whereas Medicare care physician payments have remained the same and were set to decrease by another 5 percent starting in January 2007. Furthermore, the *Daily Press* contacted 11 primary care physicians in the Hampton, Newport News, and Williamsburg, Virginia, areas, and 4 out of the 11 responded that they are no longer accepting any new Medicare patients.

This situation appears to be very bleak, but the first thing that you the solo practitioner need to consider is what kind of physician you are going to be. In my practice, I have three staff and about 750–1,000 patients. My practice is manageable. However, I cannot afford to turn down any insurance because in my patient mix no one insurance carrier predominates. In addition, by accepting some of the insurance that other providers will not, I have access to those patients that I normally would not have. I do have to be cognizant of the number of patients with low-paying insurance I accept.

Another factor that influences me to accept Medicare patients is the fact that I am a physiatrist. By definition, physiatrists see a lot of elderly patients, including those with long-standing osteoarthritis, cerebrovascular accidents (CVAs), and spinal cord injuries. If I declined to see those patients with Medicare, I would not be practicing my craft. I would therefore see only those patients with acute musculoskeletal problems and would mirror an urgent care physician practice. By serving my Medicare patients, I build a loyal patient base that is very grateful for the services that I provide, and they in turn have referred other patients to me, some of whom who are younger and well insured.

Another thing to consider is the socioeconomic environment in your geographic area. Hampton Roads, Virginia, has Norfolk and Virginia Beach as its hub cities. Norfolk is a military town with many Tricare/Champus patients, and Virginia Beach is a retirement community. In addition, there is also the naval shipyard. What this means is an area with a lot of military dependents, retirees, and blue-collar employees who will not pay for services if their insurance does not cover it. Refusing to see Medicare or insurance patients in this geographic area would be devastating for a practice.

On the other hand, there are some advantages to having a cash-only practice. The main advantage is that the middleman, the insurance company, is eliminated. Remember, medicine is the only profession where the provider (physician) does not directly contract with the consumer (patient). Eliminating the insurance component ensures that the direct contract with the patient is restored.

Another clear advantage is cash flow. There is no three- to four-week wait for Medicare or insurance checks to arrive, and there is no day that revenue will not be generated unless patients are not seen that day. The overhead is also lowered because the billing company that services your insurance claims is eliminated. Not having a billing company restores about 7 to 10 percent of your revenue to your practice as this is the typical fee that billing companies will charge.

In order to start a cash-only practice, you have to opt out of Medicare. This means that you have to agree not to reapply for Medicare provider status for at least two years. Also, a Medicare beneficiary is prohibited from submitting claims for reimbursement for services provided by the opting out provider.

Despite its advantages, I see three main drawbacks in a cash-only practice: damage to reputation of the physician; temptation of embezzlement by staff; and Medicare-related problems. In medicine, unlike other professions, reputation is everything. It can take years to build a good reputation, and only days to tear it down. The physician needs to know his patients to determine if they would patronize a cash-only practice. Some patients may actually react with offense, as though by not taking their Medicare or private insurance, you are rejecting them as patients. A succinct discussion needs to take place with the provider and patient before the provider embarks on a cash-only practice.

Like any other business where a lot of cash changes hands, such as fast-food restaurants and check-cashing stores, in a cash-only physician practice, the temptation for theft is always there. For the solo practitioner, this may not present as great a problem because one's staff is small and the soloist is hands-on; however, the temptation is still present. If you start a cash-only practice, you need to make sure that your staff have clear guidelines on how financial transactions are conducted in the office.

Lastly, Medicare is a peculiar entity in itself. Once you opt out of Medicare, you are out of the Medicare loop for two years. If the cash-only plan is unsuccessful, you cannot see Medicare patients for at least two years. Insurance companies may follow Medicare's lead and institute the same policy toward you.

Another potential problem with leaving Medicare is inquiry. Medicare may question why a physician has opted out of Medicare. Was it because the provider had something to hide? Was there fraud involved? These questions may lead to a formal audit under which the practitioner will be required to allow Medicare to have access to all charts for the last three years. If there are any irregularities, it may result in repayment of fees received from Medicare plus penalties and interest. This is a problem particularly burdensome for the soloist to have.

Below is a sample Medicare Opt-Out Notice that has to be sent by the practitioner to get out of the Medicare system.

Medicare Opt-Out Notice

Medicare carrier address:

_____

_____

_____

Attn: Provider Enrollment

I, _____ , declare under penalty of perjury that the following is true and correct to the best of my knowledge, information and belief:

1. I am a physician licensed to practice medicine in the state of_____. My address is at _____ _____ , my telephone number is_____ , and my uniform provider identification number is _____ _____. I promise that, for a period of two years beginning on the date that this affidavit is signed (the "Opt-Out Period"), I will be bound by the terms of both this affidavit and the private contracts that I enter into pursuant to this affidavit.

2. I have entered or intend to enter into a private contract with a patient who is a beneficiary of Medicare ("Medicare Beneficiary") pursuant to Section 4507 of the Balanced Budget Act of 1997 for the provision of medical services covered by Medicare Part B. Regardless of any payment arrangements I may make, this affidavit applies to all Medicare-covered items and services that I furnish to Medicare Beneficiaries during the Opt-Out Period, except for emergency or urgent care services furnished to Beneficiaries with whom I had not previously privately contracted. I will not ask a Medicare Beneficiary who has not entered into a private contract and who requires emergency or urgent care services to enter into a private contract with respect to receiving such services, and I will comply with 42 C.F.R. § 405.440 for such services.

3. I hereby confirm that I will not submit, nor permit any entity acting on my behalf to submit, a claim to Medicare for any Medicare Part B item or service provided to any Medicare Beneficiary during the Opt-Out Period, except for items or services provided in an emergency or urgent care situation for which I am required to submit a claim under Medicare on behalf of a Medicare Beneficiary, and I will provide Medicare-covered services to Medicare Beneficiaries only through private contracts that satisfy 42 C.F.R. § 405.415 for such services.

4. I hereby confirm that I will not receive any direct or indirect Medicare payment for Medicare Part B items or services that I furnish to Medicare Beneficiaries with whom I have privately contracted, whether as an individual, as an employee of an organization, as a partner in a partnership, under a reassignment of benefits, or as payment for a service furnished to a Medicare Beneficiary under a Medicare + Choice plan, during the Opt-Out Period, except for items or services provided in an emergency or urgent care situation. I acknowledge that, during the Opt-Out Period, my services are not covered under Medicare Part B and that no Medicare Part B payment may be made to any entity for my services, directly or on a capitated basis, except for items or services provided in an emergency or urgent care situation.

5. A copy of this affidavit is being filed with _____ _____ , the designated agent of the Secretary of the Department of Health and Human Services, no later than 10 days after the first contract to which this affidavit applies is entered into.

Executed on _____ [date] by

_____ [Physician name]

_____ [Physician signature]

From Shane J. Kraus, M.D. 2006. "Medicare Opt-Out Notice: A New Future with an Old Business Model." *Family Practice Management* 13 (2): 75. Used with permission.

MAINTAINING RELATIONSHIPS

You are a solo practitioner who has left the nest of group practice. You are on your own. You used to have the benefit of constant interaction with colleagues and as a result had an inside track to referrals. Obviously, as a soloist, this instant access changes. There are a couple of ways to maintain relationship with your referral sources. One way is to set aside some time to mingle in the physician's lounge. Most of the doctors on a hospital's medical staff pass through the physician's lounge for various reasons—to get a morning cup of coffee; to take time to relax and read a paper or catch up on news events; or to do research in the medical library (which is often located next to the physician's lounge). In this setting, you the soloist can approach your colleagues in a relaxed manner, and do subtle marketing for referrals without hard sell for patients.

Another approach is to attend the monthly staff meetings at the hospital that physicians are required to attend. In this setting, meals are generally served, which again allows you the soloist to approach your colleagues in a nonthreatening manner at an appropriate social gathering.

Lastly, many pharmaceutical companies sponsor dinners at local restaurants and encourage attendance by physicians in order to promote their products. The unique aspect of this medium is that the pharmaceutical representatives try to bring in new physicians to these dinners, or physicians that they do not see often, to convince them to begin using their product. This provides you, the soloist, with another opportunity to make a positive first impression with new physicians in the community, and establish potentially long-term relationships.

THE HARVEST

Once these aspects of personnel, cash flow, and bill-paying strategies have been initiated and done successfully, financial planning for your practice can begin. As mentioned earlier, the golden rule for investing is to pay yourself first. One of the ways to ensure self-payment is to protect yourself as well as your practice.

As a physician, you are at high risk for disability. You may contract blood-borne diseases such as HIV or Hepatitis B; skin contact diseases such as herpes zoster or staph aureus; and airborne diseases such as tuberculosis. If you are a surgeon, you depend on your hands for income and injury to your hands is a real threat. Any of these problems can derail a promising career and force a physician to pursue other career options. Doing so may seem fairly straightforward, as a lot of professionals make career changes. However, the transition for the physician is much more difficult because he has spent so many years in medical training, and also because medicine is so different from any other field. The training in medicine does not emphasize business, and salesmanship and marketing of medical services are still frowned upon by the community at large. In addition, other areas of employment will not likely be as enjoyable as medicine, and may not be as lucrative because medicine, unlike other professions, does not translate well into other fields.

This makes the acquisition of disability insurance paramount for the physician. There are two things to remember about disability: Obtain enough coverage to replace at least two-thirds of your practice gross income; and maintain good health at the time of acquisition of insurance, to ensure being underwritten for a policy. Unlike term or whole life insurance, the scrutiny for disability insurance is harsh. Even minor health issues will disqualify an individual from a policy to be underwritten. In particular, weight is highly scrutinized even if the individual has no other health-related issues such as diabetes and hypertension.

The other key point to remember about disability is to select a longer waiting period. Most policies are underwritten for a waiting period of 60 days; however, the longer the waiting period the higher the coverage can be obtained. Usually, a waiting period of 90 days allows for the best policy. The waiting period refers to the time you have to wait before you can start receiving payments. For example, if you were injured and unable to work on January 15, 2007, you would not be able to receive any disability payments until at least April 15, 2007 for a 90-day waiting period.

The next type of insurance to consider is mortgage insurance. A lot of practices do not obtain this, but it can be helpful. This type of insurance covers the mortgage of your practice (as well as your employees' salaries) if you are disabled or unable to practice for another reason, say because of military obligation, for a prolonged period of time. It keeps one's mortgage paid and one's staff intact while one recuperates.

The next area is to set up investing within the practice. There are essentially two options here: 401K plan and profit-sharing plan. There are other plans such as SEP and simple IRA plans, but the profit sharing and the 401K plans are the ones that most employees desire. The two basic differences between the two is that the 401K is deducted from employees' gross wages and deposited in an investment account, and allows the employee to invest a desired percentage of their wages into the account. A profit-sharing plan does not require the employee to deduct wages for investment, the employer controls the amount to be invested, and the employee's portion of the profits is determined by a vesting schedule. The amount is determined by the length of service the employee has with the employer. For example, an employee with one year of service with an employer would be 20 percent vested, meaning he would be entitled to 20 percent of his share of the profits that the practice has invested. An employee with 5 years of service would be entitled to 100 percent of his share of the practice profits. Table 1.7 illustrates the major differences between the two plans.

As reimbursement for physicians has decreased, practitioners have had to be more innovative in either increasing or maintaining their income. It has also compelled physicians to enlist skills—which previously were unnecessary—in marketing. As a solo practitioner, one of the ways to increase revenue for your practice is to take your show on the road. What do I mean by this? Those services that you provide in the office can be provided to other providers outside of the office.

For example, as a physiatrist, I usually perform about five electrodiagnostic studies in the office per week. In addition, I provide the same service to an orthopedic surgeon who orders about 15 to 20 per week. His staff does the billing and I take home a percentage of the collections per month. The range of collections is anywhere from $8,500 to $16,000 per month. Other services that can provide income outside the office are employment physicals, ultrasounds, or independent medical evaluations.

PROTECTING THE CROP

You have set up your solo practice, taken advantage of the opportunities, and met the fiscal challenges of the practice. Now you must take care of the home front. All of the hard work put into developing the practice is for naught if the psychological well-being of the provider is not maintained.

Table 1.7
Differences between 401(k) and Profit-sharing Plans

	401(k) Plan	*Profit Sharing*
Eligibility	Any employee with 1,000 hrs. of service in a year	Same
Maximum annual combined contribution the employer can deduct	25% of eligible payroll (maximum eligible pay per employee is $220,000)	Same
	Up to $15,000 year	No employee contributions allowed
Required employer contribution	One of the following • Basic match formula • Enhanced match formula	Flexible contribution allowed each year (no preset amount required) but employer must make "substantial and recurring" contributions
Vesting schedule	100% at the time of contribution	20% per year and 100% after 5 years of service
Advantages	Employee deferral of current income taxes available	Flexible contributions

One of the unique challenges of the solo practice is that, unlike large group practices with many providers, the solo provider has to be hands-on to be able to ensure that the practice is run properly. The provider can only delegate so much to an office manager, and this need to keep a finger on the pulse of the practice takes time, often at the expense of a marriage and family.

One strategy to combat this conflict is to schedule specific administrative time as part of the weekly schedule. This can be a half-day per week or a full day every two weeks. This schedule enables you the solo provider to catch up on important paperwork during regular hours, and thus allows you to get home to your family.

Another strategy to maintain good mental hygiene is leave work at work. Any discussion of medicine at home limits quality time that is spent with spouses or children. Even though we physicians may feel that our field is exciting every day, our spouses and family may not share that sentiment. It is important to adhere to the philosophy of leaving work at work as much as possible.

One creative way to reduce burnout is to perform locum tenens work. Locum tenens is an arrangement for you to provide coverage for physicians who are on leave from their practice for various reasons such as maternity leave, vacation, or illness. It reduces burnout for you because it gives you a mental break from the practice and at the same time allows you to give patient care without the administrative or political headaches that were present at your home practice. The salaries are good, in the range of $600 per day for physiatry and up to $1,200 per day for a gastroenterologist.

REFLECTION

The last most reasonable question one may ask is, "Why become a solo practitioner? It appears to be a lot of work. Where is the reward?" This is a legitimate question that needs to be addressed by anyone espousing the joys of solo practice.

I would first like to mention that most physicians who go through 12-plus years of training have had a long time to view how things operate. They see the things that work and do not work, but have little ability to influence the operations of a hospital, a school, or a clinic because they are in training.

After years of having limited authority in decision making, it is very hard for most of us to continue to hand the reins of this responsibility to others, especially when decisions made by others in a group practice setting will have a direct impact on how we practice and on our livelihood. The only way to insure that decisions made about your livelihood positively impact you is to be that provider making that decision.

You make any decision, good or bad, and you and your staff deal with the consequences. The full impact of such decisions cannot be understood unless you are the one making them. The reward for good decisions that you make is you a euphoria that few experiences can provide, and it is that so-called rush that makes solo practice so exhilarating.

Another dynamic to understand about the physician of 2007 is that medicine is no longer practiced in a vacuum, and in order to understand this change, one needs a historical perspective. In the 1960s and 1970s, physicians could practice medicine without major concern about diagnostic-related groups (DRGs), managed care, or rising malpractice costs. Reimbursement by insurance was nearly 100 percent. Marketing by word of mouth was the standard, and one could quite literally "hang up a shingle" and begin a practice. This modus operandi has long since been bypassed by the current medical climate. With Medicare and overall insurance reimbursement declining, the twenty-first-century physician is getting both a formal and an informal education in the tumultuous healthcare business; and those who choose to ignore rather than adapt will be swept away by the tide.

The fiscal pie of healthcare is smaller, and one has to make good business decisions to insure that his piece is secure, and also be creative enough to generate other revenue streams to secure the kind of livelihood that we seek as physicians.

Solo practice allows one to be on the forefront of the changes that occur in healthcare, and by being in front, allows the practitioner to forecast and prepare for the future. One of the methods to assist this is to conduct a **SWOT** analysis, that is, **S**trengths, **W**eaknesses, **O**pportunities, and **T**hreats. As a physician, and in my case a specialist, I need to ask myself, What do I have to offer? What are my skill sets? In my case, in addition to my general physiatric skills, I offer opioid pain management and electro diagnostic services.

With the emphasis by the Joint Commission on Accreditation of Healthcare Organizations (JCAHO) on pain as the fifth vital sign, I am in a good position to market myself. I also understand that many physicians, especially in primary care, do not understand how to prescribe opioids and do not want patients who may need them. Again, this puts me in advantageous position in obtaining patients. I understand how to prescribe opioids, which is a strength, and I am willing to accept patients who need this service. I also need to understand that in accepting these patients, I always have the threat of being under heavier scrutiny by the Drug Enforcement Agency (DEA) in prescribing these medicines. Moreover, accepting too many of these patients can be a weakness because it can potentially brand me as only a pain management physician, and decrease the perception of the diversity of services I offer.

I also perform electrodiagnostic services outside of the office. Other physiatrists as well as neurologists perform this same service. There is always a constant threat that any contract I hold in providing these services can be terminated and given to a competitor, so I always have to be on top of my game. Understanding these basic marketing principles can only assist the twenty-first-century physician in surviving today's healthcare market.

CONCLUSION

As a solo provider, I hope I have given the aspiring soloist insight on the incredible journey of solo practice. It does require a lot of cultivation and nurturing, but the fruit of this labor is sweet and rewarding. The only way to appreciate this fully is to follow your heart and embark on the journey. Good luck on your mission!

REFERENCES

Blanchard, K., and S. Johnson. 1993. *The One-Minute Manager*. New York: Berkley Publishing Group.

Investorwords.com. 2007. Definition of "cash flow." [On-line]. Available at: http://www.investorwords.com/768/cash_flow.html.

Kraus, S. 2006. "A New Future with An Old Business Model." *Family Practice Management* [On-line]. Available at: http://www.aafp.org/fpm/20060200/74anew.html.

Tanner, R. 2003. "Going It Alone: Solo Practice." In *Is a Group Practice or Solo Practice in Your Future?* American College of Osteopathic Family Physicians [On-line]. Available at: http://www.acofp.org/member_publications/0803_3.html.

Zonies, K. 2006. "Going Solo in a Group." *The Physician Executive* (September–October): 44–47.

FURTHER READING

Backer, L. 2006. "2500 Cash-Paying Patients and Growing." *Family Practice Management* [On-line]. Available at: http://www.aafp.org/fpm/20060200/642500.html.

"Characteristics of Different Business Entities." [On-line]. Available at: http://www.start-a-business.com/inc-category/cbe/subs.html.

Cohn, K. 2005. *Better Communication for Better Care: Mastering Physician-Administrator Collaboration*. Westport, CT: Greenwood Praeger.

"Comparing Retirement Plans." 2006. *American Funds* [Brochure]. 1–6. American Funds Service Company.

Corinaldi, R. *Financial Security Group*. [Brochure. On-line]. Available at: http://www.gofsg.com.

Ekelund, R. B., and R. D. Tollison. 1997. *Economics: Private Markets and Public Choice* (5th ed.). New York: Harper Collins.

"Higher Morale Ground: Groups Work to Build Physician Satisfaction." 2003. *Recruiting Physicians Today* 11 (3): 1–4.

Mitchell, E. R. 2006. *"Sensitive" Questions*. [On-line]. Available at: http://prodigy.net/lizmitchell/volksware/aa060401a.htm.

Oswald, S. 2001. "Business Course 7136: Strategic Management." Course taught at Auburn University College of Business, Physician Executive MBA Program.

Smith, S. 2006. "Illegal Job Interview Questions." *The Sideroad*. [On-line]. Available at: http://www.sideroad.com/Human_Resource/illegal-job-interview_questions.html.

Stone, T. 2006. "Cash-Only Practice: Could It Work for You?" *Family Practice Management* [On-line]. Available at: http://www.aafp.org/fpm/20060200/61cash.html.

U.S. Dept. of Health and Human Services. Centers for Medicare and Medicaid Services (CMS) [On-line]. Available at http://www.cms.hhs.gov/MedicareEnrpts/.

CHAPTER 2

The Logistics of Joining and Leaving a Physician Practice

Nicholas J. Giampetro

As our population ages and medical technology advances, the demand for physicians' services grows. Whether or not we are facing an impending physician shortage, the following facts remain: (a) baby boomer physicians are beginning to retire; (b) there are lengthy training requirements for new physicians; (c) reimbursement levels for physician services are under constant pressure; (d) medical malpractice risk and expenses are material concerns; (e) college graduates have opportunities at least as lucrative in other segments of our economy; and (f) there is a general disenchantment with our healthcare system. Permanency of the relationship between the associate physician and the medical practice is beneficial to all stakeholders in the healthcare process under the best of market conditions. It is even more imperative today.

This chapter deals with the various issues and methodologies regarding acquiring an ownership interest in a private medical practice ("buy-ins") that may be considered by associate physicians[1] and the private medical practices that they intend to join; and the issues considered and methodologies used for redeeming the interest of owners who voluntarily or involuntarily terminate their relationships with the practice[2] ("buy-outs"). The chapter will discuss, among other issues, preliminary matters such as due diligence by the medical practice and the associate, various buy-in and buy-out strategies, and valuation techniques.

Throughout the process—from becoming an associate to buying in and buying out—all parties should be adequately represented. Representation of each party should include an attorney and an accountant and/or an appraiser who have experience with physician transactional matters, including regulatory issues[3] and practice valuation techniques.

THE ASSOCIATE PHASE

Most physicians who seek employment in a private practice upon completion of their training and the practices that they join do so with an eye toward ownership and permanency. It goes without saying that the associate physician's initial employment with a practice provides an opportunity for the associate and the owners of the practice to evaluate whether the ownership opportunity should be offered and whether it should be accepted.

Consider the following provision in the new associate's employment agreement with an existing practice,[4] which contains a list of several criteria that both parties may consider during the courtship:

- The Employee's initial employment period represents a trial period. During this period, the Employee will be evaluating the medical practice and its personnel. The Employer will be evaluating the Employee's skills as well as the dynamics of the Employee's working relationship with the Employer.
- In addition to the Employee's clinical competence, the following specific items are essential to the Employee's overall success: (a) the Employee's acceptance by patients, staff physicians, and hospital personnel; (b) the commitment of the Employee's time; (c) the Employee's productivity and efficiency in handling patient matters; (d) the Employee's willingness and effectiveness in promoting the practice and the Employee; (e) the Employee's acceptance in the practice from an entrepreneurial standpoint; (f) a clearly demonstrated ability for the Employee and the Employer to work together with good rapport and understanding; and (g) the Employee's participation in medical staff activities at the Hospital
- Although nonbinding, it is the Employer's current intentions that, after approximately _____ years of employment, the Employee may be offered the opportunity to become an owner in the Employer on such terms and conditions as mutually agreed, provided the Employee enter into an Ownership Purchase Agreement and the Owners Agreement and Employment Agreement then in force and effect for owners of the Employer.

Although this is a good starting point, with each party acknowledging the desire for permanency, the parties should consider going further. Both the practice and the associate would be wise to consider fleshing out as many terms as possible regarding the buy-in while negotiating the associate's initial employment, and consider including them in a nonbinding letter of intent. The letter of intent would be subject to the definitive documents that are described in the above provisions that are signed at the time of the buy-in.

Aspects of the associate phase may affect the buy-in. For example, an associate may accept a lower compensation package in consideration of a shorter period of time before being offered an ownership interest. Alternatively, the owner may reduce the amount expected to be paid for the ownership interest depending upon the amount of compensation paid to the associate or the length of time the associate phase continues.

Further, there is no reason why the associate phase cannot be dynamic. For example, with physicians in short supply and demand increasing, owners may consider shortening the time to buy-in or offsetting expected buy-in amounts if associate collections substantially exceed the associate physician's incremental expenses; or the associate is an exceptional clinician, meets critical practice needs, or is difficult to replace.

The predicate for this type of effective decision-making is an understanding by both parties of what will be paid for the ownership interest (or how it will be computed), and the arrangement regarding income, equity, and management after the buy-in is complete.

In order for each party to make an informed decision, due diligence is required. From the practice's point of view, owners may make inquiry of colleagues regarding the associate's clinical skills, professionalism, and integrity from preceptors and others who have supervised the associate during training. Meetings and site visits with the prospective associate and the associate's spouse are important.

From the associate's point of view, due diligence at this stage is also important. In addition to getting comfortable with the clinical and cultural match, the associate may request financial information regarding the practice. Historically, medical practices have been reticent about sharing the level of information that is described below. In today's climate it is a matter of the market, and the extent to which the parties have other options will drive each party's decision regarding the level of information provided and accepted.

The associate should consider gathering information regarding the following:

- *Practice Entity:* The medical practice entity may take the form of a professional corporation, a partnership, or a limited liability entity. Corporations and limited liability entities provide protection against personal liability to owners from medical malpractice claims asserted against other practitioners in the practice, whereas general partnerships impose unlimited liability upon all owners. The type of entity will also affect the state and federal income tax consequences to the medical practice and its owners. For example, entities that elect to be taxed as partnerships and limited liability entities are not taxed on their income; the income and losses are passed through to their owners. On the other hand, corporations subject to tax under Subchapter C of the Internal Revenue Code (IRC) are taxable on their income. Corporations may elect to be taxed as pass-through entities under Subchapter S of the IRC, similar to partnerships and limited liability entities.[5] The use of S corporations may provide less flexibility regarding the design of compensation packages.
- Purchase Price: The price and purchase methodology, together with timing of the prospective purchase, should be disclosed. If the medical practice will be valued, the date of the valuation is important.[6]

- *Income:* Do the members of the medical practice share income equally, based upon production,[7] or utilize a hybrid approach? What do owners consider as components of compensation versus overhead; said another way, what expenses are directly charged against owners' compensation?[8] How is overhead shared? Are fixed expenses shared equally even though compensation is shared based upon production? Is income expected from ancillary services or other associates, and if so, how is that income divided?
- *Liabilities:* Having the medical practice's financial statements reviewed is a beginning (including the medical practice's payer mix). Associates should ask for explanations of loans from owners or working capital loans. Further, since most medical practices use unaudited financial statements that are not maintained in accordance with generally accepted accounting principles (GAAP), there may be off-balance sheet liabilities, which will require further inquiry. For example, depending upon the age of the owners there may be current or future unfunded buy-out liabilities, including obligations to purchase extended reporting endorsements (*tails*)[9] for professional liability coverage for owners who leave the practice. This type of information can be obtained tactfully by learning the ages of the owners, or inquiring about tail obligations if a similar provision is included in the associate's employment agreement.
- *Management:* Does the practice have an owner or representative management structure? Many progressive midsize medical practices have moved from all owners managing the practice to forms of representative management arrangements. These arrangements may include more frequent meetings of the management team and further diversification of specific management functions, and should include requirements regarding keeping other owners informed of decision making by the management team. Representative management is a good indicator of the level of trust that exists between the owners.
- *Outside Interests:* It is not uncommon for a medical practice entity to lease space from an entity that is owned in whole or part by the owners of the medical practice. Information requested about the owners' expectation regarding associate acquisition of an interest in such real estate is entirely reasonable at this stage.[10]

THE BUY-IN ARRANGEMENT

We assume that the owners and the associate physician have had a successful courtship, and the parties wish to proceed to a permanent relationship. Several of the issues that are discussed in this section may have been addressed prior to the commencement of the associate phase or may have been postponed until this point.

Purchase Price

The inquiry begins with how the medical practice is valued, and how the purchase price is determined. The type of practice and the nature of the practice's assets may drive the valuation method. For example, hospital-based practices such as anesthesia or pathology, and radiology practices that do not have office locations, have little or no tangible assets.[11] They also may have no ascertainable intangible assets[12] if their "going concern value" is predominantly based upon a short-term coverage arrangement with one hospital. Since the associate was paid less than the practice collected on account of the associate's services during the associate phase, the owners may feel adequately compensated for the transfer of an ownership interest.

Medical practices may be valued based upon the value of each asset, the assets valued as a whole by using a capitalization of earnings approach, selection of a fixed value, or a combination of approaches. Even if a fixed value approach is selected, it should either be based upon a valid valuation methodology or proven accurate by the use of recognized methodology. A rudimentary understanding of the types of assets that are owned by a medical practice, and how assets are treated taxwise together with accounting and financial principles, will be necessary.

Notwithstanding what approach is taken to valuation, federal and state laws and regulations applicable to medical practices must be considered. Generally, the purchase price should result from arm's-length negotiations between the associate and the owners, in a manner that does not take into account the volume or value of referrals or business that otherwise may be generated. The purchase price must be consistent with fair market value. The laws that have the received the most attention are the cadre of laws regarding remuneration for referrals and self-referral laws.[13]

Furniture, fixtures, and equipment are considered tangible assets. From an income tax point of view they are considered capital in nature, which means that they are acquired with after-tax dollars. The tax *basis* is the amount paid for the asset less the amount of depreciation deducted for tax purposes. These assets are customarily depreciated rapidly, or *written off*, in order to accelerate tax deductions. These assets can be valued based upon an appraisal, which is the most accurate measure but also the most costly. Alternatively, they may be valued based upon their tax basis, which is cost less depreciation. This method is the least accurate, although simple and the least costly. A compromise would be to restate the basis of the asset by using a longer life, that is, 10 years subject to a floor, that is, 25 percent of cost.

Accounts receivable represents amounts billed for services rendered but not paid. Work in progress represents amounts unbilled for services rendered. Since most medical practices are on the cash basis of accounting, accounts receivable (and work in progress) are not included in income, and have no tax basis. However, for purposes of the buy-in, accounts receivable may be treated as a "capital" asset or an "ordinary income" asset. The sale of a capital asset results in capital that is normally lower than the tax on ordinary income.[14] For example, if the associate purchases an interest in the practice, and accounts receivable are a component of the value, the accounts receivable are being treated as capital assets (being purchased with after-tax dollars) even though the receivables will result in ordinary income to the practice when collected or to the new owner when paid as compensation. It is for this reason that accounts receivable should be handled differently in most buy-in contexts.[15] Unexpected tax consequences of a buy-in amount may result from the purchase of an interest in a partnership or a limited liability entity that is taxed as a partnership with regard to accounts receivable. Whereas one would expect that a purchase of an interest would have capital gain consequences to the existing owner, if the underlying entity is a partnership-type entity which has "unrealized receivables," the IRC characterizes a portion of the purchase price as ordinary income.[16]

Goodwill is an intangible asset. It has no book value for financial accounting or tax purposes unless it was purchased as a capital asset. Goodwill represents the going concern value of a business. For medical practices, relationships with patients and referral sources, practice location, favorable payer agreements, payer mix, infrastructure, and workforce in place are components of this asset. Comparables, percentages of collections, or calculations based upon compensation paid to owners are types of methods that are used for valuation purposes.

An understanding of the accounting equation is important: assets minus liabilities equals equity. For buy-in valuation purposes, the assets of the balance sheet are restated to present a more realistic picture of the value of the practice. One approach to restatement of the balance sheet is to value each asset separately. Alternatively, if one considers an investment in a medical practice as a way to increase one's income, an approach that capitalizes earnings may be indicated; that is, a consideration of how all of the assets of the medical practice are working together to produce earnings. Consider the following provision from a medical practice's purchase agreement:

> The Purchase Price shall be the Weighted Average of the EBITDA of the Practice multiplied by _____. The "Weighted Average" shall be computed as the sum of: (i) three (3) times the EBITDA of the Practice for the most recently completed twelve (12) month period; plus (ii) two (2) times the EBITDA of the Practice for the second most recently completed twelve (12) month period plus (iii) one (1) times the EBITDA of the Practice for the third most recently completed twelve (12) month period; and then divided by six (6). "EBITDA" means the earnings of the Practice, before the deduction of interest, taxes, depreciation and amortization, as calculated by the Practice's regularly employed accountant in accordance with the Practice's past practices, which calculation shall be binding on the parties absent manifest error.

The first question is, how does one calculate earnings in a medical practice when the normal practice is to distribute all income to owners in the form of salary and benefits? The answer is that earnings must be *normalized*: that is, to the extent that the salary and benefits of the owners exceed recognized surveys of mean and median physician income,[17] the excess constitutes *earnings*. The second question is, how much is the new owner willing to invest to generate earnings that exceed the mean or median compensation that he would otherwise derive? The answer is based upon a concept of the weighted average cost of capital (WACC). The cost of capital is based upon the discount rate. The discount rate determines the level of risk of the investment in the medical practice. The capitalization rate is the inverse of the discount rate. Either of the two rates determines what the new owner expects as a return if he invests in the practice. Consider the following example:

> A medical practice is financed with a combination of debt and equity. The cost of debt is determined by using the interest rate applicable to the practice's borrowing. The cost of equity is the sum of the following: (a) the current risk-free rate of return (for example, the Treasury bond rate); (b) the equity risk premium multiplied by a Beta (volatility); and (c) the small stock risk premium. Suppose the risk-free rate is 7 percent; the market risk, which is approximately 8 percent times a Beta (between 1.1 and 1.4 for investment in the health care segment); plus small stock premium (between 4 percent and 8 percent). Hence, a medical practice's cost of equity might be: 7% + (8% × 1.2) + 6% = 22.6%. If the medical practice's debt comprises 12% of its asset value, after adjustment for accounts receivable, the calculation would be as follows:

$$.07 \times 12\% = .84\%; .226 \times 88\% = 19.88\%; .84\% + 19.88\%$$
$$= 20.3\%$$

What this means from a valuation perspective is that the new owner should expect a 20 percent rate of return to invest in this medical practice, which also means that earnings should be capitalized approximately 5 times to determine value.

A fine point in this process is the determination date. The new owner may feel that a purchase of value that was added during the associate phase is unfair, and may wish to negotiate an alternative determination date that is closer to the date that the associate phase began. Under these circumstances, the associate should be mindful of the volatility of the health care segment of our economy. For example, it is virtually impossible to predict what Medicare and the commercial payers may do with regard to reimbursement.[18] One suggestion is the use of a *call option*, which would permit the associate to lock in the price at a prior date in consideration of paying the owners an amount to hold the price at the prior date; if on the buy-in date (strike date), the value of the medical practice has declined, the associate may elect not to exercise the option, then may renegotiate the price and forfeit the amount paid for the option.[19]

Whether the individual asset or the earnings approach is used, accounts receivable deserve further attention. These assets have no tax basis and will result in ordinary income to either the medical practice or to the owners in the form of salary.

In order to assure that the new owner is getting the benefit of the bargain, certain representations, warranties, and disclosures by the medical practice and perhaps the owners are indicated, such as:

- The Practice has furnished to the Purchaser the balance sheets of the Practice and the related statements of operations as of and for the fiscal years ended December 31, 200_ and December 31, 200_ (collectively, the "Financial Statements"). The Financial Statements represent the financial position and results of operations of the Practice as of the indicated dates and for the indicated periods and have been prepared in accordance with generally accepted accounting principles consistently applied.
- The Practice does not have any liability or obligation of any nature or kind (absolute, accrued, contingent, or otherwise) that may have a material adverse effect on the Practice after the closing date that is not disclosed or that is in excess of the amounts shown on the Financial Statements of the Practice.
- The Practice has good, clear, and marketable title to all assets free and clear of all mortgages, claims, charges, liens, security interests, easements, rights of way, pledges, restrictions, or encumbrances of any nature.
- The Practice has complied and is in compliance in all respects with all Federal and state laws, ordinances, regulations, rules, requirements, and orders of all governmental entities applicable to Practice and the Practice has not received any notice of any asserted violation of and has no other basis to believe it is not in compliance in all respects with any such laws, ordinances, regulations, rules, requirements, or orders. No investigation or review by any governmental entity with respect to the Practice is pending or, to the knowledge of the Practice, has been threatened, nor has any governmental entity indicated an intention to conduct any such investigation or review.
- The Practice has correctly filed all Tax Returns required to be filed by the Practice and has paid or provided for all Taxes shown to be due on such returns. No action or proceeding for the assessment or collection of any Taxes is pending against the Practice. No deficiency, assessment or other claim for any Taxes has been asserted or made against the Practice that has not been fully paid or finally settled. No issue has been raised by any taxing authority in connection with an audit or examination of any return of Taxes of the Practice.
- Set forth on Schedule_____ hereto is a complete and accurate list of all Contracts to which any "Insider" is a party. Insider means any owner, manager, director, or officer of the Practice, and any Affiliate or Relative of any of the foregoing.
- Schedule_____ sets forth a complete list of all interests in real property used by the Practice in connection with its business. All leases set forth thereon are valid and, to the Practice's knowledge, without any default under such lease by the Practice or by the lessor beyond the applicable notice and cure period.
- Schedule_____ sets forth a list and brief description of all pending and, to the knowledge of the Practice, threatened suits, actions, investigations,

grievances, and proceedings affecting the Practice since _____ 20__. Except as set forth in Schedule____, there is no suit, action, investigation, grievance, or proceeding pending or, to the knowledge of the Practice, threatened against, by, or affecting the Practice.

- Schedule_____ is a list of all malpractice, casualty, liability, business interruption, and other insurance policies held by the Practice, together with a list of all parties listed (or required by any contract to be listed) as additional insureds under such policies. All such policies are in full force and effect and there is no threat, to the knowledge of the Practice, by any of the insurers to terminate, or increase the premiums payable under, any of such policies. The Practice is in full compliance with the conditions contained in such policies.
- In connection with the conduct of the business of the Practice, to the Practice's knowledge, (i) the Practice is in compliance with all applicable Environmental Laws and has obtained and is in compliance with all permits, licenses and other authorizations required under any such Environmental Law for the conduct of the Practice; (ii) there is no past or present event, condition, or circumstance caused by the Practice that is likely to interfere with the conduct of the Practice in the manner now conducted or which would interfere with the compliance with any Environmental Law or constitute a violation thereof, and (iii) the Practice has not leased, operated, or owned any facilities in connection with the business with respect to which the Practice is subject to any actual or potential proceeding under any Environmental Law.
- Set forth on Schedule___ is a list of all accounts receivable, promissory notes, contract rights, commercial paper, debt securities, and other rights to receive money reflected as assets of the Practice in the Financial Statements or otherwise related to the Practice (the "Receivables"), in each case showing the name of the account debtor, maker, or obligor, the unpaid balance, the age of the receivable, and, if applicable, the maturity date, the interest rate, and the collateral securing the obligation. All Receivables are legal, valid, and binding obligations of the obligors and are collectible in accordance with their terms.

The following is a type of provision that protects the new owner from a breach of any of the representations or warranties that surface after the closing of the sale:

- From and after the Closing, the Practice shall protect, defend, indemnify, and hold harmless the Purchaser from and against all losses, liabilities, indebtedness, damages, actions, causes of action, debts, dues, judgments, penalties, fines, costs, obligations, taxes, expenses, and fees, including all reasonable attorneys' fees, and the reasonable fees of any experts, contractors and consultants, and court costs, incurred by the Purchaser resulting from, arising out of, relating to, or caused by any inaccuracy or misrepresentation in or breach of any of the representations, warranties, and covenants to the Purchaser set forth herein by the Practice.

Compensation

The primary purpose of a compensation sharing methodology is to align the individual physician with the practice's compensation philosophy—maximize income, reduce expense, and provide quality outcomes. Owners may share compensation equally, base compensation on production, or elect a hybrid approach. No matter which approach is utilized, the first step in computing compensation is to determine the aggregate component of compensation that will be shared among the owners of the practice during the relevant computation period. In order to do so in a fair and equitable fashion, the owners need to decide what expenses are directly charged against each owner's share of compensation and which expenses are considered to be overhead of the practice. Generally, expenses that directly benefit the owners, and are susceptible to variability in amount between owners during the computation period, are charged back against the owners' share of the compensation component. What is important is that the owners reach an understanding on which expenses will be charged back.

For purposes of determining how the aggregate component of compensation will be divided among the owners, overhead expenses may be characterized as fixed or variable expenses. In lieu of reviewing individual expenses and deciding which are fixed and which are variable, some practices assume that a certain percentage of expenses are characterized as one or the other. Even if the compensation component is divided based upon production, fixed expenses could be divided equally; conversely, if the compensation component is divided equally, variable expenses could be divided based upon production.

Finally, if any portion of the compensation component will be divided based upon production, the owners need to decide upon the measure of productivity they will use to develop the production fraction.

- *Charges* have the advantage of being easy to track. However, if charges are based upon a hypothetical, outdated fee schedule, they may be an unrealistic measure of production.
- *Collections* have the advantage of administrative ease, and are probably the most prevalent form of measurement in most medical practices. Collections have the advantage of directly correlating to income. The disadvantage of collections is that they will vary based upon payer mix and the level of reimbursement.
- *Encounters* measure work effort and are easy to track. Encounters fail to measure the time and intensity involved in the delivery of care, and they are useless when comparing specialties and subspecialties.
- *Relative value units* (RVUs) are the standard applied by Medicare and most commercial payers. RVUs are based on the level and intensity of physician work, and thus are not as subject to variability as collections.

The RVU value for a particular service is standardized and dependent on the intensity and time involved in furnishing the service. The disadvantages of RVUs are that they are not connected to cash flow, and are more complicated to administer than charges (which explains in part why they are not used more frequently by practices).

RVUs deserve more attention. The Medicare fee schedule for physician services is based upon the Resource Based Relative Value System (RBRVS).[20] The RBRVS determines the relative value of physician services and the resources consumed. The RBRVS will permit the medical practice to compare physician services across payers and physician specialties; for example, evaluation and management services and surgical procedures can be compared using this system.

There are three types of RVUs for each CPT (Common Procedure Terminology) code:[21] physician work level, practice expense, and medical malpractice expense. The number of RVUs for each RVU component is multiplied by a Geographic Practice Cost Index (GPCI). A conversion factor, which is the perceived cost of 1 RVU, is multiplied by the total number of RVUs for the service to calculate an allowed fee.[22]

Owners who share income based upon production may consider it more equitable to share income or loss from associates[23] equally. Consider the following example:

The associate's collections are $200,000 and the associate's incremental expenses are $150,000 within a computation period. The practice's total collections are $1,000,000 and practice expenses (including associate incremental expenses) are $600,000. Owner A's collections are $500,000 and Owner B's collections are $300,000. Owner A's and Owner B's compensation method is entirely production based.

- Associate's Profit Shared Based Upon Owner Production: $1,000,000 − $600,000 = $400,000

  - Owner A's share: 5/8 × $400,000 = $ 250,000;
  - Owner B's share: 3/8 × $400,000 = $ 150,000

- Associate's Profit Shared Equally: $800,000 − $450,000 = $350,000

  - Owner A's share: 5/8 × $350,000 = $218,750 + $25,000 = $243,750
  - Owner B's share: 3/8 × $350,000 = $131,250 + $25,000 = $156,250

The owners may desire to share the income from ancillary services based upon the physician who ordered the service. Stark[24] and state self-referral laws place significant limitations on the ability to benefit directly the physician who referred certain ancillary services. Many medical practices will qualify for the in-office ancillary service exception to Stark,[25] which allows intragroup referrals of Stark services. However, even if the medical practice qualifies for the exception, Stark does not allow income from Stark services to be divided among the physicians in the group practice based upon the volume or value of referrals. The regulations under Stark provide that the income from these services may be paid as productivity bonuses based upon: (a) total RVUs; (b) allocation of revenue from non-Stark services; or (c) a profit share based upon: (i) per capita; or (ii) revenues from non-Stark services.

Income paid to owners from pharmaceuticals, ancillary services, or associate physicians (including physician extenders) could cause adverse federal income tax consequences depending upon the type of entity that provides the medical services. In *Pediatric Surgical Associates v. CIR*,[26] a medical practice provided pediatric surgical services. It employed four shareholder physicians and two associate physicians on fixed salaries. The practice entity was a corporation taxed under Subchapter C of the Internal Revenue Code and operated on the cash basis of accounting. At the end of each fiscal year, the medical practice distributed the remaining net income of the corporation equally as additional salary to its shareholders. The IRS took the position that the salary of the shareholders, to the extent that it represented profit from the personal services of the associates, represented dividends to the shareholders and was not deductible to the corporation as salary expense. This determination caused the income to be subject to a 35 percent rate at the corporate level and a second tax was imposed at the shareholders level for the dividends—together with interest and penalties. This is a very bad result.

The Court's rationale was based upon Section 162(a) (1) of the Internal Revenue Code, which provides that salary is deductible if it is reasonable and is *payment solely for services rendered*. This decision was based on the theory that a portion of the distribution to the owners was a return for their entrepreneurial efforts, that is, a dividend. This result would not have occurred if the corporation had elected to be taxed under Subchapter S of the Internal Revenue Code. As mentioned earlier in this chapter, S corporations are pass-through entities, and not subject to tax.[27]

MANAGEMENT AND GOVERNANCE

The types of governing documents for a medical practice depend upon the practice entity. If the practice entity is a corporation, the governing documents will be found in the bylaws, the employment agreements between the owners and the practice entity, and the shareholders agreement. If the practice entity is a partnership, the partnership agreement will control the actions of the members; the analog in the limited liability entity is referred to as the operating agreement.

The new owner should become familiar with her voting rights and requirements, and what is required for a quorum. Some buy-ins postpone equal voting rights until the purchase price is fully paid if paid over time or some arbitrary period. More and more medium to large physician practices are moving toward representative types of governance arrangements, to streamline decision making and respond efficiently to changes in the health care climate. A technique that will tend to assure continuity in governance is a board with staggered terms. As mentioned earlier, using representative governance requires the trust of the non-participating owners, which can only be maintained by effective communication of board actions to the other owners.

Under these representative arrangements, certain decisions may require super-majority approval by the governing board, or require that the ownership at large approve the decision. For example, many practice entities permit associate physicians and owners to be terminated without cause. Who is permitted to take this action, and what is required to take it, are obviously very important issues. Other actions that may require approval by more than a majority of the governing board or by the owners at large are organic changes to the practice entity, large expenditures, long-term commitments, or payer agreements that are outside certain reimbursement corridors.

Smaller practices face different problems. The biggest hurdle is what is done if irreconcilable differences arise between the owners, resulting in a deadlock. If the owners are unable to resolve their differences, they may end up using a costly judicial dissolution procedure.[28] Alternatives include agreeing on what occurs in the event of a deadlock,[29] having the senior owner make the ultimate decision, or using a technique referred to as "Russian roulette."[30]

THE BUY-OUT

The same principles that apply to the valuation and purchase price for purposes of the buy-in will likewise apply to the buy-out. These issues should be addressed prior to the associate becoming a new owner, if not discussed before the associate phase began.

Off-balance sheet liabilities that were discussed earlier should be considered, such as medical malpractice tails. If the new owner is required personally to guarantee debts or other liabilities such as leases of the medical practice, the practice and the new owner should address release or indemnification upon departure.

Differences in the amount paid to a departing owner may be attributable to the event that gives rise to the buy-out—the trigger event. The trigger event is most times something that results in a termination of employment: death, disability, retirement, voluntary separation from service, or termination with or without cause. Today, with the physician population aging, many older physicians are relinquishing their ownership and management rights and re-engaging with the practice in an associate role.[31]

If the trigger event results in a hardship to the practice, some practices reduce the purchase price. For example, if the physician voluntarily terminates employment and leaves the practice without affording the practice adequate notice to replace the lost production or is terminated for cause upon short notice, the remaining physicians are forced to incur a larger portion of the fixed expenses.

Also, with regard to multiple simultaneous buy-outs, total yearly payouts may be capped, with amounts payable in excess of the cap postponed.

OTHER BUY-OUT CONSIDERATIONS

Practice Location, and Practice Telephone Numbers

In practices where the departing physician will continue to practice in the area, it is normal for the senior physician to retain the practice location and telephone numbers. These issues should also be addressed if a potential for deadlock exists.

Custody of Medical Records

The departing physician should have rights to access the medical records in the event of claims of professional malpractice or erroneous billing. The methodology for transferring medical records if a patient requests that the departing physician continue her care should be clear (for example, who keeps the records, and who pays the copying charges). State and federal confidentiality laws need to be considered. In some jurisdictions, patients are required to be notified when a treating physician leaves the practice.

Patient Abandonment

The physician-patient relationship may be terminated without cause or for reasons related to retirement, or separation of service with the medical practice, with sufficient notice to allow the patient to identify another provider. The practice and the departing physician may consider sending neutral/nonsolicitous letters to patients, advising them that the physician has left the practice; if the physician is continuing in practice, the letters should advise the patient of the departing physician's location or telephone number, and include a statement that the practice is able to continue the patient's care, if that is so. The patient should also be advised of the location of her medical records.

Posttermination Restrictions

If state law permits, posttermination restrictions regarding practice location and solicitation of patients are typical in buy-outs. Even in jurisdictions that permit these types of restrictions, the courts do not favor them, and generally any ambiguity will be construed against the party seeking to enforce the restrictions. Some states permit the court to rewrite the provision if it is overly broad; others will completely invalidate the restriction if any aspect is deemed unreasonable.

The general rule for posttermination restrictions is reasonableness with regard to the medical practice, the departing physician, and the public. With regard to the medical practice, the proprietary interest of the medical practice is considered. The medical practice has the right to protect relationships with patients, referral sources, and employees. The restriction should not impose undue hardship on the ability of the departing physician to earn a living; hence, any restrictions should be reasonable as to time and geographic scope. In addition, the restrictions cannot impede the ability of the public to access health care services. For example, shortages of medical professionals or vital services may be considered by a court to determine enforceability of posttermination restrictions. Prohibitions against treating a patient and geographic limitations that may affect the ability of the patient to use the services of the physician at a hospital are not favored. Finally, nonsolicitation provisions may conflict with legal and ethical requirements to notify a patient when a physician leaves a practice.

CONCLUSION

In conclusion, there are numerous issues attendant to buy-ins and buy-outs in physician practices. Valuable time and money will be wasted by the associate physician and the medical practice—and patient relationships may be disrupted—with a bad match. Full disclosure and consideration of as many buy-in issues as possible at the time the associate phase commences will increase the chances that the relationship will be permanent. It would be unfortunate and expensive for each party if after a successful courtship a contentious negotiation ensues regarding ownership and results in the parties going their separate ways.

NOTES

1. This chapter will refer to a physician as an *associate* until such time as the physician becomes an owner of the practice, at which time the physician will be referred to as a *new owner*. The physicians who have an ownership interest in the practice other than the new owner will be referred to as *owners*.

2. The term *owner* may take different forms depending upon the type of medical practice entity, that is, shareholders of professional associations, partners of partnerships, or members of limited liability entities. However, the bundle of rights that are included in "ownership" are generally the same—income, the value of the owner's interest, and the owner's right to manage and control the practice entity.

3. The American Health Lawyers Association is a source for attorneys who have experience in and who specialize in the representation of physicians and physician practices.

4. The author wishes to thank Michael Schaff, Esq., with the law firm of Wilentz, Goldman and Spitzer, P.A., in Woodbridge, New Jersey, for his permission to use the sample provisions in this chapter. Mr. Schaff is a past chair of the American Health Lawyers Association's Physician Organization Committee.

5. Some of the tax differences for buy-ins and buy-outs depending upon the type of entity will be discussed later in this chapter.

6. The importance of the date that value is determined will be discussed later in this chapter.

7. Production approaches include billings, collections, encounters, or relative value units. The differences between these approaches will be discussed later in the chapter.

8. To the extent that an associate's production exceeds the associate's incremental expenses (additional expenses that the practice incurs on account of employing the associate), the production reduces the fixed expenses of the practice. The reduction of fixed expense will increase the owner's compensation. In a production-based model of compensation for the associate, the associate's request to share collections in excess of incremental costs is legitimate.

9. *Claims made* professional liability insurance policies respond to claims asserted during the policy period. These policies typically require coverage for claims that are asserted after the physician's relationship with the practice terminates. This is typically referred to as *tail* coverage.

10. This also includes interests in ambulatory care facilities.

11. Tangible assets are furniture, fixtures, and equipment, and will be discussed later in this section.

12. Goodwill, which is an intangible asset, will be discussed later in this section.

13. The Medicare Fraud and Abuse statute (42 U.S.C. Sections 1320a-7(b) (1), (2)) prohibits the offering/paying or receiving/soliciting of any remuneration to induce or in return for the referral of a person for an item or service payable by Medicare, Medicaid, or any other federal program. This is an intent-based statute, which if violated imposes both civil and criminal penalties on each party, including potential decertification from the federal programs. There are several statutory and regulatory safe harbors applicable to various transactions that fall within the scope of the proscription by the statute—none apply to the sale of an interest in a practice when the seller remains a participating owner. However, a technical violation of the statute with no safe harbor does not necessarily mean that the Office of Inspector General (OIG) will take enforcement action against the parties to the transaction. Certain letters from the OIG raise the OIG's concerns regarding what is being paid for and the continuing compensation arrangement in connection with practice sales. What is clear from the letters is that the volume and value of referrals must be excluded from the valuation. Letter dated December 22, 1992, from D. McCarty Thornton (Associate General Counsel of the OIG) to T. J. Sullivan (Office of Associate Chief Counsel, Internal Revenue Service); and letter dated November 3, 1993, from D. McCarty Thornton to John E. Steiner, Jr., Esq. (Assistant General Counsel to the American Hospital Association). The parties also need to consider state self-referral laws. http://oig.hhs.gov/fraud/docs/safeharborregulations/acquisition110293.htm; and 122292htm.

14. Conversely, one is required to use after-tax income to acquire a capital asset.

15. For example, the interest in accounts receivable may be acquired by the new owner deferring receipt of a share of compensation in an amount equal to the interest in accounts receivable for some mutually acceptable period. Alternatively, the new owner's post buy-in compensation may exclude amounts collected by the practice on account of services rendered prior to the buy-in date. Even if the interest in the practice is based upon the value of the practice as a whole, the accounts receivable may be carved out and treated on a pretax basis.

16. This will also apply to certain depreciation deductions that the medical practice may have taken with regard to tangible assets.

17. For example, the Medical Group Management Association conducts annual physician compensation surveys, and publishes reports that include mean and median

survey information. Other recognized physician compensation surveys are conducted by Sullivan, Cotter and Associates, Inc.; Hay Group; Hospital and Healthcare Compensation Services; ECS Watson Wyatt; and William M. Mercer.

18. Medicare is considered the "gold standard" with regard to reimbursement and reimbursement methodology. Commercial payers have a tendency to follow Medicare's lead, and oftentimes they tie their reimbursement rates and methods of determining reimbursement to Medicare.

19. Martin, D. G., T. K. Ross, and F. Akinci. 2006. "Analyzing the Efficacy of Physician Practice Acquisition Using Real Option Theory." *Journal of Health Care Finance* 32 (4): 46–54.

20. The RBRVS was developed by researchers at the Harvard University School of Public Health. The number of RVUs for each CPT code is relative to a patient visit of approximately 15 minutes (CPT code 99213), which was originally assigned one RVU.

21. Common Procedure Terminology or CPT codes are copyrighted by the American Medical Association. The American Society of Anesthesiologists has developed its own set of CPT codes, which are now used by Medicare.

22. RVUs can also be used to negotiate managed care agreements. By knowing the number of RVUs for a procedure, the medical practice can ascertain what a health plan is using as its conversion factor. By comparing the plan's conversion factor with the medical practice's "cost" per RVU, the medical practice can determine whether it will make or lose money on delivering the service. For a complete discussion of how RVUs can be used in a medical practice see: Kathryn P. Glass, *RVUs Application for Medical Practice Success* (Englewood, CO: Medical Group Management Association, 2003).

23. See footnote 8, infra, for a discussion regarding how associate collections may increase owner compensation. This issue also applies to physician extenders (such as physician assistants, nurse practitioners, and physical therapists) whose services may be billed either incident to the physician services or under their personal provider number.

24. Stark is a federal law that restricts referrals of certain designated health services with regard to beneficiaries of federal health programs—Medicare, Medicaid, and Tricare—to entities with which the referring physician has a financial relationship. Designated health services include radiology, clinical lab, pathology, and so forth. (*Ethics in Patient Referral Act of 1989,* Omnibus Budget and Reconciliation Act of 1989, codified at 42 U.S.C. Section 1395nn; amended by the Omnibus Budget and Reconciliation Act of 1993, codified at 42 U.S.C. 1395nn(a)(1)).

25. There is an in-office ancillary services exception under Stark for referrals of certain designated health services within a group practice. However, the exception does not permit the revenue from such services to be divided among the physicians within the group practice based upon the volume or value of referrals. Income from these services may be divided other than equally (42 C.F.R. Section 411.355(b)). The exception addresses who provided the service; where the service is performed, and who billed for the service. Who?—The referring physician, another physician in the same group practice as the referring physician or a person supervised by the referring physician or a physician in the group. Where?—The same building as the location of the group practice. Who bills?—The group practice.

26. *Pediatric Surgical Associates v. Commissioner of Internal Revenue,* 81 TCM (CCH) Dec. 54,296 (M) (2001).

27. A conversion from a C corporation to an S corporation is possible, but the methodology is beyond the scope of this chapter.

28. This might be the best alternative. Faced with this possibility, the owners may be more apt to resolve their differences.

29. For example, who remains in the practice location, retaining the phone numbers and work force in place.

30. Each owner submits a sealed bid to purchase the practice from the other owner. The highest bidder is required to buy and the lower bidder is required to sell.

31. This arrangement has its own set of problems, particularly where the older physician is slowing down and the practice is production-based, but all expenses are production-based as well.

CHAPTER 3

Measuring Performance in a Medical Practice

William S. Reiser

The success of a medical practice is dependent on performance in four key areas, which may be termed *business imperatives*: clinical quality, service quality, physician productivity, and financial viability. For those medical practices intent on remaining successful over the long term, every decision, every investment, and every policy and procedure must increase, facilitate, or at very least not detract from these four imperatives. They are the filters that help physicians and managers stay within the bounds of correct operating principles for successful medical offices.

Ideally, performance measurement and continuous performance improvement in each of these areas should form the foundation for strategy development and for daily operations. Unfortunately, the state of performance measurement in the areas of service quality and clinical quality, particularly in medical practices, is in its infancy, at best. Until recently, there has not even been a consistent set of clinical indicators for practices to measure. Several organizations offer measures of service quality (at least for patient satisfaction), but with little or no consistency and no national benchmarks.

The current state of productivity and financial indicators is much more advanced, thanks to annual surveys that have become more sophisticated and reliable over the last decade. The Medical Group Management Association (MGMA) and the American Medical Group Association (AMGA) have made significant contributions to the industry in terms of national benchmarks, by publishing their annual surveys. The results are available for purchase by both members and nonmembers.

The state of performance measurement in medical practices is the topic of this chapter. By some standards, the measures we will discuss are relatively unsophisticated, although many practices have not even implemented these simple approaches. We will discuss that current state of performance measurement for each of the four business imperatives.

CLINICAL QUALITY

Good clinical quality is good business. Very few would argue the point. Appropriate medical practice yields appropriate outcomes, which is good for patients, reduces medical malpractice liability, and ultimately enhances financial viability. The challenge over the past few decades has been to define, measure, and improve clinical quality. That challenge is particularly acute in ambulatory settings, where physicians and staff scramble to address patient and referring physician demand for services while meeting a payroll in an environment of decreasing reimbursement. Daily operations pressures are often so intense that they crowd out anything more than rudimentary efforts at quality measurement and quality improvement.

Several organizations have been involved in trying to define quality by developing clinical practice guidelines, sometimes supported by evidenced-based practice, sometimes supported by common sense, and sometimes simply supported by consensus among providers. These organizations include the following:

- American Medical Association Physician Consortium for Performance Improvement
- IPRO, Inc.
- National Committee for Quality Assurance (NCQA)
- Institute for Clinical Systems Improvement
- The Centers for Medicare and Medicaid Services (CMS)

The efforts of these and other organizations have yielded certain quality indicators that have been recently summarized as the "2007 Physician Quality Reporting Initiative (PQRI) — Physician Quality Measures" that have been promulgated by CMS. This list involves some 74 clinical quality measures across a variety of illnesses and chronic disease. CMS has also defined how these indicators will be measured in medical practice, which involves four steps:[1]

1. A patient is identified as eligible for reporting during the office visit based on the clinical condition.
2. The eligible professional (physician or other provider) documents the condition and the measurement requirements in the medical record.
3. The quality code associated with the measure is captured for claims submission.
4. The billing staff enters the codes as part of the coding and billing process.

The CMS program is a "pay for reporting" initiative rather than a "pay for performance" effort at the present time. Physicians who are able to comply with the reporting process 80 percent of the time are paid a bonus or premium that is a percentage of the eligible revenue they received during the designated time period. (There are obvious exceptions, payment caps, and other factors that are detailed on the CMS web site, and will likely be modified.)

This effort to pay for *reporting* creates the potential opportunity for significant revenue in those situations where physicians are able to track diagnoses, discipline themselves and their staff members to document properly, and organize their operating systems to institutionalize the measurement process. Obviously, as these clinical indicators are tracked more closely, physicians and their staffs will likely work not only to report, but to improve the management of patients according to the indicators. It would be a short leap, then, from *reporting* the findings to *improving* the indicators and implementing a true "pay for performance" approach.

Still, as of this writing, the process of measuring and reporting performance remains challenging for those who are attempting to take advantage of the CMS initiative, let alone the challenge of changing behaviors and meeting the proposed criteria. Nevertheless, it is a victory to have a standard set of clinical indicators against which performance can now be measured.

Given the busyness of most medical practices, success in measuring, reporting, and improving clinical quality will likely require two key elements. First, for a busy physician, seeing 20 or 30 or more patients a day, an electronic health record with appropriate flags or reminders is the likely solution to improvements in clinical quality measurement and reporting. Second, charging the clinical assistant with the responsibility to focus on the relevant indicators as she updates the clinical record during the patient workup is already proving successful at improving reporting in several busy medical practices. Engaging the clinical assistant in such activities appears to improve documentation, patient satisfaction, and employee satisfaction as nurses and medical assistants become more than traffic cops.[2]

SERVICE QUALITY

While offering appropriate clinical quality is critical, it is not enough in competitive environments. In fact, clinical quality is assumed in most cases and is, therefore, not a differentiating factor among most physicians. It is the service experience that makes the difference in patient retention—and in most patient referral decisions made by primary care physicians and other providers. While a few specialists bristle to admit their dependence on primary care physicians, even fewer would want to survive only on the word-of-mouth referrals from the few patients who understand their specialty scope of services.

Given the nature of medical practice, even the most sophisticated patients have a hard time discerning whether or not they experience quality clinical care—particularly cognitive care. Certainly, patients know when their pain has been assuaged, when their laceration is repaired, or when their screening test has been performed. But, rarely do they have the training and experience to understand clinical performance. Instead, they use surrogate measures to determine their *satisfaction* with most of the services that physicians provide. Those surrogate measures often have more to do with what patients "experience" in physician offices than with the technical competence of physicians and their clinical staff. That *experience* includes what happens at the appointment desk, at the reception desk, and in the reception room, as well as what happens in the examination room.

Critically, specialty physicians must also consider the service quality they deliver to their referral sources. The days of a primary care physician (PCP) "scrubbing in" to assist a surgeon and personally witness her technical skill are long gone. In fact, new primary care physicians will often make their initial specialty referral decisions the same way Mrs. Smith selects her primary care physician—by word of mouth from a peer. They will approach an established partner or associate to ask where to refer a patient for orthopedics, ENT, and other services. Subsequent referrals are likely to be a function of the service experienced by the PCP, even more than technical competence, which is difficult to measure/prove. Otherwise, the most competent technician in town would have all the patients and others in her specialty would starve to death.

Managing service quality provided to primary care physicians is so critical because patients rarely understand *when* they need a specialist, even if they understand the specialist's scope of practice. Most patients are very (often totally) dependent on their PCP to recommend *which* physician to choose among those of the same specialty. When a choice is available, primary care physicians tend to refer to those specialists who provide access to their referred patients, who provide feedback to the PCP, and who are respectful of both.[3] Obviously, a physician who is not technically competent will soon be discovered and shunned by referring physicians. In addition, a specialist who is not responsive or who is arrogant will lose referring physicians, even if he is the most technically competent provider in town, as soon as an alternative provider is available.

Measuring service quality to patients can be as simple as a self-administered set of questions periodically mailed or distributed to patients as they exit after an appointment (see Figure 3.1), or it can be professionally administered by national firms such as Gallup or Press Ganey, with comparatives to their proprietary benchmarks by specialty. Several local/regional firms also develop and administer patient satisfaction surveys for medical practices. Medical Group Management Association, some professional associations, and others also make survey documents available for purchase by their members. Payers, including CMS, have been experimenting with ways to consistently measure patient satisfaction as part of pay-for-performance initiatives.[4] Professionally administered surveys will likely be too expensive for smaller practices. Due to the challenge of processing large numbers of surveys, however, larger groups and networks will likely benefit from such vendors. Regardless of the method used, all practices should measure patient satisfaction and then act on the feedback they receive. We recommend that questions relate to specific components of the office visit, such as appointment scheduling, reception, wait time, clinical assistance, the physician's services, and ancillary services provided as part of the visit. Even the cashier and billing activities might be surveyed profitably.

Measuring referral source satisfaction is still woefully lacking in most specialty practices. Nevertheless, it is just as critical to the success of a specialty practice as

Figure 3.1 Patient Satisfaction Survey

[Date]

Dear Patient:

The [Healthcare Facility Name] is an organization committed to meeting its customer's needs. As a result, we are always trying to identify ways we can better serve our patients by implementing appropriate changes. This process is called Continuous Quality Improvement, and it requires us to always work toward raising the level of efficiency and effectiveness with which we care for you. Please take a moment to respond to the following questions by circling the response that best indicates your opinion.

[Provider Name]

1. [Provider Name] spent enough time with me	Strongly Agree	Agree	Disagree	Strongly Disagree
2. I understood the explanation of my care/illness	Strongly Agree	Agree	Disagree	Strongly Disagree
3. Overall, I was satisfied with the medical care that was provided to me	Strongly Agree	Agree	Disagree	Strongly Disagree
4. I am able to get an appointment when I need care	Strongly Agree	Agree	Disagree	Strongly Disagree
5. I was seen by [Provider Name] within a reasonable period of time	Strongly Agree	Agree	Disagree	Strongly Disagree
6. [Provider Name] and his office staff were courteous and helpful	Strongly Agree	Agree	Disagree	Strongly Disagree
7. The office is clean, neat, and comfortable	Strongly Agree	Agree	Disagree	Strongly Disagree
8. There is adequate parking when I visit the office	Strongly Agree	Agree	Disagree	Strongly Disagree
9. I am satisfied with the office's handling of my billing and financial matters	Strongly Agree	Agree	Disagree	Strongly Disagree

Please include any additional comments:

Please return the completed survey in the enclosed postage-paid envelope by [Date]. Thank you for your assistance.

patient satisfaction. Our firm has developed a "Specialist of Choice" questionnaire to assist specialty physicians and their office staff members to identify the performance criteria necessary to meet the needs, wants, and priorities of primary care physicians and other referral sources. That questionnaire is presented with permission as Figure 3.2. The increasing use of hospitalists in many markets today creates a significant barrier for specialists trying to maintain relationships with PCPs whom they used to see in the medical staff lounge or in the hospital hallways. We encourage specialty physicians to maintain a profile on each referring physician detailing when (under what circumstances) and how (e.g., letter, fax, phone call) the PCP prefers to receive feedback on referred patients. Some PCPs are so busy that they prefer not to be bothered by phone calls unless they involve a significant untoward event while the patient is under the specialist's care. Others are pleased to accept a telephone call from a specialist at any time. Asking the PCP how and when he prefers to be contacted demonstrates respect for this important customer. Periodically asking how the specialty practice is performing for the PCP and his patients is the best way to gather that critical intelligence—especially if the specialist is doing the asking.

Figure 3.2 Specialist of Choice Questionnaire

Halley
Consulting
Group
Strategy and Performance Improvement for Physician Networks

Specialist of Choice
Practice Evaluation

[Client Name]
[City, State]

[Date Conducted]

Conducted by:
[Team Member's Name]

"*SPECIALIST OF CHOICE*" PRACTICE EVALUATION

REFERRAL SOURCE KNOWLEDGE	● Yes ○ No
1. We have identified all of the potential referring physicians in our defined geographic marke	○
2. We track volumes by referring physician each month and identify any significant changes.	○
3. We have a written profile for each of our referring physicians and other providers documenting their contact information, any preferences or unique practice characteristics, their office manager or clinical coordinator and other key contacts, and their preferred method and timing for receiving feedback from us.	○
4. We send a brief satisfaction and information gathering survey to the office manager along the practice holiday gift each year.	○
5. Our physicians, management and staff routinely discuss the results of our surveys and develop action plans to address practice problems and to take advantage of positive suggestions.	○
REFERRAL SOURCE KNOWLEDGE: Total Capabilities Identified = (Count each ● Yes)	

REFERRAL SOURCE ACCESS	● Yes ○ No
6. We have a designated telephone line(s) for referring physicians and other providers to use when contacting our practice or physicians.	○
7. We have assigned an experienced and service-oriented staff member to answer the referr physician line(s) and respond to inquiries from referring physicians and their staff members.	○
8. We accommodate all requests for non-acute appointments within three days.	○
9. We accommodate all referring physician/provider requests for acute appointments each d	○
10. We have privileges at the hospitals and facilities preferred by our referring physicians.	○
11. Our payer participation matches that of our referring physicians.	○
12. Our office is accessible during all normal business hours, whether the physician is present or not.	○
13. Our call coverage network is comprised of competent associates who share our customer philosophy toward patients and toward our referring physicians and other providers.	○
14. Our physicians respond to every call from a referring physician's office within the same day.	○
15. Our physicians provide their pager numbers to key referring physicians for "quick consults."	○
16. We accept all patients and payers from our referring physicians and other providers.	○
17. We provide our fair portion of care for the uninsured and underinsured.	○
18. We provide all pre-authorization services for our patients and referring physicians.	○
19. We have the ability to assist patients in identifying and obtaining alternative funding if they are not insured.	○
20. Our partners and/or mid-level providers handle acute cases that our physicians cannot work into their schedules.	○
21. In regional settings, we provide outreach services to satellites in small communities with primary care physicians and a community hospital.	○
REFERRAL SOURCE ACCESS: Total Capabilities Identified = (Count each ● Yes)	

REFERRAL SOURCE EXPECTATIONS	● Yes ○ No
22. We provide quality patient education materials for our referring physicians and other provi use in educating and informing patients about common ailments or conditions specific to c specialty.	○
23. When possible and clinically appropriate, our referring physicians and other providers are of the routine ancillary tests we need in order evaluate their patients. They have the optior provide those tests themselves, in which case we always acknowledge and request those results.	○
24. For patients whose physicians do not provide ancillary services, we will take responsibility schedule and facilitate the testing prior to the first visit, if necessary.	○
25. We make an information package available to referring offices to share with patients. The package includes maps, welcome information, and instructions for patients who are referr us.	○
26. We provide the ancillary services routinely expected of our specialty according to the community standard of care.	○
REFERRAL SOURCE EXPECTATIONS: Total Capabilities Identified = (Count each ● Yes)	

CUSTOMER SERVICE TEAM	● Yes ○ No
27. We hire outgoing, friendly staff members who view "customer" service as part of their personal mission in life, whether that customer is a patient, a family member, a referring physician (member.	○
28. Our current staff members recommend new hires they think will "fit" our customer-focused culture.	○
29. Staff members are trained to respond to physicians and their staff members as very critica customers.	○
30. Each of our staff members receive formal training in customer service techniques.	○
31. All staff members go through a formal customer service training process annually.	○
32. Customer service is one of the critical factors in every staff member's performance appraisal.	○
33. All of our staff members are well trained in their technical role within the practice. Trainees identified for our retail customers and do not manage the referring physician telephone lin	○
CUSTOMER SERVICE TEAM: Total Capabilities Identified = (Count each ● Yes)	

RELATIONSHIP MANAGEMENT	● Yes ○ No
34. According to the referring physician's profile and preference, we teleconference and/or provide written feedback on each new referral within 24 hours of initial evaluation.	○
35. We acknowledge the referring physician or other provider to the patient during each patient encounter.	○
36. Whenever possible, and according to the referring physician/provider profile, we refer our patients back to their primary care physician for follow up care. This verbal "referral" is accompanied by a referral form copied to the referring physician's/provider's office.	○
37. We acknowledge the role of non-physician primary care providers and value them as cust	○
38. We offer to conference with the referring physician while the patient is in the examination according to the physician's profile.	○
39. We communicate with the referring physician or other provider within 24 hours after any significant event, surgery or procedure. According to the physician's profile, this communication may be a telephone call, email or letter.	○
40. We routinely communicate with the referring physician or other provider during the course of treatment of a chronically ill patient according to the profile.	○
41. We ensure that there is adequate coordination of each patient referred to us either through their primary care physician, hospitalist, or our office. This coordination includes, at a minimum, pain management and medication management.	○
42. We include complimentary specialty physicians in our relationship development and mana activities, to ensure that we function as a team to meet the needs, wants, and priorities of our referring physicians/providers and their patients.	○
43. Our profile contains each referring physician's/provider's preferred hospital and we contact that physician or provider before performing a procedure in any other facility.	○
44. We chart and initial every interaction with a referring physician/provider's office.	○
45. We survey each referred patient and obtain their permission to share the results with their referring physician.	○
46. We participate in leadership positions to strengthen the local medical staff of hospitals where we have active staff privileges. As part of our leadership role, we acknowledge and protect the interests of our referring physicians.	○
47. During telephone contact with a referring physician/provider or their staff, we routinely ask "how" our service to them and their patients could be enhanced.	○
48. Any negative feedback received from a referring physician/provider or referred patient is addressed in regular meetings with a written response going to both the referring physician/provider and the patient, as appropriate.	○
RELATIONSHIP MANAGEMENT: Total Capabilities Identified = (Count each ● Yes)	

EDUCATION/PROMOTION	● Yes ○ No
49. We support our referring physicians/providers by making available high quality educational information for their patients regarding common ailments or conditions specific to our practice specialty.	○
50. We volunteer to provide lectures and education to assist primary care physicians/providers in becoming more knowledgeable and effective in their clinical practice in our area of expertise.	○
51. We acknowledge our referring physicians/providers and their office staff with an additional token of our appreciation during the Holiday season.	○
EDUCATION/PROMOTION: Total Capabilities Identified = (Count each ● Yes)	

"SPECIALIST OF CHOICE" PRACTICE EVALUATION SCORES (Transfer totals from previous sections)	
Referral Source Knowledge	
Referral Source Access	
Referral Source Expectations	
Customer Service Team	
Relationship Management	
Education/Promotion	
Total	
OVERALL SCORE ÷ 51 x 100 = (Rounded to the nearest whole number)	

Source: The Halley Consulting Group, LLC, used with permission.

Surveying customers is only half the battle, perhaps even less than half. No survey is complete without an action plan to improve performance in areas identified by customers as failing to meet their expectations. A performance improvement action plan should include all the initiatives being pursued by the practice and they should remain active on the plan until they are resolved. As illustrated in Figure 3.3 each initiative should include the following:

- *Priority*—because we cannot do everything at once. Focusing on a few priorities (as opposed to a lengthy, although impressive, list of issues to be addressed) is critical to performance improvement in any practice setting.
- *Person responsible*—because every project needs one person to become the champion and to be held accountable, although many may be involved in its accomplishment.
- *Date added*—to remind us that this issue will not go away until it is resolved, whether or not it is a priority at the current time.
- *Target completion date*—to establish a commitment to accomplish the initiative.
- *Notes*—to document barriers to performance and progress being made.

The action plan should be formally reviewed at least monthly, by practice leadership with responsible parties expected to report on progress and barriers. Responsible parties should be held accountable weekly by their supervisors in order to ensure that these critical matters are not lost in the rush of operating urgencies.

Figure 3.3 Performance Improvement Action Plan

Performance Improvement Action Plan

DATE		NEXT MEETING			
PRIORITY	PERFORMANCE IMPROVEMENT ACTION	PERSON RESPONSIBLE	DATE ADDED	TARGET COMPLETION	NOTES
1.					
2.					
3.					
4.					
5.					

PHYSICIAN PRODUCTIVITY

The physician, or other provider, in a medical practice is the revenue-generating engine. In most ambulatory settings, the physician(s) personally generates charges for the majority of the personal services rendered, and orders the ancillary services associated with those services. Physicians generate revenue when they are interacting with patients in the examination room, the procedure room, or the operating room. There is an opportunity cost associated with physician involvement in any other activity. Maximizing patient interactions and the efficient use of the time associated with those interactions should be the driving force behind measures of productivity.

The most common productivity indicator used among primary care and internal medicine subspecialties has traditionally been visit volume. Private practice physicians knew how many patients they had to see in a morning in order to pay their share of the overhead, and how many patients they had to see in the afternoon to pay themselves. In recent years, this simple but effective measure has been enhanced by also measuring Work Relative Value Units (WRVUs) attached to each CPT code, which provide an indication of the intensity of each patient visit. The coding index (WRVUs divided by the number of office visits) provides justification for those physicians who claim that they see less visit volume because their patients are sicker. A family practitioner may see 25 to 30 patients per day and have an average coding index of 1.0 WRVUs per visit. A general internist may have a coding index of 1.10 WRVUs per visit, but only see 23 or 24 patients per day. The combination of measures enhances the manager's understanding of the patient profile and the physician's coding patterns as compared with others in his or her specialty.

Failure to achieve appropriate levels of productivity according to these measures of noninvasive services may indicate inadequate new-patient volume, poor time management, or inappropriate coding. Low new-patient volume may be a function of inadequate promotion, poor customer service, or market saturation for the specialty. If patient volume is available, but access is inadequate due to poor time management, the physician, the clinical assistant, and the appointment scheduler must be engaged in the performance-improvement process. Once an appropriate number of appointment slots are made available and the scheduler is trained to schedule appropriately, the management of physician productivity falls largely to the clinical assistant. He or she must be authorized and held accountable to manage the physician's time with each patient and to ensure that the workup and follow-up for each visit are handled appropriately. (In order to accomplish these tasks, clerical issues such as referral calls must be delegated elsewhere.) Finally, the physician must be disciplined to keep the visit to issues surrounding the chief complaint and the patient's chief objective for the visit. Other issues must be scheduled for a subsequent visit (unless, of course, the patient is also complaining about chest pain and numbness in the left arm). The physician should always complete procedure coding and the accompanying appropriate documentation. Annual training for physicians and key personnel and periodic documentation audits are more than adequate to improve performance in most instances.

For invasive specialists, the number of cases tends to head the list of productivity indicators. While admittedly not a measure of procedural efficiency, it is an indicator of how busy a physician is during a given month. A busy obstetrics practice, for example, may have 15 deliveries and another 15 surgical cases each month. A reasonably busy orthopedic surgeon specializing in total hip replacement may have 20 to 25 cases a month. Invasive specialists will also track WRVUs and visit volumes during clinic days. Again, these measures of productivity are limited and fairly unsophisticated, but they are effective management tools when comparing physicians within the same group or using national benchmarks (subject to the benchmark warnings discussed later in this chapter).

Again, failure to achieve appropriate levels of productivity in terms of case volume may be a function of poor service quality to patients (which gets back to referring physicians), poor service quality to PCPs, or market saturation for the specialty. Assuming that the specialist is technically competent and has a desire to provide high-quality care and caring, even these challenges can be overcome. Market saturation is the most difficult issue to address and may require a move or involvement in a more regional market strategy.

The efficiency of physicians in terms of time spent per encounter, time spent per work RVU, or other similar measures has not been a significant factor in measuring productivity. The variability in training and in personality, skill, style, and motivation of providers across this personal service industry makes comparisons a significant challenge. However, the combination of visit volumes, cases, WRVUs, and time available tend to identify productivity issues that must be addressed in order to ensure practice viability.

FINANCIAL INDICATORS OF PERFORMANCE

A monthly income statement or profit and loss statement is fairly common for even the smallest of medical practices. A balance sheet listing assets and liabilities, common in many industries, on the other hand, is rarely part of the monthly reporting cycle for physician practices. If the income statement is based on an MGMA or AMGA general ledger footprint, it can be a very useful managerial tool. In our experience, the most useful statements provide managers with several comparative views detailing both dollars and ratios. Revenue factor ratios use gross charges as the denominator (assuming an accrual accounting model). Expense factor ratios use net patient revenue or collections (in a cash accounting environment) as the denominator. Effective income statement analysis includes the following comparisons (while the following factors may be simplistic, we find that many managers fail to carefully analyze income statements in this manner):

- Current month dollar results are compared to average monthly results. This first analytical cut forces management to explain aberrations in revenues or expenses, potentially leading to corrective actions or additional emphasis related to positive variances.

- Comparing current month ratios to year-to-date ratios also highlights significant variations from the annual norm.
- Comparing current year-to-date dollars and ratios with prior year-to-date dollars and ratios can also yield significant insights into the revenue profile (e.g., changes in gross revenues, net revenues, ancillary ratio, contractual write-off ratio, capitation contract performance) and changes in cost structure that might otherwise go unnoticed.
- Dollar and ratio comparisons to budget, especially on a year-to-date basis, can be helpful, assuming that the budget was properly prepared. Unfortunately, many organizations manipulate the budgeting process with unrealistic demands to achieve arbitrary goals. This process is common in some hospital or health system-owned medical practices and shifts ownership for financial performance from those who must manage the budget to the finance department. Explaining the resulting budget variances then becomes management's focus, rather than owning and meeting challenging but realistic performance objectives. This is not to say that stretch goals and performance improvement should not be part of every budgeting process. However, goals must be based on realistic objectives and clear tactics.

In addition to a careful analysis of the income statement, we have found several useful performance indicators that should be observed on a monthly basis:

- *New Patient Ratio:* This ratio is simply the number of new patients divided by the total number of patient visits, and is an indicator of the vitality of the practice. The new patient ratio for healthy established primary care practices may range between 5 percent and 10 percent depending on the specialty and patient profile. Since every primary care practice experiences attrition, every practice needs to add new patients to remain viable over time. A lower ratio may be an indication of poor customer service, lack of access, or market saturation and should be explored in more depth.
- *Surgical Cases:* Since multiple procedures may be performed in each case, surgical cases are the most meaningful gross measure of performance in an invasive specialty practice. Comparing revenues per case and WRVUs per case are significant measures of performance within a practice across physicians of the same specialty, for the same physician over time, and for comparison with national benchmarks available for most specialties through AMGA or MGMA.
- *Scheduled Hours:* Scheduled hours as a percentage of available hours are a measure that is available on some of the more sophisticated practice management and billing packages. The ratio provides a simple measure of the practice's capacity utilization.

- *Labor Ratio:* The labor ratio is simply nonprovider labor costs divided by net revenue. It is a more meaningful measure than the traditional full-time equivalent (FTE) support staff per physician because busier practices tend to require more support staff than others. Limiting staff based on an FTE ratio will limit the productivity of physicians who end up escorting their own patients because the clinical assistant is on the telephone or completing paperwork that could be completed by others and approved by the physician. A family practice physician with median productivity (as measured by visits or WRVUs) may require three staff members to accomplish the work associated with the practice. A busy family practitioner, functioning at the 75th percentile may require an additional staff member, but will likely have a lower overall cost of support staff as a percentage of net patient revenue.
- *Building Occupancy Ratio:* The third most significant cost in most medical practices is the cost of space. Although it appears on the income statement, comparing this significant fixed cost to national benchmarks and striving to achieve those benchmarks is critical to the long-term success of the practice. In the case of long-term leases, adding providers or services per square foot may be the only interim performance improvement tactic.
- *Coding Index:* It has been our experience that most physicians under-code and under-document relative to the level of service they actually provide. Sometimes this under-coding is a function of potential audit anxiety, sometimes it is lack of coding knowledge, and at other times it is simply unwillingness (or lack of motivation) to fully document for billing purposes. The coding index (mentioned earlier) is an indicator of trends in coding among physicians of the same specialty and over time. As training is implemented and documentation audits/education occur, the coding index will change quickly, particularly if the physician's compensation is a function of revenues or of WRVUs.

Although a balance sheet is not frequently produced in a medical practice, current assets and current liabilities are frequently reviewed. The most important current asset to manage for the success of a medical practice is accounts receivable. Billing, even in the smallest practices, is usually automated (using internal software, a web-based vendor, or a billing company) and most billing software on the market today provides common analytical tools to track days in accounts receivable and aging categories or "buckets." Once again, these indicators of billing performance can be compared internally, over time, or with external benchmarks. In addition, we recommend the careful measurement of performance at the front desk to ensure verification of demographic and insurance data and to drive collection of required copayments, as well as measurement of cashier performance in terms of collecting patient due balances. Data verification can be monitored quite easily by the manager, who should examine the reasons for any claims that do not survive a claims "scrubber" found on many software packages, or claims that are rejected by carriers. We also recommend that the reception and cashier incumbents report their performance to the office manager on a daily basis in terms of dollars collected and the number of patients from whom copayments or balances were collected as a percentage of those who presented with copayments or balances. This focus on data verification and on point-of-service collections (both copayments and patient due balances) has a dramatic effect on the cost and success of receivables management efforts.

COMPARATIVE ANALYSIS: APPROPRIATE USE OF SURVEY DATA

The term *benchmark* is often confused with the term *best practice*. Utilizing survey data as a reference point against which to compare practice performance is certainly an appropriate application of industry benchmarks. However, it is important for all users to understand that the survey data is *not* necessarily an indication of *the best practice*. Most survey documents are, in reality, a census of survey participants, who may or may not represent the practice ideal. Census data is useful to make sure that performance is within the ballpark for a specialty, but the benchmark may or may not be a useful performance target depending on a current practice situation.

As valuable as external data can be in assessing relative performance on key indicators or ratios, it is never as relevant to a practice situation as the practice's own internal data either across physicians of the same specialty or over time. Unfortunately, managers eager to "score" their practice performance in order to justify their current position often overlook this critical concept. External data is just that, *external* to the specifics of any particular practice and therefore it has no bearing on the actual performance of the practice. Any analysis or time spent modifying or seeking survey data to better fit a manager's specific practice situation is a distraction that does nothing to improve the performance of a practice. By contrast, astute managers will assess the validity of comparative and benchmark data to their practice and will then utilize the comparative information to identify realistic gaps in performance that will help focus management decisions and efforts to effect operational change.

THE PITFALLS OF PERCENTILES

Survey data is often reported in percentiles, which are extremely valuable if not overinterpreted. For example, each data element represented in the MGMA Physician and Compensation Survey reports the 25th percentile, mean, median, and 75th percentile of survey responses. Table 3.1 illustrates three common data elements reported within the MGMA Compensation and Production Survey report.[5]

Each of these data elements individually can provide management with valuable comparative data. These data elements, when inappropriately interpreted or correlated, can lead management to draw inaccurate conclusions with potentially devastating financial results. A common temptation of managers is to assume that

Table 3.1
MGMA Compensation and Production Survey—Family Practice

Data Element	Providers	25th Percentile	Median	75th Percentile
PCPS Table 19.1 Physician Work RVUs (CMS RBVS Method) All Physicians	2,737	3,354	4,053	4,844
PCPS Table 21.1 Physician Collections per Work RVU (CMS RBVS Method) All Physicians	1,524	$71.23	$79.66	$91.44

Source: Reprinted with permission from the Medical Group Management Association, 104 Inverness Terrace East, Englewood, Colorado 80112. Copyright 2006.

the percentiles for one data element (or table) correspond to and align with the data elements from another data element (or table). For example, a manager may have a physician who generates 4,000 work RVUs. Referencing the table above, this value corresponds closely to the median. A common misinterpretation of the data would be to then assume that the anticipated collections per RVU for those generating 4,000 RVUs would be about $80 per RVU, and that with increasingly higher levels of RVU productivity one should expect increasingly higher collections per unit.

The appropriate interpretation of the data represented above is that each data element (or table) reports the percentiles *for that data element only.* The 25th percentile to the 75th percentile for work RVUS is reporting the percentile rankings for work RVUs, and the 25th percentile to 75th percentile for collections per work RVU is reporting the percentile rankings for collections per work RVU, *not* the percentile rankings of collections per work RVU *at* specific work RVU levels. Failure to comprehend this distinction has led many managers or physicians to inappropriate conclusions regarding performance, especially relating to compensation for high-producing physicians.

GAP ANALYSIS

In our early consulting experience, we made the mistake of assuming that we could cost control our way to success in the medical practice business. We were working with practices that were losing money, so we applied the ratio analysis described above. Table 3.2 illustrates a simplified analysis of key performance indicators for a primary care practice losing $150,000 per year. We used ratio analysis to identify key problem areas:

We assumed that this table illustrated an expense control problem. The provider cost was 7 percentage points higher than our benchmark for the same specialty.

Table 3.2
Key Expense Ratio Analysis

	Actual	% Revenue	% Revenue Benchmark
Net Revenue	$1,234,805	100	
Provider Cost	595,706	48	41
Staff Cost	395,138	32	26
Building Occup.	123,481	10	7
Clinical Supplies	$98,784	8	4
Other Expenses	176,200		
Total	−$154,504		

Our staff cost was high by 6 percentage points and our building occupancy and clinical supplies were both higher than our benchmark by 3 and 4 percentage points, respectively. We then calculated the dollar impact of these variances by subtracting the actual percentage from the benchmark percentage as illustrated in Table 3.3.

Based on this interpretation of the data, it appeared that eliminating the $150,000 in losses would be an exercise in expense control. We began to reduce expenses by cutting hours, eliminating staff, and reducing inventory levels of clinical supplies. Much to our chagrin, the rate of financial losses in the practice increased.

Our experience illustrates one of the potential pitfalls of a simple ratio analysis based only on expense ratios. We learned that while expenses must be managed in a medical practice, success or failure in our business is found on the revenue side of the income statement.

Extending the gap analysis to view these expenses from the perspective of revenue illustrates the benefits of a ratio analysis based on appropriate income. The benchmark net revenue for this primary care practice, given the number of physicians, is $1,612,500. The current net revenue is $1,234,805, or more than $377,000 below the benchmark net revenue.

Table 3.4 illustrates a more appropriate interpretation of the ratios, basing the gap analysis on benchmark net revenue. Table 3.4 will lead management to a very different interpretation of the underlying performance issues. If the practice

Table 3.3
Key Expense Ratio Financial Impact

	Actual	% Revenue	% Revenue Benchmark	Impact
Net Revenue	$1,234,805	100		
Provider Cost	595,706	48	41	−$89,436
Staff Cost	395,138	32	26	−74,089
Building Occup.	123,481	10	7	−37,045
Clinical Supplies	$98,784	8	4	−$49,392

Table 3.4
Gap Analysis—Expense Ratios at Benchmark Revenue

	Actual	% Revenue	% Revenue Benchmark	Impact	Value at Benchmark	Difference to Actual
Net Revenue	$1,234,805	100			$1,612,500	–$377,695
Provider Cost	595,706	48	41	–$89,436	661,125	65,419
Staff Cost	395,138	32	26	–74,089	419,250	24,112
Building Occup.	123,481	10	7	–37,045	112,875	–10,606
Clinical Supplies	$98,784	8	4	–$49,392	$64,500	–$34,284

net revenue were nearer the benchmark, we could potentially afford to pay our physicians more money and our support staff costs come right in line. Building occupancy would be much closer to reasonable levels. Our clinical supplies (our only short-term variable expense in the illustration) would still need some attention from a cost control standpoint compared to benchmark.

SUMMARY

The success of a medical practice is ultimately based on high clinical quality, high service quality, and high physician productivity, all of which ultimately yield financial viability. As we analyze struggling practices, one or more of these business imperatives is always implicated. The solutions to poor performance always lie in the correction of aberrations in these business imperatives.

Performance improvement starts with performance measurement in all four areas. In an era of consumer-driven healthcare, evidence-based medicine, and pay-for-performance, just having a medical degree will not be enough to demonstrate value. Providers of medical services will increasingly be held accountable to prove their value by measuring their performance against indicators or benchmarks identifying acceptable performance levels and then reporting that performance to payers and to the public. More importantly, the success of every practice in the face of reduced reimbursement and increasing costs depends on successful implementation of tactics for all four business imperatives.

Incorporating the new PQRI indicators, patient service indicators, referral source satisfaction indicators, physician (and other provider) productivity indicators, and financial indicators into the normal reporting process will be critical for the successful medical practice of the future. These indicators do not have to be overly complex, but must be reported consistently and interpreted correctly, and poor performance must be addressed appropriately. Physician leaders and managers should use the four business imperatives as filters for every policy, every procedure, every capital investment, and every operating decision in the practice setting.

NOTES

1. Centers for Medicare and Medicaid Services. April 5, 2007. *2007 Physician Quality Reporting Initiative (PQRI), National Clearinghouse Call*. Available at: http://www.cms.hhs.gov/PQRI/30_EducationalResources.asp#TopOfPage. Accessed May 24, 2007.

2. Anderson, Peter B. 2005. *Liberating the Family Physician: The Handbook of Team Care for 21st Century Family Medicine*. Newport News, VA: Riverside Health System.

3. Halley, Marc D. 2007. *The Primary Care—Market Share Connection: How Hospitals Achieve Competitive Advantage*. Chicago, IL: Health Administration Press.

4. Guadagnino, Christopher. 2003. "Role of Patient Satisfaction." *Physician News Digest* (December): 9.

5. Medical Group Management Association. 2006. *Physician Compensation and Production Survey, 2006*. Englewood, CO: Medical Group Management Association.

CHAPTER 4

Building a Culture of Accountability in Physician Practices

Marc D. Halley

The challenges to a successful medical practice include lower reimbursement, shortages of qualified labor and the associated labor costs, higher malpractice premiums, an increasing administrative burden, and many others. These challenges are felt in solo settings, in small group practices, and in large multispecialty groups. Many practices struggle along, month after month, just to make payroll and to provide the physicians with a reasonable income. Few medical practices reserve enough excess cash to cover even their depreciation, let alone to invest in strategic opportunities.

Many practices have difficulty funding retirement savings or providing competitive benefits for physicians and staff. Some practices succumb to these challenges. Others limp along, with physicians working harder and harder just to maintain past earnings levels. There are a few medical practices, however, that seem to weather these storms without losing ground. In fact, they are exceptional in terms of clinical performance, customer service, physician productivity, and financial outcomes. They may be located in the same communities, even in the same office buildings, and have the same specialty as their less successful peers. Nevertheless, there is something significant about these exceptional practices. After years of experience consulting with numerous practices we have found that the most significant factor influencing exceptional practices is what we call *a culture of accountability*.

WHAT IS A CULTURE OF ACCOUNTABILITY?

Several factors that define a culture of accountability were discussed by this author in a 2005 article:[1]

- *Effective sponsorship:* Sponsorship is a term used by Daryl Conner to describe those organizational leaders who can support and push through organizational change.[2]

- *A common purpose:* Exceptional medical groups have a very clear vision and purpose that is compelling enough to engage not only physicians, but also staff members despite potential differences of opinion around tactical implementation.
- *Clear performance targets, timelines, measurement, and consequences:* A compelling vision is not enough without short-term targets, timelines, and measures. In turn, without consequences, targets, timelines, and measures are useless exercises.
- *An effective implementation team:* In an effective practice, physician leaders set direction and approve policy. They then hire competent managers to implement (at a lower cost than a physician implementer).
- *"A" players:* Exceptional practices hire and retain only "A" players. They hire deliberately to make sure they get the best-qualified staff for the dollars they can pay.[3]
- *Frequent accountability:* The most successful practices frequently hold people accountable to deliver the targeted results within the timeline. Without frequent accountability, important tactics leading toward the common purpose are lost in the myriad of urgencies and emergencies that burden all of us on a daily basis.

These characteristics, indeed, do set exceptional organizations apart from their peers. The logical question, then, is how do practices become exceptional? This chapter further defines accountability, identifies common barriers to accountability in medical practices, and discusses implementation tactics.

ACCOUNTABILITY TO WHOM?

We often think of accountability only in terms of "the boss," a parent, or someone else in authority. Ultimately, however, all of us who offer products or services are accountable to our customers. In fact, successful individuals and organizations understand, intrinsically or otherwise, that meeting the needs, wants, and priorities of their customers is essential to their success in a competitive setting.[4] For a primary care medical practice, the customer is usually the patient. If the patient requires a parent or guardian to participate in decision making, that individual is also a customer.

Understanding and meeting not only the clinical *needs* of these customers, but also their reasonable *wants* and *priorities,* is the focus of effective customer service and should be the basis for building a culture of accountability. A specialty medical practice certainly has the same patient and parent or guardian as customers. In addition, the specialist is likely to have a referring physician whose needs, wants, and priorities must be acknowledged and consistently met if the practice is going to prosper in a competitive environment. We are ultimately accountable to our customer.

ACCOUNTABILITY COMPONENTS

An accountability culture includes three major components: assigning responsibility, enabling, and an accounting. All three components must be focused on meeting the needs, wants, and priorities of customers in a successful medical practice.

Assigning Responsibility

Allocating the work is one of the fundamental responsibilities of management. The way work is allocated has a great deal to do with the success of the incumbents. For example, certain tasks, such as greeting patients or answering the telephone, require repetitive, largely automatic actions on the part of staff members. Other activities, such as completing a performance appraisal form or researching a rejected insurance claim, require a level of focus, concentration, and thought. Mixing activities that require concentration with those that require an automatic response is likely to result in an inadequate response, reduced productivity, and a higher error rate.

For example, a receptionist's responsibility often includes greeting patients and answering the telephone. If we also assign that same receptionist a stack of rejected claims to research by day's end we will likely end up with alienated patients and research errors—not to mention a frustrated staff member who is being asked to accomplish the impossible. Holding people accountable to accomplish impossible or conflicting tasks is a prescription for poor performance and low morale. It is the fault of management rather than the fault of the employee.

Properly assigning tasks and responsibilities also requires an understanding of the primary and support roles found in a medical office. Primary roles are those that directly affect the patient's treatment or experience in the office. Those roles are receptionist (or patient service representative), the physician, and the clinical assistant. All other roles, including the manager, are support to the primary roles. Jobs should be designed and tasks allocated in such a way as to promote the success of the primary roles.

For example, a wise manager will keep the receptionist in a busy practice focused on greeting patients, verifying insurance information, completing paperwork, and monitoring the reception area. Tasks that can distract the receptionist from these duties are shifted, if possible, to other practice staff. As a primary role, the clinical assistant should be focused on greeting patients, taking vital signs, monitoring examination rooms, and managing the physician's productivity. All other duties should be delegated where possible, including referral calls, which can each take several minutes to complete. Finally, the physician should do what only physicians can do and should delegate all other tasks to less expensive resources. With these three primary roles properly focused on the customer and on delivering quality service, the patient's experience is enhanced, as is the productivity of the physician—the most expensive resource in the practice. Simply having the clinical assistant near the examination room each time a physician opens the door, rather than on the phone, has a very positive impact on patient flow and physician productivity. We call this process "highest and best use staffing."

Effective delegation of tasks and short-term assignments also falls under the responsibility component. Selecting appropriate tasks to delegate, matching the human resource to the task in terms of ability, properly assigning the task, engaging the delegate in defining the process of completing the project, and establishing timeframes are all essential components of delegation.

Enabling

Enabling people to carry out their assigned responsibilities is another critical component of a culture of accountability. Enabling includes authorizing people or giving them the authority or permission to act. Authorizing is external to the job incumbent. Authorizing includes letting others know that the delegate has been assigned a particular task, which facilitates its accomplishment. Enabling also includes training to ensure that the delegate has the skills necessary to succeed. Enabling also includes empowerment, which is an overused term that connotes ownership of a task by the delegate. Empowerment comes from within: I am authorized by my boss, but I *feel* empowered to take ownership of a task. Of necessity, enabling usually requires a level of decentralization, placing the authority at the point of service. Enabling also includes performance tracking, which is best done and reported by the delegate.

An Accounting

Accountability requires an accounting.[5] Most often what passes for an accounting is merely "story telling"—an explanation of the variance between actual performance and the expected outcome, with precious little focus on corrective action. An accounting requires a defined outcome and a timeline. It may also require an accounting of process or activity. An accounting is facilitated by regular opportunities to return and report. More complex projects may require action plans and a formal reporting of one's stewardship. An accounting asks, "If not, why not, and by when?" It records critical incidents of exceptional or inadequate performance, which ultimately contribute to the delegate's performance appraisal, as well as to rewards or consequences for behavior and accomplishments.

BARRIERS TO ACCOUNTABILITY

There are a number of common barriers to accountability in a medical practice setting. These barriers are often caused, intentionally or otherwise, by the physicians, support staff, or management. Common barriers include the following:

- *Short-term financial focus:* The focus of many group practice administrators is maximizing the quarterly bonuses of the physician owners. Exceptional practices have the discipline to forego some short-term gratification in favor of pursuing their mutual purpose. A short-term financial focus can, and often does, keep physicians and management from identifying and pursuing the right vision and targets.

- *Playing favorites:* Sometimes personal relationships undermine an accountability culture. Physicians may authorize managers to act until a favored employee complains or threatens to leave the practice. Then they undermine the manager and shatter morale of other staff members who are not so favored. Thereafter, it becomes very difficult for the manager to hold anyone else accountable for fear of reprisal.

- *Failure to act:* A major barrier to accountability, particularly in larger practices, is failure to act. Fear of change, political fallout, or failure may prevent the timely implementation of strategies, tactics, new policies, procedures, or projects. Without action there are no targets, timelines, or meaningful measures. Failure to act among organizational leaders is often manifest in calls for additional analysis, more planning meetings, and endless debates over potential outcomes. Such "leaders" focus on aiming rather than pulling the trigger in order to avoid the risk of making a mistake. (Unfortunately, there are also consequences for failure to act.)

- *Political, financial, or administrative bullies:* Organizational "bullies" are a major barrier to the accountability process in many types of organizations including medical practices. These bullies may have knowledge power, political power, or financial control, or they may have legal authority resulting from their position. Potential bullies include the surly surgeon who knows that he is responsible for putting millions of dollars on the practice and hospital books, which, in his mind, makes his opinion more important than his primary care peers who provide his patients. The list of bullies may also include the practice controller who depends on accrual accounting and control of the purse strings to support his preferred position. Bullies are sometimes so cantankerous that both physician peers (in the case of physician bullies) and managers (in the case of administration and support staff) are fearful of holding them accountable due to the emotional strain on the entire organization. Bullies stomp their way around organizations, killing innovation and driving out their talented peers. It is "their way or the highway" in meetings where little progress is made. Everyone, even the owners, is (or should be) accountable for his or her performance.

- *Data rich, information poor:* Thanks to computers, some organizations have reams of paper with numbers, charts, and graphs containing little meaningful information. Some managers are so focused on multiple ways of measuring where the organization has been (including color slides) that they never get around to helping physicians and staff members measure and improve their current daily performance.

- *Unrealistic expectations:* Closely related to the proper division of tasks and responsibilities is the barrier of unrealistic expectations. Physicians or managers who make unrealistic demands of their subordinates in terms of timeframes or who ask for performance miracles without providing resources violate the principles of a healthy accountability culture. This is not to say that leaders cannot occasionally ask staff members to rise to meet some significant challenge, but living a life of excessive demands and unrealistic expectations is disheartening and contributes to a culture of cynicism rather than accountability.

- *Program of the month:* Those who manage change in organizations often see employees and others hold out, hoping that the change will pass by with any accountability for implementation. Some physicians are the same way, ignoring the performance objectives, policies, and new procedures they approved in the last staff meeting. Some employees have become conditioned to give lip service to change initiatives while sabotaging their implementation by simply ignoring them. Consequently, potentially valuable initiatives like Total Quality Management or Six Sigma are simply forgotten once the initial training and hoopla are over.

- *"C" Players:* Bradford Smart discussed the concept of "C" players and the damage they cause in organizations.[6] Many organizations harbor "C" players rather than implementing consequences for their failure to perform. Some "C" players make their way into management positions, further limiting the organization's ability to develop a culture of accountability. "C" players don't deliver because they are not capable of and/or not interested in delivering the desired result.

- *Story telling—no rigor:* Where there is no rigor, there is no accountability. An accountability culture is rigorous at setting objectives and measuring performance. While line managers we interview can usually tell us *who* holds them accountable (i.e., they can point to their "boss" on an organization chart), many cannot tell us *what* they are currently being held accountable to accomplish or specifically *how* they are held accountable. Our question about the *what* often elicits a response that includes reference to the budget and coming up with a better story to explain the variance each month, instead of specific actions to correct performance problems and timelines for accomplishment. Responses to our question about *how* managers are held accountable rarely includes a discussion of regular formal reporting process and almost never includes clear consequences for failure.

- *Nice and fair (leniency bias):* Some physicians and managers prefer to be liked or to be nice, and perceive that holding others accountable might offend. Most of us want to be viewed as fair, and we prefer to be lenient with others and ourselves. Holding people accountable does not require one to be mean or nasty. It does, however, require one to be intellectually honest and motivated by correct principles. Exceptional practices are full of nice doctors, managers, and staff who have high expectations of each other and who hold each other accountable to meet those expectations.

- *No return or report:* Holding people accountable takes time and effort. Many managers will not invest that time because they feel that they are too busy themselves. Consequently, those who receive assignments are not required to return and report on their stewardships. Without frequent and formal reporting there is no accountability—only disappointment when the task is not completed on time or at all. A key to holding people accountable is taking time to ask them for a report of their progress. Asking for the report helps managers understand the effort or lack thereof, the barriers being encountered, and the expected outcomes. Formal reporting is an investment in the future of the employee for the benefit of the manager and the organization.

- *No target timeline, or consequence:* Failure to establish specific targets or clear timelines will undermine any form of accounting. Even if such targets and timelines are established, they are of little value if there is no consequence for failure to perform.
- *Conflict avoidance:* A major barrier to accountability is conflict avoidance on the part of organizational leaders. Failure to discuss the elephant in the room or to question the emperor's new wardrobe will contribute to lack of performance and lack of accountability.

CREATING THE CULTURE

Overcoming the barriers and building a culture of accountability starts with the leadership in a medical practice setting. Those who lead and govern (or *sponsor*) within the organization must have the courage and integrity to govern well. They must articulate a vision that will be compelling enough to engage every physician, manager, and staff member. They must always make decisions based on correct operating principles rather than on whim or personal agenda. As leaders, their motives must be unquestionable, even on those occasions when they make tactical errors.

If practice leadership is viewed as consistently trying to do the right thing for the practice and those it serves, it will be much easier for that commitment to filter down through the rest of the organizational hierarchy. Sponsors must be willing to ask the hard questions about tactics, policies, procedures, and direction. They must ensure that every decision improves or maintains quality clinical care, customer service, provider productivity, and financial viability. Fundamentally, sponsors must live the vision they articulate. Their personal actions and words must demonstrate their personal commitment to the direction and vision.

Case Study: Vision

The four new physicians at County Internal Medicine have developed strong practices over the past five years. They are located in a developing area of the community and have a solid clinical reputation on the medical staff of their local hospital. During their first few years of practice their focus has been on growth and meeting payroll. Now that their practices are very busy, the challenges of continuing to provide high-quality care and caring have surfaced. Physicians and staff members are sometimes overwhelmed with the sheer volume of patients and paperwork. In recent months, the doctors have received several complaints about poor access, long waits, and grouchy staff members. They and their practice manager have emphasized the importance of "being nice" in every staff meeting, but the complaints continue. The manager recently reported several chart requests for patients who have transferred to the new hospital-owned internal medicine practice in the area. The doctors decide that it is time to take action to protect their future.

County Internal Medicine has established a vision to capitalize on their reputation for clinical quality and to become the premier internal medicine practice in the community. They have defined their future in terms of practice size, locations, patient access, financial viability and, most importantly, *customer* experience. This vision has been documented in writing, and support staff have been asked to enhance the vision to ensure that their "fingerprints" are on the document.

The physicians have been very clear about their commitment to the vision, with each other, with their manager, and with their support staff. They have expressed their commitment to leave no stone unturned in pursuit of that vision, including spending capital dollars to facilitate improved performance. They will examine policies, procedures, and processes to ensure that they are all supportive of their written vision. Every individual has been asked to personally contribute ideas and effort to the cause.

Once a compelling vision has been established and communicated, the entire organization, every department, and individual must consider their contribution to achieving that vision. The practice managers play a significant role to ensure that each individual and department defines and understands its contribution to the vision, and develops tactics as well as performance targets and timelines to support those tactics. Once targets and timelines have been developed, individuals and departments are asked to develop measures of their progress.

Case Study: Practice and Individual Objectives

The physicians and office manager of County Internal Medicine have selected certain practice-wide initiatives they believe will help achieve the vision (e.g., opening the office at 8:00 A.M. rather than 8:30 A.M.). The office manager has been instructed to work with each individual to ensure that he or she understands the vision and the practice-wide initiatives, and has established one or more performance targets in his or her areas of responsibility in support of those objectives (e.g., the receptionist attempting to call each patient by name). Each target must be accompanied by a timeline and a clear method by which the employee will measure and report his or her own performance. The manager records the practice-wide initiatives and the individual commitments on an action plan for weekly review by the physicians.

Fortunately, the front office staff members have a wonderful esprit de corps and are very excited about setting and achieving objectives to help their practice continue to prosper. The receptionist has set a goal to call each patient by name as he or she arrives at the front desk. This seems like a daunting task given the 80 to 100 patients who visit the practice each day. The manager and the front office staff members work together to discuss barriers to achieving this customer service objective. Recognizing the critical customer service role played by the receptionist, the switchboard operator, the cashier, the appointments specialist, and medical records clerk all offer suggestions to overcome the barriers, including removing certain tasks that distract the receptionist from her primary responsibility. The receptionist uses the appointment schedule to help determine the patient's name and develops scripts to "apologize" when she makes a mistake (turning lemons into lemonade). The receptionist keeps track of her successes and reports them to the manager and to her front office peers at the end of each day. The patient suggestion box in the reception room also provides objective feedback on the results of her efforts.

We have found that weekly follow-up is a critical part of the accountability process. Why weekly? The answer is simple. We are all so busy reacting to the myriad of *urgent* activities, assignments, responsibilities, and challenges of the normal workday that we often fail to think about issues that are the most *important* to our future. Weekly accountability is a reminder of those *important* items and our commitments to make progress on critical initiatives to secure our future. It is also an opportunity for the manager to check on barriers being encountered by the incumbent and to help facilitate removal of those barriers to successful implementation. Importantly, it is also a critical opportunity to make sure that the employee is on the right track toward achieving the objectives he or she has selected.

Case Study: Weekly Accountability

The County Internal Medicine physicians have decided to meet with their office manager on a weekly basis to ensure that the critical practice-wide and individual initiatives contained in their action plan remain on track. (Once they are confident that adequate progress is being made, they may choose to meet less often.) They have instructed their manager to visit with each staff member on a weekly basis to ensure that progress is being made on their individual contributions to the success of the whole. The manager is expected to report progress on each action item each week.

As the implementation process continues, progress is carefully monitored by the manager and the physicians. Accomplishments are openly celebrated in monthly staff meetings, with physicians expressing their thanks for the progress being made. Lack of progress and failures are carefully evaluated to determine whether the source is systemic (e.g., a policy/procedure, job design, or staffing), technical (e.g., facilities or equipment), a challenge with the human resource (e.g., training, capability, or motivation), or some combination of these barriers. Actions are identified to rectify the barriers encountered and recorded on the action plan along with a timeline and responsible party. Those actions may include changes in any or all of the factors involved, including the human resource.

Case Study: Action Orientation

The manager of County Internal Medicine has determined that the person selected to manage the telephones for this busy office is struggling to keep up with this significant responsibility. Several programming changes have been made to ensure that the telephone system is efficient, user-friendly, and customer-friendly. It has been suggested that the office switch to an electronic attendant to help route the calls, but the physicians feel strongly that this option is in conflict with their vision of customer service. Even with training and system changes the incumbent is unable to keep up with the increasing pace of the office. Another receptionist is asked to try the switchboard role and proves to be much more effective than the incumbent. The roles are adjusted, correcting the telephone issues, but creating other performance concerns at the front desk. After careful consideration, it is determined that the former switchboard operator is no longer a good fit for the busy office and she is terminated according to practice human resource policies.

Weekly "stand-up" staff meetings are held for a few minutes once each week before the office opens. During these sessions support staff members literally stand in a hallway and raise any significant performance barriers or customer service issues that have surfaced. Stand-up staff meetings may take only a few minutes, and may only focus on one practice-wide initiative, but they can improve the performance of staff during the entire week. All-staff meetings are held at least monthly with the physicians, the manager, and support staff members all in attendance to review performance, action plan progress, and other critical issues that arise. There is a spirit of cooperation and mutual respect, with physicians and the manager listening carefully to the suggestions of even the least experienced staff member. The manager facilitates the meeting and all attendees participate without fear of reprisal for sharing a minority opinion.

Case Study: Communication

The physicians and office manager of County Internal Medicine have established formal communication channels to keep the vision and objectives in front of all members of the team. Through weekly stand-up staff meetings, the manager listens to current feedback on performance and barriers to practice success. The manager is also sensitive to small irritations that often appear between departments, which, if unaddressed, can fester until they become very apparent to patients and damaging to productivity. At least once each month the physicians, the manager, and the staff meet for an hour-long session to openly celebrate successes and to discuss challenges and failures. The physicians and manager are introspective, each looking first at him or herself regarding his or her potential contribution to performance problems. The physicians and manager have also learned to listen carefully to those who do the work, realizing that the staff often have the answers to perplexing challenges in the medical office setting. No one is bullied or censored for expressing an opinion, especially if it varies from the majority thought. As the holders of knowledge power in the practice, the physicians are careful to protect the open communication they have fostered. The group openly reviews their successes and failures, identifying opportunities for individual and organization learning.

Success is always acknowledged and, where feasible, accompanied by rewards ranging from a simple "thank you" to small gifts such as movie tickets or gift cards, as well as occasional performance bonuses. Likewise, consequences (including termination) for consistent failure to perform are fairly and consistently administered.

Case Study: Rewards and Consequences

As performance improves at County Internal Medicine the physicians are careful to express their gratitude to the group. They also acknowledge individuals for their contribution to the whole and for their individual achievements. The action plan document helps ensure that physicians recognize the contributors to their success. Acknowledgments include personal thanks, notes copied to the employee's file (which reappear at appraisal time), movie tickets, gift cards, and other trinkets. The physicians have established a small bonus pool based on the success of the practice. The bonus pool target is $500 per employee. The pool is distributed just before the holidays as a special acknowledgement of group and individual effort. During years when the practice is extremely successful, the physicians may choose to increase the pool. Other years, the physician owners may reduce or eliminate the pool. The physicians always include their accountant (as an outside objective counselor) to help them determine the size of the bonus pool each year.

As illustrated earlier, the physicians and management are not unwilling to make the difficult decision to remove "C" players from the practice in order to protect their customers and their "A" players. These consequences are always carefully but consistently applied so they are perceived to be fair and equitable.

INDICATORS OF A CULTURE OF ACCOUNTABILITY

A healthy accountability culture is not achieved quickly. Cultural change can take months or years, even in a small practice setting. Regardless, the practices that pursue a culture of accountability begin to benefit almost immediately from the effort. Figure 4.1 presents a Culture of Accountability Self-Assessment that we have applied to many of our physician practice clients. It focuses on 6 primary

Figure 4.1 Culture of Accountability Self-Assessment

Halley Consulting Group
Strategy and Performance Improvement for Physician Networks

CULTURE OF ACCOUNTABILITY

A SELF ASSESSMENT

Indicator	Evidence	Action Step
We Have Adequate "Sponsorship" Of Organizational Initiatives	1. Sponsorship is evident at all levels within the organization.	
	2. We set realistic performance targets based upon sound analysis.	
	3. Our leadership is publicly committed to our initiatives, including the establishment of a performance target, a timeline for achievement and a consequence for failure.	
	4. Our leadership identifies and eliminates barriers to performance improvement as identified by implementers.	
	5. Our leaders actively hold themselves accountable on a monthly basis consistent with the financial cycle.	
We Delegate Effectively	6. Our managers can be absent with only limited effect.	
	7. Our implementers are not all managers.	
	8. Our managers have trained their replacements	
	9. We retain our "A" players.	

Culture of Accountability
A Self Assessment

© The Halley Consulting Group, LLC
www.halleyconsulting.com
Page 1 of 3

Indicator	Evidence	Action Step
	10. The organization benefits from innovative work the management team did not personally accomplish.	
	11. We achieve measurable results.	
We Are Results-Oriented	12. We have clearly defined outcomes that are understood by all stakeholders.	
	13. Our leadership meetings focus on progress toward results, rather than process or structure.	
	14. Our progress reports include root causes of barriers to performance.	
	15. We strictly avoid "story telling."	
	16. We are introspective in success or failure.	
We Measure for Accountability	17. Our desired results have been quantified for individuals, for teams and for the organization as a whole.	
	18. We have identified internal and external benchmarks for performance comparison.	
	19. We are rigorous in tracking our actual performance against benchmarks.	
	20. We track and frequently report our progress and barriers to our sponsors and stakeholders.	
We Ask For An Accounting	21. We all expect to work for a living and to be held accountable for our performance.	
	22. We have a formal mechanism for asking implementers whether or not they have achieved the desired results.	

Culture of Accountability
A Self Assessment

Source: The Halley Consulting Group, LLC, used with permission.

indicators and 30 specific pieces of evidence by which a practice holds itself and its members accountable. Such a checklist can be useful in providing an initial baseline, as well as a measure of progress.

CONCLUSION

A culture of accountability is achieved by the best-performing practices through consistent commitment to the effort. The results for customers, physicians, management, and staff members are well worth the effort in terms of clinical quality, service quality, provider productivity, and the resulting financial performance. In my experience, employee morale is higher in a busy top-performing office where staff members feel committed, are held accountable, and are appreciated for their performance.

NOTES

1. Halley, M. 2005. "A Culture of Accountability: What Distinguishes an Exceptional Medical Group." *Group Practice Journal* 54 (3): 11–14.

2. Conner, D. R. 1992. *Managing at the Speed of Change: How Resilient Managers Succeed and Prosper Where Others Fail.* New York: Villard Books.

    3.   Smart, B. D. 1999. *TopGrading: How Leading Companies Win by Hiring, Coaching, and Keeping the Best People*. New York: Prentice Hall.
    4.   Halley, M. 2005. "A Culture of Accountability: What Distinguishes an Exceptional Medical Group." *Group Practice Journal* 54 (3): 11–14.
    5.   Ibid.
    6.   Smart, B. D. 1999. *TopGrading: How Leading Companies Win by Hiring, Coaching, and Keeping the Best People*. New York: Prentice Hall.

CHAPTER 5

Managing Difficult and Disruptive Physicians

Larry Harmon and Susan Lapenta

Disruptive, intimidating, or abusive behavior may increase the likelihood of errors by leading nurses, residents, or colleagues to avoid the disruptive physician, to hesitate to ask for help or clarification of orders, and to hesitate to make suggestions about patient care.... Consequently, disruptive behavior by physicians not only threatens patient safety but has a corrosive effect on morale, making life miserable for the nurses and residents who work closely with these physicians.[1]

In a survey conducted by the American College of Physician Executives in 2004, 95 percent of the physician leaders who responded to the survey reported that they "routinely" have to deal with the behavior of disruptive practitioners.[2] Physician leaders often identify disruptive behavior as a great distraction and a source of incredible frustration. In addition, these disruptive practitioners drive away valuable nurses and negatively affect both the operation of the organization and patient care.[3]

Physician and hospital leaders have long struggled with effective ways to turn around disruptive practitioners, frequently without any long-lasting success. This chapter describes pitfalls that physician leaders can avoid and reviews various approaches for managing and rehabilitating disruptive physicians, using a case presentation that follows. (See Table 5.1 for an overview.) Recommendations include the use of formal workplace assessment and annual physician feedback reports. These can also be used to provide behavioral education and monitoring.

WHO IS THE DISRUPTIVE PRACTITIONER?

Behaviorally, disruptive practitioners have much in common.[4] Irritable and snappy, they scream at health care staff and sometimes at colleagues. Arrogant

Table 5.1
Top Six Steps for Dealing with Disruptive Physicians

1. Implement prevention programs
   a. Create a Code of Conduct
   b. Prepare annual physician survey feedback reports
   c. Train leaders on how to deal constructively with behavioral issues
2. Try informal intervention
   a. Review documentation and history of prior actions and incidents and actions taken
   b. Prepare for and perform a collegial intervention
   c. Consider taking progressive disciplinary measures
3. Perform a formal workplace assessment
   a. Interview complainants and witnesses; prepare investigative report
   b. Conduct structured workplace behavior assessment with team members and prepare report and recommendations
   c. Impose Personalized Code of Conduct with clearly articulated expectations and consequences
4. Require remedial action
   a. Basic educational program—physician feedback survey assessment and/or anger education program
   b. Group psycho-educational interactive program
5. Continue to monitor compliance with Personalized Code of Conduct
   a. Passive monitoring: watch and wait for complaints
   b. Active monitoring: ongoing, periodic physician survey feedback program
6. Take disciplinary action
   a. Follow bylaws in taking disciplinary action, including investigation, hearing, and appeal
   b. Personalized Code of Conduct may narrow rights
   c. Continue to review quality concerns raised by disruptive practitioner

and obnoxious, they often upset others with their bad manners and rudeness. They can be passive-aggressive when asked to do things such as returning a document or signing a letter. They are typically defensive about even the most constructive of criticism and can quickly overreact to a team member's smallest mistake. They almost never admit to being wrong, frequently blame others for their own mistakes, and always think they are right.

When the disruptive practitioner undergoes psychological personality testing, the findings often reveal a practitioner who has compulsive, histrionic, or narcissistic features.[5] Some of the most common words to describe the disruptive practitioner are: arrogant, tenacious, energetic, controlling, charismatic, intimidating, and explosive. At the same time, the disruptive practitioner may be perceived as one of the best and brightest in the hospital, and may have one of the largest practices.[6]

PROBLEMS IN MANAGING DISRUPTIVE PHYSICIANS

Rule No. 1: Do Not Treat the Disruptive Physician Like an Impaired Physician.
Disruptive physicians differ from impaired physicians because their main problem is not caused by an underlying disorder but, rather, they display unacceptable

workplace behavior.[5] Therefore, instead of clinical evaluations, management of disruptive physicians involves assessing and addressing their behavior, both for prevention and for remediation.

Two mistakes are often made when managing disruptive physicians. First, leaders treat the disruptive physician like an impaired physician without documentation of any specific disorder. Second, they use informal, undocumented means to address the problem.

The first approach is followed because, historically, physician leaders used the impaired practitioner model to address concerns about disruptive conduct.[6] This approach usually included requiring the disruptive physician to undergo a clinical mental health evaluation, typically performed by a psychiatrist in the community. The problem with this approach is that often the evaluator had only a few, if any, documented incident reports on which to rely. Therefore, the disruptive practitioner could easily counteract the evaluator's limited background information by painting a distorted but persuasive picture of himself—minimizing disruptive conduct and presenting himself as a caring, but demanding, physician who just wanted the best for his patients.

Even when the evaluation is more comprehensive (e.g., two to five days) and is performed at a well-established, specialized program, the program can still be handicapped without detailed documentation or a formal, objective workplace assessment. Thus, these programs are still vulnerable to being "snowed" by the bright, articulate, difficult, and disruptive practitioner.

Even experienced evaluators may have difficulty finding a clinical diagnosis, or only vague subclinical levels of personality disorders, like narcissistic features. Thus, as a general rule, clinical evaluations are discouraged when dealing with a disruptive practitioner who presents no evidence of impairment such as psychiatric disorder, substance abuse, or physical health conditions.[1]

An exception to this general rule of avoiding clinical evaluations is when there is evidence of a disorder or when there are clear warning signs of acute impairment. Physical violence or threats are almost always associated with impairment. Other examples of possible impairment include rapid personality changes; bipolar disorder, which might be demonstrated by accelerated talking or extreme grandiosity, followed by sluggishness, depression, or tearfulness; and alcohol or drug abuse. These complaints can be handled initially through the medical staff's Practitioner Health Committee and are typically followed up by a referral to the state's Physician Health Program. When in doubt about whether the issue is the result of conduct or condition, a discussion with corporate counsel or with your state's physician health program may help determine the appropriate route to take.

Rule No. 2: In Dealing with a Disruptive Physician, Remember to Document, Document, Document.

The second mistake in managing disruptive physicians is failing to document both concerns and the progressive steps taken to address those concerns. Often, physician leaders ignore behavioral issues or handle them in such a way that the message to stop the bad behavior gets muffled and lost in the translation. Even when physician leaders do take appropriate action, they may be reluctant to document that action. When leadership turns over, the disruptive physician gets a new lease on life and often the cycle of difficult behavior repeats itself.

PREVENTING DISRUPTIVE BEHAVIOR: START WITH A CODE OF CONDUCT

Traditionally, hospitals and medical staffs assumed that every physician appointed to the staff understood the culture of the organization and would play by the rules. Over time, it has become clear that even the most basic expectations about conduct are not universally shared.[7] The Code of Conduct Policy is an effective way to define unacceptable behavior, and thus establish community expectations. As many organizations have discovered, it is easier to deal with behavioral issues when there is a policy in place. Then, a determination of whether conduct is unacceptable is less subjective, and thus less personal. No one gets singled out, and everyone is expected to conform to clearly articulated behavior standards.

In addition to providing clear examples of behavior that is not acceptable, the Code of Conduct Policy addresses how incidents of disruptive behavior are reported, what is included in the report, and who receives the report. The Code of Conduct Policy also outlines the process for addressing reports of disruptive conduct.

PREVENTING DISRUPTIVE BEHAVIOR: AN ANNUAL "PHYSICIAN LEADERSHIP FEEDBACK REPORT"

Once a Code of Conduct has been established, compliance with this code can be assessed and feedback given to physicians with a Physician Leadership Feedback Report. These report cards, generated by periodic 360-degree survey feedback assessments, provide an early warning system that enables both the physician and leadership to recognize and resolve conduct problems *before* more serious incidents occur, thus serving a preventative function. They also document any existing disruptive behavior problems.

Feedback reports provide an additional benefit. Since it is often difficult to find methods to identify and the time to acknowledge the "delightful docs," the feedback report validates those who exemplify positive teamwork and leadership skills that inspire and motivate others to do their best work. Formal physician feedback is an important tool to help identify what these physicians are doing right and motivate and encourage them to continue as facility role models.

Through the use of behavioral surveys and feedback, these report cards provide a formal monitoring system. When generated on an annual or more frequent basis, they can serve preventative, educational, and assessment functions.

There are a number of online survey companies that a facility may use to create a customized survey, administer it at low cost, and then use the results to help prevent, identify, and monitor disruptive behavior, as well as develop physician leadership and teamwork skills. Alternatively, some firms, for example, the Physicians Development Program with which one of the authors is associated (Larry Harmon), have developed an automated 360-degree protocol in which physicians are reminded annually to enroll online. The protocol updates their list of team members providing feedback, and surveys physicians and their team members, automatically generating a report and e-mailing it to the physician several weeks later.

TRAIN LEADERS TO DEAL WITH BEHAVIORAL PROBLEMS

Physician leaders typically have an intuitive sense of how to deal with their colleagues who exhibit clinical problems. However, behavioral problems can be more challenging. As mentioned above, it is important to have an institutional Code of Conduct Policy to serve as a guide to leaders in defining disruptive behavior and providing steps to follow in addressing concerns.

The use of a Physician Leadership Feedback Report will also make addressing behavioral concerns more routine and at least make behavior a factor to consider in granting reappointment and renewal of privileges.[8]

THE COLLEGIAL INTERVENTION

The collegial intervention is typically the first step used to address a disruptive incident. These interventions can be difficult with the disruptive practitioner and are best conducted with planning and practice. The following format provides an overview of steps for you to consider as part of the collegial intervention.

Preliminarily, it is helpful to interview the individual(s) who prepared the incident report or complaint. This will help you have a better understanding of what actually happened. It is also useful to review the physician's file to determine if there have been previous complaints and what, if any, action was taken in regard to them.

The next step is to review the record with the disruptive physician, describing the documented incidents, as well as any corrective efforts the facility has required as a consequence of these incidents. Expect defensiveness at this point. The physician is likely to vent her frustrations and blame others. Make a record of her complaints by writing them down at this time.

Make an effort to restate her complaints, letting her know that you have heard her frustration and concerns by repeating a summary of the complaints from her perspective. For example, "You're frustrated because x, and y, and z." Reading from notes may be the most convenient way to mirror back the frustrations. It may also be helpful to ask if there are any more concerns. At this point, the physician leader should transition from the physician's frustrations to the incident that, of course, is the primary focus of the meeting. The leader may want to indicate that the physician's frustrations are important to the leader and that another meeting for that topic may be scheduled.

In the meantime, it is important to refocus the conversation to the purpose of the meeting, which is the incident and the requirement that the physician alter behavior in the future. The leader must define this purpose, indicating that the leader and physician must come up with a plan of action to avoid any further complaints.

Since the physician may still be defensive, it is important to reassure her that she is valued and that the goal is to keep her on staff, but without any additional complaints. Acknowledging the physician's technical or professional strengths at this point can reduce tension. Overall, the success of the collegial intervention is often tied to the degree of planning and preparation, along with patience and support. It is important to remember that the physician's initial reaction of defiant denial often gives way to a later response of reluctant compliance.

To sum up:

1. Review the record.
2. Restate the physician's complaints.
3. Focus on the purpose of the meeting, which is to encourage the physician to alter future behavior.
4. Reassure the physician.
5. Refer for assessment or educational intervention.

FORMAL INTERVENTIONS FOR THE CHRONIC DISRUPTIVE PHYSICIAN

The collegial intervention process is typically repeated, sometimes involving other leaders within the organization, and may include an educational referral to an anger management program, a behavioral coach, or an educational group program for disruptive physicians. If the physician's disruptive behavior continues, it is recommended that the facility follow a four-step model, including: (1) assessment; (2) feedback; (3) education; and (4) monitoring.

INDIVIDUAL ASSESSMENT PROTOCOL FOR PHYSICIANS DEMONSTRATING DISRUPTIVE BEHAVIOR

One method for objectively intervening when a physician's behavior continues to be disruptive is to enroll the physician in a physician feedback program (PFP). A good PFP will provide an objective survey assessment of both the disruptive behavior and its negative impact on the healthcare team. One example of a PFP is the P.U.L.S.E. (Physicians Universal Leadership-teamwork Skills Education) program, developed by one of the authors (Larry Harmon), which uses an assessment method similar to the 360-degree survey feedback approach widely used for management development. The survey's feedback report was also designed to help the physician more clearly understand the nature and impact of her disruptive behavior, and to increase leadership and teamwork skills.

The P.U.L.S.E. survey was developed and validated by having nurses, residents, physician assistants, and other health care staff identify and rate the behaviors of physicians and other leaders that *motivate* them to do their best work and behaviors that *disrupt* them in doing their best work. Their feedback generated a survey with 42 items that measures motivating (e.g., "Treats team members with respect") and disruptive behavior patterns (e.g., "Gets sarcastic when asked important questions") plus items that assess their impact on the healthcare team (e.g., "Discourages others from asking important questions").

The most common method to conduct the program for an individual physician is to use an on-line, three-phase process. The first step in the process is enrollment—the allegedly disruptive practitioner enrolls in the program, rates himself on the survey, and then creates an initial list of the names of nurses, supervisors, and colleagues with whom he works. The hospital and medical staff leadership then review and validate the list, adding any missing individuals to create a more representative sample of the physician's work teams and supervisors.

Second, surveys are e-mailed to the individuals on the final rater list, along with an explanation of the physician's participation in a physician leadership development program. The raters are invited to provide honest feedback and the surveys are anonymous, which helps ensure candid responses.

Third, all the surveys are scored compared to physician norms, and a detailed feedback report is prepared. The report graphically displays how the practitioner scores herself, comparing her score to how each group (for example, hospital staff and other physicians) collectively rates the physician in question. Individual behavior items are also color-coded for clarity and emphasis. For example, disruptive behaviors in critically high ranges are highlighted in red and behaviors in favorable ranges are highlighted in green. A more detailed interpretive report analyzes the degree of disruptive behavior and identifies which behaviors are creating a hostile work environment for the healthcare team. Specific recommendations can be offered to improve workplace conduct.

APPLICATION OF A PHYSICIAN ASSESSMENT REPORT: CREATING A PERSONALIZED CODE OF CONDUCT FOR THE DISRUPTIVE PHYSICIAN

One of the tools that can be used to manage a disruptive physician is a Personalized Code of Conduct. The goal of the Personalized Code of Conduct is to outline and prohibit specific behaviors that have been problematic in the past. Since background documentation is often vague, unsystematically collected, or poorly written, the feedback report can provide a detailed evaluation. Using the language from the assessed behaviors listed in the feedback report, the practitioner can be placed on notice to stop the specific, measurable behaviors that are inappropriate and unacceptable. For example, Dr. Disruptive's Personalized Code of Conduct included a requirement that he avoid any the following behaviors: Yelling and swearing at others, overreacting to small mistakes, threatening retaliation when angry, and insulting others over minor problems. In addition, any educational or other corrective actions, such as the ones described below, should be specified.

It can also be helpful to build behavioral coaching or mentoring into the Personalized Code of Conduct, which should be scheduled from weekly to monthly at the beginning of the process and perhaps less frequently as sustained behavior improvement occurs. The frequency can be adjusted to help address any backsliding, reinforce positive changes, and provide feedback on the surveys. The goal is not to turn the physician into a charming or popular Dr. Delightful, but rather to teach the practitioner how to behave appropriately and stay, so to speak, under the radar.

Another important component of the Personalized Code of Conduct is to identify for the practitioner the consequences if he fails to abide by the terms of the code. In all but the most extreme situations, the final discipline imposed following a breach of the Personalized Code of Conduct should be tailored to fit the "crime." However, the Personalized Code of Conduct can identify a range of options that may result, including short-term suspension, long-term suspension, or termination of privileges.

The Personalized Code of Conduct should also make it clear that any fair hearing and appeal that would follow a violation would be limited in scope to the particular violation at issue. Thus, the focus of any hearing would be on whether the current conduct in question breached the Personalized Code of Conduct. This kind of limited focus can help ensure that the hearing does not get off track and take on a life of its own.

EDUCATIONAL RECOMMENDATIONS

It is important to articulate in the Personalized Code of Conduct or other corrective action any specific requirements for rehabilitation. For example, the practitioner may try to fulfill a vague requirement of "anger management" by finding a one-hour reading assignment on the Internet that provides a certificate of completion. It is generally recommended that the disruptive practitioner participate in a training program designed for physicians and which includes an examination component to ensure that the practitioner actually understood and learned the materials.

Educational training to develop leadership, teamwork, anger management, and motivational management skills can be done remotely by the physician watching videotapes at home on evenings, weekends, or holidays. Some physicians prefer this approach because it avoids travel time, and that time can be applied to learning the materials more efficiently. One such program, developed by one of the authors, is called T.E.A.M. Training (Techniques for Emotional and Anger Management). Depending on the findings of the initial survey assessment, the T.E.A.M. Training may include: anger management, emotional self-discipline, skills for dealing with difficult people, and constructive management of medical mistakes. At the conclusion of the program, the physician can take a test on the

Physicians Development Program Web site and provide the referring facility a certificate of completion.

OTHER FORMAL INTERVENTIONS

The kind of training offered in a T.E.A.M. take-at-home educational format may be considered a first-line intervention because it does not involve the more interpersonal one-on-one contact that may be more intensive and necessary for some physicians to improve. If the remote survey assessment model has not worked, more intensive psycho-interactive programs as offered by some universities, like the three-day program for disruptive physicians at Vanderbilt's Center for Professional Health and the Health for the Healer program at the University of Alabama School of Medicine, may be worth considering.

If disruptive workplace behavior is severe enough to indicate the possibility of impairment, clinical evaluations may be warranted. Clinical evaluations are not recommended as a first-line intervention before attempts at behavioral assessment and education are made; however, behavior that may, for example, endanger patient safety should result in referral of the physician to the state's Physician Health Program. Clinical evaluations could result in a recommendation for outpatient or inpatient treatment. Outpatient treatment options typically include psychotherapy, group therapy, and/or medication management, while inpatient treatment might include psychiatric hospitalization and/or residential treatment.

FOLLOW-UP MONITORING OF THE PHYSICIAN'S PROGRESS WITH THE P.U.L.S.E. SURVEY

After the Personalized Code of Conduct is put in place, medical staff leaders often become distracted by other new and emerging problems and typically forget to monitor the practitioner's compliance with the code on an ongoing basis. Passively waiting for additional complaints is a poor practice because it doesn't ensure that the bad conduct has actually ceased, especially since staff often tire of reporting practitioners when they do not see any action being taken. Thus, without ongoing monitoring, while the situation may appear to have improved, the problem may still be simmering.

One of the critical components of any physician survey feedback program is to ensure that after the anger management or related training, the practitioner's compliance with the Personalized Code of Conduct is monitored by some active process, such as *ongoing* surveys. Healthcare team members can be asked to complete a survey on the practitioner periodically, a process called behavior monitoring or simply the physician's feedback program. The ongoing monitoring through the use of surveys continues until the practitioner has achieved a sustained period of acceptable feedback reports. *Acceptable* is defined as a feedback report in which all significant behaviors have been within normal ranges with no significant disruptive behaviors or negative impact on others.

GROUP PHYSICIAN FEEDBACK PROGRAMS

Physician feedback programs can be conducted with several physicians, a healthcare team, a department, or with the entire facility. Annual feedback, for example, to physicians serves preventative, educational, and assessment functions. On the preventative end, it provides an objective, early warning system, identifying potential problematic physicians prior to their behavior becoming chronic and entrenched. Physicians and their leaders can be alerted to emerging difficult, discouraging, and disruptive behaviors. Educationally, it functions as an early intervention program identifying those physicians who could benefit from improved leadership skills, and providing target behaviors for educational tools and interventions.

For assessment, it enables the chief of staff or other physician leader to conduct a collegial intervention with the support of objective documentation, thereby avoiding the typical "he said—she said" dilemma. If leadership wants to avoid singling out a particular physician, then a group or department can be surveyed. Once completed, a scatter plot can be prepared designating where each physician falls compared to his colleagues, thereby identifying the so-called bad apple.

An additional benefit is that objective, formal feedback provides physician leaders with the ability to provide collegial acknowledgment. The chief of staff or hospital leader can contact physicians scoring in motivating or highly favorable ranges, and she can provide the always-important pat on the back, encouragement, or recognition for being a strong leader or team player. Physicians especially value this feedback because it can be peer-based.

Ongoing annual use of a physician feedback program has further benefits. When the program is conducted over several years, it can provide a mechanism by which leadership can monitor improvement or backsliding, enabling leaders to either acknowledge the progress or warn the physician of chronic dysfunctional conduct or relapse. Finally, this kind of feedback program also educates and reinforces the Code of Conduct Policy, as well as communicates to each and every nurse, supervisor, and physician receiving the survey the set of behaviors this facility implicitly expects from its community members and healthcare team.

There are a number of ways of initiating an annual feedback program. A hospital can begin with employed physicians and later expand to community doctors. Other protocols could include physicians first giving feedback to nurses, and then vice versa. For example, the P.U.L.S.E. program has been used with individual physicians, single departments, and multiple departments in the same facility.

Physician feedback programs that do not require the physician to travel may be more user-friendly for the physician and the physician is probably more likely to agree to participate. For instance, nearly all physicians referred to the P.U.L.S.E. program survey assessment have agreed to participate. In spite of several collegial interventions, many physicians were genuinely unaware of the disruptiveness of their behavior. Either they believed the survey results would vindicate them or they were curious to find out what team members really think of them. If a physician is highly resistant, it may be because he has some questions or misconceptions about the protocol, and may first require some clarification about the mechanics before enrolling.

However, even if the practitioner refuses to participate, a workplace assessment can be done without his involvement by identifying the relevant supervisors, staff, and physician colleagues and then surveying these individuals. The results of the survey can then be used as a tool to help gain the physician's compliance with follow-up recommendations or could form the basis for a request for a more in-depth investigation.

Case Study: Introduction

Dr. Disruptive is an excellent cardiovascular surgeon with a stellar reputation for his clinical competency. He is also known for a history of disagreeable, discouraging, and difficult conduct over the past 10 years. Two or three times a year, the nurses and other health care staff either verbally complain or file written incident reports when Dr. Disruptive has outbursts of screaming and swearing. These behaviors often occur in situations where an "incompetent" nurse has supposedly overlooked a minor patient care task, when a lab result is "missing," or when Dr. Disruptive has been awakened late at night for what he labels a "stupid reason." He has never threatened or demonstrated physical aggression, but he can look flushed and red-faced, intimidating some nurses and technicians.

Over the years, Dr. Disruptive has had a number of informal collegial interventions with various chiefs of staff. His behavior typically improves for about two to three months. Almost always, this improvement is followed by a relatively minor incident, and then by a more serious one resulting in a formal incident report.

On several occasions, Dr. Disruptive has been asked to make his complaints directly to the nurse manager or director of nursing. So far, he has been reluctant to comply with this request, perhaps since he had a screaming match with the last director of nursing after his second collegial intervention. Some nurses have reported that Dr. Disruptive becomes so intensely enraged that, on occasion, his hands shake during surgery.

Over the years, Dr. Disruptive has been sent a letter of general warning and been called before the medical executive committee (MEC) several times to explain his behavior. The MEC also discussed referring him to the state's physician health program, but no action was ultimately taken. Additionally, at one point, the MEC wrote Dr. Disruptive a letter requesting him to attend an anger management program; however, the request was polite and vague, and no effort was made to follow up on whether he had actually done so. The chief executive officer (CEO) has also had two documented discussions with him to no avail.

There have been several consequences of Dr. Disruptive's behavior. Many nurses have said they are nervous and intimidated working with him. Some of the top operating room (OR) nurses have apparently quit and sought employment at the competing hospital, citing in their exit interviews Dr. Disruptive's abusive behavior as one of the chief reasons they left. Nurses have also said they have called in sick on the days Dr. Disruptive has cases. However, other, seasoned nurses brush off these complaints, saying, "That's just the way he is and he's never going to change. He does good work. Either accept him or get out."

When confronted with his behavior and the disruptive impact it has had on staffing and morale, Dr. Disruptive typically blames the nurses, defensively stating that if they were competent, he wouldn't get so mad. He frequently changes the topic to veiled threats of reporting the nurses to the board of nursing or reporting the hospital to Medicare. When confronted with his yelling, he insists that he did not yell, but rather he "spoke firmly." He denies that he has ever sworn, even though several nurses witnessed him saying "you stupid s***." When threatened with suspension, Dr. Disruptive angrily and defiantly challenges, "Go ahead and suspend me. I'll just go to the other hospital and I'll see you in court."

Case Study: Intervention

The medical executive committee reviewed Dr. Disruptive's history of inappropriate and abusive behavior toward nursing staff, and it decided that his behavior violated the hospital's Code of Conduct and standards of physician professionalism. They agreed to refer him to a physician feedback program in order to conduct an objective assessment to determine the nature and extent of any disruptive behavior, as well as the disruptive impact of his behavior on the healthcare team. Surveys were sent out to all healthcare team members and a feedback report was prepared which indicated the behaviors in critically high ranges, such as yelling and swearing at others, overreacting to small mistakes, threatening retaliation when angry, and insulting others over minor problems. A "watch-at-home" series of videotape modules on anger management, emotional intelligence, managing difficult people, and handling medical mistakes constructively was suggested. In addition, it was recommended that he participate in ongoing survey feedback until he achieved sustained reports indicating minimally appropriate conduct.

Upon reviewing his feedback report with the chief of staff, Dr. Disruptive was surprised at its level of negativity and was defensive, stating, "I'm the best surgeon in the OR. All I really care about is patient care. Doesn't anyone else think that's important? I'm not there to hold people's hands or sweet talk them. I'm there to save patients." The chief of staff pointed out that the disruptive impact caused by his abusive behavior—such as making nurses afraid to ask important questions or making them avoid working with him—may be one of the reasons they are more prone to misunderstandings and mistakes. Dr. Disruptive began to see that his behavior had been causing the very problems that frustrated him, and he also began to realize that applying contemporary motivational tools, for which he got low scores in his feedback report, might actually help motivate his team to perform better for him. He slowly understood that treating team members with respect, for example, by pointing out mistakes in a helpful way and trying to work out conflicts in more productive ways, might actually improve his relationship with the healthcare team, as well as help him reach his stated goal of providing the best care for his patients.

Dr. Disruptive grumbled about having to spend time watching videotapes, but appreciated that he could watch them at night and on weekends, and that he did not have to leave his practice to complete the training component. He decided to watch some of the videotapes with his wife, and she reinforced the importance of using the frustration management tool and the conflict techniques provided in the videotape modules. He said he found the tape on "managing medical mistakes constructively" very helpful and practical.

By the time he received his first follow-up survey feedback report a few months later, his behavior had dramatically improved. For example, the number of disruptive behaviors in critical ranges decreased from 18 behaviors to 4. In large part, this was due to simply withholding some of his condescending or demeaning comments or stating requests in softer and more constructive ways, for example, by asking, "In the future, would you arrange my instruments this way?" He continued to be a somewhat negative and sour personality, but managed to suppress the more hostile and abusive behaviors that get him into trouble. His feedback report was full of comments from his healthcare team that he had been more calm and agreeable, as well as less hostile and demeaning. His numerical ratings improved by almost 100 percent.

During subsequent survey follow-ups, his ratings did not improve much more, but he was able to achieve several acceptable feedback reports in a row and graduate from the program. When asked if he felt the program was valuable, he said, "It's all common sense. It's nothing I didn't already know. In fact, I probably learned it all in elementary school. All I need to do is keep my mouth shut and remember, 'If you don't have anything nice to say, don't say anything at all.'" He continues to think disparagingly about the state of nurses, hospitals, and managed care, but admits that he is happier these days with his healthcare team and that there is less turnover in the operating room. Follow-up one year after he graduated from the program with his chief of staff indicated that there was an occasional grumpy day, but that there have been no additional formal complaints.

HOW SUCCESSFUL HAS THE P.U.L.S.E. PROGRAM BEEN IN CHANGING BEHAVIOR?

A data analysis of the administration of the P.U.L.S.E. program to 117 disruptive practitioners in hospitals and clinics in the United States and Canada demonstrated a 91 percent improvement in conduct as measured by Leadership Index changes between the baseline and first follow-up survey, about three to nine months later. The Leadership Index score is a calculation derived from the physician's ratings on both motivating and disruptive behaviors. Improvement in a physician's Leadership Index score reflects an increase in average motivating behavior ratings and a reduction in average disruptive behavior ratings. These improvements were generally sustained for all physicians over several follow-ups, with some physicians followed for as long as three and a half years. Many of the physicians were referred by their hospitals' MEC, while others were required to participate by their state physician health programs. All but two of the physicians monitored by the P.U.L.S.E. Program improved.

Additional analysis of the worst 25 percent of the physicians referred for disruptive conduct by both state physician health programs and community hospitals shows a 572 percent improvement over baseline after four P.U.L.S.E. survey administrations. Further, those disruptive physicians who received both P.U.L.S.E. feedback and the T.E.A.M. Training described above improved at a greater rate than those receiving the P.U.L.S.E. feedback alone (242 percent versus 75 percent improvement).

WHAT IF THE PRACTITIONER STILL DOESN'T IMPROVE?

At some point—whether it is after a long history of informal attempts to improve behavior or after a physician feedback program such as the P.U.L.S.E. program—the facility leaders might reach the conclusion that there has been no sustained improvement and more formal disciplinary action needs to be taken. No matter what kind of discipline is imposed, it is essential, of course, that the applicable bylaws or policies be followed. It is helpful to keep in mind that disruptive practitioners are more likely than other physicians to sue, and courts are most likely to intervene if the bylaws have not been followed.

There are two goals to keep in mind when considering disciplinary action for the disruptive practitioner. First and foremost, the goal is to get the practitioner's attention and convince the practitioner to reform his behavior. A secondary goal is to create a record so that, in the event there is litigation, it will be clear that lesser sanctions were tried and were not successful in achieving the necessary change in behavior.

In many instances, a letter of counsel or warning, followed by a letter of reprimand, would be the first disciplinary actions taken. These actions are typically followed by a short-term suspension and, if this is unsuccessful, a longer-term suspension. The final action is likely to be revocation of the practitioner's appointment and clinical privileges. Depending on the applicable bylaws, these disciplinary actions may trigger a right to a hearing and appeal.

It is important not to overreact to the disruptive practitioner. Instead make sure that the incident that leads to discipline adversely affects or has the potential to adversely affect patient care. Suspending a practitioner for stealing an envelope, parking in the chief of staff's space, or raising a mild complaint in the medical record about broken equipment may not be compelling enough to convince a hearing panel or judge that suspension or revocation was reasonable.

WHAT ARE THE LEGAL ISSUES FACING LEADERSHIP REGARDING THE DISRUPTIVE PRACTITIONER?

Physician leaders face numerous legal pitfalls when they attempt to confront disruptive physicians. First, disruptive practitioners tend to be adept at diverting attention away from themselves and onto others. A common ploy of the disruptive practitioner is to deflect criticism by claiming that his actions are a response to quality problems. With this approach, the disruptive practitioner tries to shield himself from discipline by claiming to be a whistle-blower. It is critical to take this shield away from the disruptive practitioner by investigating, addressing, and resolving any legitimate quality of care concerns he might raise.

It is important to remember that even the most disruptive practitioner can raise a legitimate quality concern.[9] A legitimate quality concern should not be ignored because the messenger happens to be a disruptive force.

A separate legal issue involves the use of mental health evaluations for the disruptive physician. In addition to the reasons mentioned above concerning the lack of workplace behavioral evidence to back up clinical findings, clinical evaluations are typically not recommended because many disruptive physicians do not have a diagnosable underlying condition. However, referring the physician for a clinical evaluation opens the door to allegations that leadership thought the physician was impaired, which in turn allows the physician to argue that any subsequent action was based on his or her disability. Thus, a good faith effort to detect an impairment is often turned around on leaders and they are left to defend a claim of discrimination under the Americans with Disabilities Act.

Nevertheless, if there is any evidence of a psychiatric, substance abuse, or other medical disorder, it is recommended that a referral for a clinical evaluation be made. Most states have physician health programs that are knowledgeable and experienced in coordinating these evaluations.

Due to these legal pitfalls, the need for proper documentation in dealing with a disruptive practitioner cannot be overstated. Documentation provides the institutional memory of what happened, when it happened, and what the response was. As with all peer review documents, documentation pertaining to a disruptive practitioner should be labeled "confidential, peer review" and should be maintained in the practitioner's credentials or quality file. The practitioner's response to any documentation generated by hospital or medical staff leadership should also be maintained in the file.

SUMMARY

Disruptive practitioners present special challenges. They often strain everyone's patience, persistence, and perseverance. Leaders must develop a well thought-out, progressive strategy for dealing with the disruptive practitioner. In developing that strategy, it is helpful to use currently available objective and structured approaches. Coupling a formal physician survey feedback program with the more familiar approach of a Personalized Code of Conduct provides the components of a win-win strategy—practitioner participation, feedback, documentation, ongoing monitoring, and clear communication of consequences. This approach is likely to either get the practitioner to change or provide all the necessary documentation to take disciplinary action.

The first action physician leaders can take to manage disruptive physician behavior is to have preventative measures in place, like a written Code of Conduct. This creates community expectations of acceptable workplace behavior and provides the blueprint for the documentation of disruptive conduct. However, if disruptive physician behavior already exists and informal or collegial discussions with the physician have failed to result in sustained improvement, then a formal workplace assessment is recommended. A physician survey feedback program can provide objective documentation of unacceptable behaviors by involving the healthcare team in generating feedback for disruptive physicians. The finding can identify the behaviors that the physician needs to target and address, as well as the recommendations for specific educational interventions. Annual or follow-up feedback assessments enable ongoing monitoring of disruptive physicians' conduct improvements and reinforce the improvement so that it can be sustained.

KEY POINTS

- Disruptive physician behaviors are a problem for physician leaders because arrogant, bullying behavior disrupts teamwork and can potentially affect patient care.
- A series of progressive interventions is required to manage and rehabilitate disruptive physicians.
- Formal interventions like physician feedback programs and anger management training can be successful in assessing disruptive conduct, measuring its potential disruptive impact on the healthcare team, designing a customized anger-people management program with behavioral targets, and improving and maintaining more motivating behavior patterns.

REFERENCES

1. Leape, L. L., and J. A. Fromson. 2006. "Problem Doctors: Is There a System-level Solution?" *Annals of Internal Medicine* 144: 107–15.

2. Weber, D. O. 2004. "For Safety's Sake, Disruptive Behavior Must Be Tamed." *Physician Executive* 30 (5): 16–17.

3. Rosenstein, A. H., H. Russell, and R. Lauve. 2002. "Disruptive Physician Behavior Contributes to Nursing Shortage: Study Links Bad Behavior by Doctors to Nurses Leaving the Profession—Doctors, Nurses, and Disruptive Behavior." *Physician Executive* 6: 12–13.

4. Pfifferling, J. 1999. "The Disruptive Physician: A Quality of Professional Life Factor—Physician Anger." *Physician Executive* 25 (2): 56–61.

5. Harmon, L., and R. Pomm. 2004. "Evaluation, Treatment, and Monitoring of Disruptive Physician Behavior." *Psychiatric Annals* 34 (10): 770–74.

6. Piper, L. E. 2003. "Addressing the Phenomenon of Disruptive Physician Behavior." *The Health Care Manager* 22 (4): 335–39.

7. Thompson, R. E. 2004. "Misbehaving Physicians and Professional Ethics." *Physician Executive* 30 (5): 32–36.

8. In the 2007 Joint Commission on Accreditation of Healthcare Organizations (JCAHO) Medical Staff Standards, special emphasis is placed on interpersonal and communication skills and the professional. See JCAHO MS.4.10. It is also important to keep in mind that physician leadership training programs, which all hospitals should provide, should include modules on disruptive behavior since these problems seem to be on the rise.

9. Linney, B. J. 1997. "Confronting the Disruptive Physician." *Physician Executive* 23 (7): 55–58.

CHAPTER 6

Developing and Promoting a Physician Practice

Marc D. Halley

Not so many years ago, physicians, like other professionals, would complete their professional training and hang out a shingle, letting their selected communities know that they were available to provide services. Most physicians practiced alone, sharing after-hours call with others in their specialty. In those days, physicians were paid 95 percent or more of what they charged for their services. Most used a pegboard and ledger cards to keep track of their accounts receivable. Beyond a simple newspaper announcement for new practices and a brief listing in the telephone book, there was very little in terms of advertising for medical practices, or any other profession for that matter. Other physicians were not viewed as competitors and most medical practices appeared to succeed financially and otherwise.

Oh, the good old days...

Today, the intensity of medical practice competition in many communities has dramatically changed the landscape. Long gone are the ledger cards and the 95 percent reimbursement. Solo practices have merged to become single-specialty or multispecialty groups, with many physicians preferring employment to entrepreneurship. Hospitals have entered the medical practice arena by employing physicians in many communities and competing with members of their own medical staffs. Physicians have returned the favor, capitalizing on new technology and capital to compete directly with hospitals for lucrative diagnostic and therapeutic services. The shingle has been replaced with billboards, television advertisements, Web pages, radio spots, direct mail, large Yellow Page ads, lighted signs, and more. In many communities, medical professionals "compete" for the attention of patients and referring physicians, whether they admit it or not. Building and maintaining a viable medical practice in competitive settings have become more difficult with each passing year.

Thankfully, the fundamentals of growing a medical practice are still very much in place. The majority of new patients selecting a primary care practice come via word-of-mouth referral from a friend or relative. New physicians will often select the same specialty referral patterns as their more established partners—again, word-of-mouth. However, in today's highly competitive markets, attracting and maintaining those word-of-mouth referrals and referral patterns have become increasingly difficult and cannot be left to chance.

Having started and grown several practices over the last two decades, the author has discovered the value of applying fundamental marketing principles to the challenge of developing medical practices in competitive settings. This chapter identifies those marketing fundamentals and their application in primary care and specialty practices. The chapter will define the term *marketing,* document the development process for a new medical practice, and discuss ways in which promotional activities can facilitate practice growth. Finally, the chapter emphasizes the critical nature of understanding our medical practice "customers" and meeting their needs, wants, and priorities more effectively than our competitors.

TRADITIONAL VIEW OF MARKETING

The traditional view of marketing taught in business schools has included what are often termed "the four Ps," namely *p*roduct, *p*rice, *p*romotion, and *p*lace. All four of these components are so interrelated that it is difficult to discuss one without including the others. Products offered to a customer may be tangible goods, such as an automobile or a refrigerator. Products may also be less tangible, such as a radio signal or electronic information. Products include a variety of services, which may have both tangible and intangible components and benefits. Some products address necessities that ensure our comfort and survival. They are "must haves," such as food and shelter (or video games for teens). Other products cater to our egos—to our wants and our priorities, such as the latest fashions or tickets to the opera. Businesses spend millions of dollars each year in research and development to create products and services that can compete effectively in the marketplace. In many situations, product also includes the packaging necessary to deliver the product to the ultimate consumer.

The pricing of products and services affects, and is affected by, the other three marketing components. Ideally, the pricing strategy for a particular product or service is high enough to cover the costs of its development, production, promotion, and delivery, plus a reasonable profit, while still offering enough perceived value to enough customers to ensure its success in the marketplace. Some great ideas are so costly to develop and produce that they must be shelved because too few potential consumers can afford them. Other ideas that reach the market in the form of products or services are so inexpensive and easy to duplicate that they cannot generate enough profit to warrant their continuation. Successful products and services have enough customer-perceived value that they can be offered at a price that includes the profit necessary to attract the resources required (e.g., human resources, capital) to continue offering those products and services. Some products, such as gasoline, are so essential that prices can increase dramatically before customers reduce their consumption. This phenomenon is called low price elasticity. The slightest change in pricing of other products, such as commodities, can immediately cause customers to reduce their consumption or to change to a substitute product. Such inelasticity in pricing dramatically affects the potential pricing and profitability of the product or service being offered.

Promotion is the process of educating our targeted customers about our product offering, our pricing, and our delivery options. It also involves the critical component of motivating behavior on the part of our targeted customers to seek out and purchase our product or service. Promotion includes a variety of tactics such as general advertising to establish an image, product-specific promotion, product packaging, product sales, pricing discounts, and rebates. It includes high-cost media buys, newspaper advertisements, and billboards. It even includes simple thank-you notes and phone calls. Most importantly, promotion includes the personal word-of-mouth referral—a testimonial of sorts—from one satisfied customer to another. Effective promotion places our product or service top-of-mind when a customer need or want arises. Effective promotion establishes our "brand" in the minds of current and potential customers. Effective promotion encourages action on the part of the customer to fill a need and to address a want or a priority.

Place is broadly defined as not only where, but the way in which the product or service is delivered. In fact, sometimes the term *delivery* is used instead of the fourth P. Delivery may include the complexities of a product supply chain stretching from raw materials manufacturers, to end-product manufacturers, to wholesalers, to retailers and to thousands of customers. On the other hand, it may be as simple as a personal service provided by a professional to several dozen clients. Place strategies certainly include well-defined channels for distributing products nationwide or even worldwide. They also include access, timing, and customer service requirements. Successful distribution or place strategies focus on the point of service or product delivery and the needs, wants, and priorities of targeted customer(s). Consider the "C" store phenomenon with its focus on *convenience* for busy customers who work and live in a certain geographic area. Successful "C" stores in the right locations, offering a few key products, for extended hours 365 days a year, can even charge a premium price, which customers gladly pay for the convenience. Likewise, customer service is a critical place or delivery strategy driving (or driving away) repeat business.

The four Ps provide a useful platform for exploring the development and promotion of a medical practice. Before launching into that discussion, however, we must first understand the target of our marketing efforts—the medical practice customer.

WHO IS MY CUSTOMER?

Ideally, our products and services, our pricing, our promotion, and our delivery are driven by (or should be driven by) the needs, wants, and priorities of our targeted customers. As in most business ventures, it is critical to note that not all

medical practice customers are created equal. Sometimes our customer is the re-
cipient of our medical services. At other times, our customer may be the parent or
guardian of our patient. Oftentimes the needs, wants, and priorities of close family
members must be taken into account, making them customers, as well. Early in his
or her practice development, a primary care provider recognizes the critical nature
of these relationships and the powerful effect word-of-mouth referrals have on the
growth and development of his or her practice.

Specialists have the same challenges meeting the needs, wants, and priorities
of multiple customers. In addition, specialists must pay particular attention to the
needs, wants, and priorities of their referral sources. Even in settings where patients
can select their own specialist, most are unprepared to do so. Experience indicates,
and logic supports, the fact that most will depend on a trusted primary care provider (the "doctor" to most patients) to recommend when to see a specialist and
which specialist to see. Invasive specialists, in particular, must have a constant flow
of referrals in order to maintain a viable medical practice. A wise specialist understands that he or she must effectively meet the needs, wants, and priorities of
the patient (or the patient's parent or guardian). He or she also understands the
importance of addressing the different needs, wants, and priorities of the referring
physician. Failure to perform on either front risks the loss of the referral relationship and future business—the lifeblood of any medical practice.

It is a well-documented fact that women use a majority of health care services
and make the majority of health care purchasing decisions for their families.[1]
Women are, therefore, the critical target for medical practices in most communities. Obviously, the needs, wants, and priorities of women vary based upon a
variety of factors such as life stage, employment status, children, marital status,
household income, and education level. For example, experience indicates, and zip
code analysis confirms, that a majority of patients selecting a family physician in
an urban or suburban setting do so within a few miles of their homes.[2] Naturally,
these findings have tremendous implications for primary care physicians trying to
develop and promote their medical practices. Expensive billboards across town
are not likely to have the same impact as much less expensive flyers delivered to
selected neighborhoods within a ten-minute drive of a new primary care practice.
More importantly, the marginal cost of a referral from a satisfied patient is zero!

Understanding our targeted customer and the fact that we may have more than
one type of customer (multiple customer segments) is essential in designing effective promotional strategies.

DEFINING THE PRODUCT OR SERVICE

Effective promotion of a product or service also requires a clear understanding
of the product or service itself and those characteristics or features that are likely
to be important to each of our customer segments. Automobile dealers have long
understood the importance of product features in selling their wares to a variety
of customer segments. Horsepower, paint colors, size, vehicle purpose (e.g., a
pickup truck for a contractor), ease of use, safety, comfort, controls, and myriad

other factors are considered in the design, packaging, and promotion of automobiles. Even fast food retailers boast of their ability to custom design their burgers, hot dogs, and sandwiches to meet the needs, wants, and priorities of a variety of customers.

Purveyors of services, even professional services, should be just as cognizant of their "product" as automobile dealers and restaurateurs. Healthcare professionals, in particular, sometimes find it difficult to focus beyond *clinical need* to address the wants and priorities of their patients and referral sources. From the customer's perspective, the features of medical services go well beyond the Common Procedural Terminology (CPT) or International Classification of Diseases (ICD) definitions, most of which our customers do not understand or even appreciate. The "product" features most appreciated by our patients/customers might include the following:

- An appointment today, because I feel terrible
- Extended medical practice hours because I cannot afford to take off work to get Junior to the doctor
- A pleasant reception when I enter the office
- Great staff with a caring attitude
- Help with my medical insurance questions
- Lab and x-ray services right in your office so I don't have to go (or drag my child) to another location
- Easy parking and access to your medical office
- A short wait time in your reception and examination rooms
- A physician who listens to me before diagnosing
- A clear understanding of my unique situation (even though you have seen six other cases of the same diagnosis today)
- Taking over scheduling diagnostic tests, specialty physician visits, and therapeutic services that I cannot pronounce
- Help me get you paid by my insurance company
- A clear explanation of your bill for the services I receive.

Paying attention to these features helps address the *wants and priorities* part of the patient service equation. In many cases, these features help attract (largely through word-of-mouth referrals) and retain patients in primary care settings, including family medicine, general internal medicine, pediatrics, internal medicine/pediatrics, and obstetrics. In specialty settings, attention to these same features ensures that delighted patients will return to their referring physicians with positive feedback about their experience.

Speaking about referring physicians, wise specialists recognize primary care physicians (PCPs) and other referral sources as a very important market segment with their own unique *needs, wants,* and *priorities.* Features that could be of interest to these referral sources include:

- Ease of access when the PCP wants to refer a patient, regardless of the patient's insurance carrier

- Respect for the PCP as a medical professional
- Confirmation of the PCP's initial diagnosis or respectful feedback and education if the diagnosis ultimately differs
- Rapid response when a consult is requested
- Feedback according to the PCP's preference (e.g., immediate phone call, letter, and email)
- A thank you for each patient referred
- A patient returned to the PCP for follow-up
- Positive feedback from patients referred by the PCP to the specialist.

Understanding the desired customer segment and building the features into our services to meet their *needs, wants,* and *priorities* is the basis for effective promotion and successful practice development.

THE ANATOMY OF PRACTICE DEVELOPMENT

Long gone are the days of physicians routinely graduating from training programs to hang out a shingle as solo practice entrepreneurs. Today's new physicians are more likely to seek an employment opportunity, often in a group practice or in a hospital-owned medical practice, rather than the solo practice standard of their predecessors. Many graduating physician residents express concern about the additional debt and risk that would be required to start up a medical practice. Most want a better quality of life than those physicians who have gone before. (Older physicians often lament the relative lack of commitment to practice on the part of younger physicians now entering the field.)

Regardless of differences in career objectives, practice ownership, or legal structure, there are certain factors that attend and potentially drive the development of a new medical practice. Indeed, some of these factors are found in the physicians themselves. Others are outside of the physician and his or her direct control. The most critical factors in each group are listed below:

Factors within the Physician

- *Learning to practice:* Residency training helps physicians develop the skill and expertise to practice clinically. Graduates can boast hands-on experience, with a variety of clinical skills having been mastered. Due to the nature and purpose of residency programs, speed and efficiency are not necessarily acquired during the training process. We have often worked, for example, with primary care physicians, right out of residency, who dropped exhausted after seeing 4 to 6 patients in a morning. The thought of seeing 4 to 6 more in the afternoon was almost overwhelming. Then to learn that 12 patients a day only pays the overhead and not the physician can be a cause of great consternation on the part of the new recruit. New physicians are clinically competent, but they still need to learn to *practice* medicine. It takes time to develop the skills, processes, experience, and confidence to see 24, 26, 28, or more patients a day and still practice quality clinical care and caring. Without a mentor, it can take months for new physicians, even with the right motivation, to develop the ability to see higher patient volumes. Hiring or moving an experienced physician to start a new practice in a new location can shortcut this barrier.

- *Personality:* A physician with an engaging personality will build a practice more quickly than one who is more reserved.
- *Communication skills:* A physician who can listen intently, reflect understanding, and explain clearly will have the advantage in acquiring patients and developing a viable medical practice.
- *Gender:* Female providers tend to develop a practice more quickly than their male counterparts do in the same specialty because women typically prefer a female provider if one is available.
- *Motivation:* Physicians who are financially motivated and who have the opportunity to benefit from a growing practice will tend to increase practice more quickly than their less motivated counterparts.

Factors outside the Physician

- *Supply and demand:* When the demand for services exceeds the supply of providers, new practices will grow more quickly. When the opposite occurs, new practice development will become protracted, even with effective promotion and a willing physician.
- *Warm start:* Particularly in primary care specialties, adding a new physician to an established practice will enhance the growth of a new practice. The new physician will benefit from the patient volume and word-of-mouth referrals of the established provider, and can benefit from established processes and systems that support higher productivity.
- *Competitive alternatives:* Part of the supply and demand equation is the availability of competitive options. Other physicians in the same specialty or perceived substitutes (e.g., chiropractors) can dramatically reduce the development of a new practice.
- *Location:* Location is always a factor in developing a practice. For a primary care provider, locating in or near vibrant neighborhoods and a growing population will positively affect the growth, payer mix, and prosperity of the practice. For the specialist, locating near the "right" hospital and within referral range of several primary care physicians is essential to survival.
- *Hospital affiliation:* What is the "right" hospital? Several factors make an acute care facility the hospital of choice. First is its competitive position in the marketplace. Attaching your practice to a sinking or marginally profitable hospital can have a dramatically negative effect on your success. Beware of recruitment deals that are too good to be true—they might just be desperate last-ditch efforts to survive. Instead, the hospital

partner of choice is likely to have a clear vision, access to adequate capital to achieve that vision, experienced leadership, integrity, and a reasonable share of the market. For specialists, selecting a hospital partner whose primary service lines coincide with your expertise is a real plus.

- *Payer participation:* The opportunity to participate with a variety of payers in the community is critical to the success of any practice. Most patients in most communities have some type of insurance coverage. In order to attract those patients, primary care providers have to participate in the right panels. In order to accept referrals from those PCPs, specialists must align their payer mix with that of their referrals sources.

- *Promotion:* Letting your targeted customers know that you are available and interested in their business is critical to the survival of every new practice. Newspapers, fliers, referral acknowledgment, speeches, presentations, church attendance, and social functions, all contribute to the growth of the new primary care practice. Orchestrated meetings and educational opportunities, as well as breakfast in the physician lounge, can help specialty physicians gain practice development traction. Unfortunately, fewer primary care physicians are rounding at the hospital these days, so wise specialists make the rounds of primary care offices, often assisted by hospital liaisons or by their own office managers.

- *Customer service:* New patients have already had several opportunities to form opinions about a new practice and/or physician before they ever meet the doctor. The word-of-mouth referral, the first appointment call, the receptionist's greeting, the paperwork, the nurse, and the wait time either place the physician on a pedestal or in a deep dark pit from which there is little chance of escape. The entire service experience reflects on the physician.

In our experience, when there is reasonable demand for service, when we place a gifted and motivated physician in a great location, when the staff we hire is personable and enthusiastic, and when the promotion is appropriate, it still takes 18 to 24 months for a new primary care practice to approach financial viability. Specialty practices vary in their start-up experience, ranging from as little as 6 months for many high-dollar surgical practices to 18 months or more for some less invasive specialties. (Some internal medicine specialists find that they must spend a portion of their time practicing primary care medicine in order to survive.)

FACILITATING PRACTICE DEVELOPMENT THROUGH PROMOTIONAL ACTIVITIES

The mere mention of advertising or promotion in some physician circles used to conjure up a repulsive image of the sleazy used car salesman in a bright-colored sport jacket trying to pawn substandard vehicles off on unsuspecting dupes. This was hardly the image physicians wanted to portray. Just a few years ago, it was difficult to find more than a line or two in the Yellow Pages alerting patients to the telephone number and address of doctors in their communities. Today, most professionals, including physicians, recognize the importance of advertising and promotion. Newspaper space, Yellow Page ads, billboards, and even radio and television spots are common tactics used by physicians in many competitive markets. Consumers have so many choices and they are bombarded with so much information on a daily basis that the opening of a new medical practice can easily become lost in a cacophony of marketplace noise.

What role does promotion play in the growth and development of a new medical practice? How can a physician determine which promotional tactics to employ?

First, let us define *promotion* for our purposes as activities designed to promote a medical practice to both current and potential patients/customers. Within our definition, we will find tactics such as educational activities, mass media advertising, direct advertising, relationship development, sales, and even the Internet. A brief definition of these tactics, again for our purposes, follows:

- *Educational activities:* This tactic includes membership in the local healthcare speaker's bureau, opportunities to address the medical staff regarding the physician's expertise, providing medical education segments for local media, brief talks given at local schools and day care centers, and articles written for local papers or newsletters.
- *Mass media advertising:* This tactic includes the newspaper, Yellow Pages, billboards, radio, television, and any other vehicle that reaches large numbers of current and potential customers.
- *Direct advertising:* This tactic includes selected letters, announcements, fliers, brochures, refrigerator magnets, and other vehicles that target specific households or referring physicians.
- *Relationship development:* This tactic includes active participation on the medical staff, memberships in the Rotary Club or the Chamber of Commerce, church attendance, meet and greet visits, dinners, and luncheons. It even includes golf (thankfully), membership in the country club, and other places where relationships can be developed. It has been said, "Referrals follow relationships."[3]
- *Sales:* Satisfied patients and referring physicians become a passive sales force. They are passive, because they only "sell" or recommend our services as the occasion arises rather than actively soliciting business on our behalf. It is largely the practice's service level that creates and maintains this passive sales force.
- *Internet:* "Everyone who is anyone has a Web page!" Not so, but almost. This electronic communication medium is becoming so pervasive that many of our customers are likely to use it. Every organization of any size must consider its use to both develop and maintain relationships with customers.

Second, in order to use the promotional tactics/tools effectively, we must first identify our target market(s) and determine our promotional objectives for reaching each market. Then we can determine which tools—or combination of tools—will most likely reach our targeted audience and achieve our objectives. Failure to match our tactics with our target market and promotional objectives can be an expensive lesson. For example, a neurosurgeon hoping to generate new surgical business by using direct mail to reach a neighborhood near his practice is not likely to see much of a return. A family physician, on the other hand, may benefit tremendously from the use of direct mail to alert new households in a new neighborhood within a three- to five-mile radius of her practice location of her interest in meeting their primary care needs. One of her promotional objectives may be to alert the neighborhood of her special interest and expertise in women's health issues, which can be included in the selected advertising piece.

Third, tools or tactics must be designed around the needs, wants, and priorities of the target market. The closer the match, the better will be the return. For example, some years ago I learned a valuable lesson when advertising two new solo practice general internal medicine physicians. Both doctors were to start practice on the same Monday during the month. The same size newspaper advertisement for each physician was placed on the same page of the same Sunday paper. Both physicians were men and both physicians had an office in the same medical office building. One physician wanted nothing more than the bare facts about his board eligibility, address, and telephone number. The other physician listed these same facts and, in addition, noted a few of his areas of clinical interest. Monday morning brought a flurry of telephone calls for the physician who had been more specific in his advertising. Patients with migraine headaches and his other areas of clinical interest saw the ads and said to themselves, "I've got that problem!" They called. The nonspecific ad resulted in far fewer telephone inquiries.

Fourth, given the competing noise, medical practice promotion is most successful when it involves a variety of tactics over a period of time. Most members of our target audience need a physician only infrequently. Therefore, they might pay little attention to a newspaper advertisement, even if it runs for a few weeks in their local paper. The key is to be top-of-mind or the first referred when they *do* need a physician.

Fly fishermen, trying to get the attention of a trout in fast moving water, will sometimes use what is called a "dropper" fly—a second fly tied 12–18 inches behind the first hook. This rig increases the opportunity to interest and attract a wily trout to strike one of the artificial lures. Likewise, multiple attractors will potentially increase our opportunity to interest and attract our targeted audience. For new primary care providers, we usually recommend the development and implementation of a promotional plan using multiple tactics and implemented over several months. Such a plan may include initial newspaper advertising to reach a broad audience and alert them to the availability of a new physician in the area. The newspaper ads might be followed with high-quality fliers hand-delivered to targeted neighborhoods near the practice. Refrigerator magnets might be developed with local emergency phone numbers and the physician's telephone number. These can be distributed by mail or along with the fliers previously mentioned. Participation in health fairs and health screenings (also distributing the refrigerator magnets) can attract interested parties. Public speaking on relevant healthcare topics to church groups, nursing homes, day care centers, school classes, and clubs will often result in new patients being attracted to the practice.

Asking new patients how they were attracted to the practice and creating a referral log will help identify those promotional techniques that yield the greatest return in your local market area. The referral log also notes the names of patients who, by word-of-mouth, send their friends and relatives to our practice. Thanking those who refer, without violating patient confidentiality, is a nice gesture and likely motivates additional referrals.

A referral reward system or process takes very little physician and staff time. This technique is often used successfully by those in the dental profession to thank patients who refer new patients to the practice. Most often, a referral reward is simply a thank-you form letter, tailored by a mail merge, to patients who have referred others for care. Naturally, the letter should not mention the referred patient's name, but might just thank our established patient for keeping us in mind.

Specialty physicians will likely use a different set of promotional tactics, but should not leave promotion to chance. Alerting the community to a new specialist's availability is certainly a reasonable objective, especially if patients can self-refer to the specialist for certain ailments (e.g., allergy services, dermatology services). More critical to the specialist, particularly invasive specialists, is developing relationships with primary care physicians and other potential referral sources. As noted earlier, referrals follow relationships. In my experience, many relationships can be interrupted because relationships tend to atrophy or grow stale over time. A new specialist may have the advantage over busy competitors who find it more difficult (or who have simply quit paying attention) to maintain their current relationships with their referral sources. Meeting and greeting primary care physicians or going to dinner with them can immediately begin to yield returns. Providing education to referring physicians in support of their practices is a huge benefit, whether that education is provided in formal settings or through high-quality educational materials provided for their use with patients.

CUSTOMER SERVICE AS PROMOTION (MAINTAINING AND MOTIVATING OUR SALES FORCE)

As mentioned earlier, it is our customer service level that builds and maintains and motivates our established patient sales force. Promotional activities are of only limited value if the physician or the practice fails to consistently deliver the anticipated service results. Frustrated patients will likely tell their story more often than happy patients—and the story gets more graphic with every telling. They are likely to include their referring physician among those who have to endure the tale. It is critical to remember that primary care customers are unlikely to fully understand the value of the cognitive and procedural services they receive. Their assessment is likely to use surrogate measures such as the responsiveness of the appointment desk, a pleasant greeting by a receptionist, a clean and nicely appointed office, a friendly nurse, recent magazines, wait time, and other measures.[4] Even the billing clerk and the billing process influence the patient's view of the practice, and by association, the physician. Yes, a friendly and favored physician can counter failure in the other areas for a period of time, but many patients ultimately become frustrated and leave if the practice culture is not customer friendly. Frustrated patients become a negative sales force that is not so passive. So much for promotion.

Frustrated physician customers (and other referral sources) will likely respond with their feet by referring to another provider and practice without ever saying a word to the offending specialist. PCPs will not long suffer the negative feedback from patients who are offended by a referent physician. Nor will they long endure the disrespect shown by specialists who are not responsive or accessible. As soon as an alternative becomes available, referral patterns will change.

The challenge for the most successful practices is remaining accessible, responsive, and service-oriented when the practice becomes busy. It is much easier to "be nice" at the front desk when we are new and checking in three patients a day (the two-hour lunches were great!). However, when we are checking in three patients every 15 minutes, it is hard to smile and be nice unless that service orientation is part of who we are.

Assuming that we understand the needs, wants, and priorities of our various customer segments (e.g., patients, guarantors, referring physicians), we must prepare the entire organization to meet those needs, wants, and priorities automatically. Physicians and management must consider the impact of each of those items (listed in Table 6.1) from a service perspective.

Table 6.1
Customer Service Considerations

Physician commitment	The first and foremost influence on customer service is the physician's attitude as displayed in his or her words and actions. A willingness to work in that 4:30 P.M. patient or to respond to that urgent call from a referring physician will demonstrate a level of commitment that will be shared by the support staff.
Facility design, furnishings, and equipment	Designing the facility around patient service and physician productivity is critical. Offering, for example, privacy at the cashier's desk is very important. Such privacy involves design rather than the bulletproof glass found at many reception desks.
Telephone system	Select a phone system that can grow with the practice with features that facilitate responsive service. Add a special line for referring physicians and for pharmacies.
Computer technology	A user-friendly practice management system is essential. Patient service representatives should be able to use the software as a performance-enhancing tool, whether they are verifying patient information, scheduling follow-up appointments or referrals, collecting co-payments and cash, or answering insurance questions. The best software is just as important as the best clinical equipment.

Table 6.1
Customer Service Considerations *(continued)*

Hiring support staff members	Hire for service. Friendly, smart, competent, pleasant "A" players are the people we want in our practice. Quickly (and appropriately) remove those who fail to live up to service requirements.
Policies and procedures	Make sure that every policy and procedure established in the practice passes four important filters. First, does it enhance or maintain our ability to deliver quality clinical care? Second, does it enhance or maintain our ability to deliver high-quality customer service? Third, does it enhance or maintain physician productivity? Fourth, does it enhance or maintain practice financial viability? Even the smallest policy or procedure at the front desk or in the billing department must pass all four filters to survive.
Staff training	There is nothing more frustrating for all parties than having competent, caring, and poorly trained support staff. Patients, physicians, fellow employees, even the incumbents are frustrated. Too busy to train? Don't worry. You won't be for long!
Division of tasks	Organize the work in the office with the four filters previously mentioned in mind. Keep nurses off of the referral phone and hire a referral coordinator so that the nurses can manage physician productivity. Let the receptionists greet patients, collect co-payments, verify insurance data, and manage the reception room rather than forcing them to do data entry. Don't add staff until you have examined and fine-tuned processes. Otherwise patients will enjoy another episode of the Keystone Kops through the wide-screen TV we call a reception window.
Staffing	The busiest medical practices tend to employ slightly more staff per FTE physician. However, they generate so much more revenue that the additional staff is not an expense issue. Remember, the medical practice "game" is won on the revenue side of the income statement.
Performance standards	Articulating and documenting our performance standard is critical to establishing a service culture. "Be nice" is just not compelling enough to inspire supportive standards for each position and staff member. A clearly articulated service vision should be supported throughout the organization as each person is asked to develop his or her own performance standards in support of the vision. For example, the receptionist who decides to try greeting each patient in an extremely busy practice by name is certainly doing more than being nice.
Performance measurement	The organization should rigorously measure overall performance against the service vision. Effective patient satisfaction surveys can be implemented rather inexpensively. The specialist can solicit referring physician satisfaction formally and through telephone calls. Individuals should be asked to measure their own performance rigorously against their standard and to report that performance to management and the physicians.

Table 6.1
Customer Service Considerations *(continued)*

Performance recognition	Strong performance by the organization and by individuals should be celebrated on an ongoing basis in staff meetings and in other small ways. Bonuses are not necessary (although an occasional "thank you" check certainly does not hurt). Personal recognition, movie tickets, peer recognition, and occasional pizza parties are all welcome reminders that service is a part of our culture.
Managing exceptions	Service exceptions (usually identified through patient complaint or through patient satisfaction surveys) are openly discussed in physician meetings and in staff meetings. The group analyzes these exceptions, with ideas solicited to ensure that such failures do not reoccur. Physicians are not exempt from the discussion. In fact, they should lead it!

SUMMARY

Product, price, promotion, and place, the traditional concerns of marketing, are still relevant today in the development of a new medical practice and the maintenance of an established one. Understanding our customer segments, their needs, wants, and priorities, is the first step. Defining our product or service in terms of their needs, wants, and priorities is the next step. Organizing around high-quality clinical care and high-quality caring is a critical area of focus to ensure our ability to deliver automatically and consistently the service we have promised. Finally, letting our prospective customers know about our service using multiple tactics, including our established patient sales force, will help ensure our ability to develop and promote a physician practice.

NOTES

1. Braus, P. 1997. *Marketing Health Care to Women.* Ithaca, NY: American Demographic Books.

2. Halley, M. 2007. *The Primary Care—Market Share Connection: How Hospitals Achieve Competitive Advantage.* Chicago, IL: Health Administration Press, 37.

3. Ibid., 120.

4. Halley, M. 2004. "The Case for a Medical Practice Retail Strategy." *Journal of Medical Practice Management* (November/December): 164.

CHAPTER 7

Creating a Simplified, Integrated, Practice Marketing Plan

Debra R. Murphy

Whatever you build must begin with a solid foundation or you will be faced with a structure that requires constant maintenance and repair. Creating a solid marketing plan requires similar diligence. Jumping directly to program execution without producing the necessary foundation increases your risk of missing your target and wasting your marketing dollars. The fundamental information and tools that must be in place before any marketing campaign will be successful need to be assembled with as much care as the foundation of a building.

The VistaPlan Framework is a simplified, integrated marketing plan process designed to help you focus on the key elements that will make a difference in your business (Figure 7.1). Starting at the bottom, the figure takes you through the process one step at a time, ensuring you have the information you need before you go to the next step.

As you work your way up the figure, you systematically develop your marketing strategy for each segment of the market you wish to target. Once you have the strategy in place, you can then start to execute marketing activities.

This chapter will walk you through the figure as follows:

- Situation analysis
- Target market and segmentation
- Positioning, differentiation, and messages
- Vision, mission, and goals
- Marketing strategy
- Brand image and identity
- Sales tools

Figure 7.1 A Marketing Plan Framework

We will conclude with developing the marketing budget that corresponds to the plan. The appendix provides a sample marketing plan for an orthopedic group.

SITUATION ANALYSIS: LAYING THE FOUNDATION

Market Review

Healthcare marketing continues to evolve and many professionals still feel uncomfortable doing it. In today's competitive marketplace, hospitals, private practices, and other healthcare facilities have to market in order to win their share of patients and keep their practices solvent. To ensure that you market your practice effectively and in good taste, you need a marketing plan. A market analysis is a critical first step in market investigation and development of your marketing plan. You need to understand the market forces that influence patients' choices of healthcare providers by thoroughly examining the market for your services. The analysis will help you define your target market, determine its requirements, and understand factors that can affect the success of your practice. The market analysis has you look at the pool of potential patients and understand what these people need that you can provide. Think about your practice in terms of whom you wish to attract and use this analysis to determine how you want to focus your marketing efforts. By evaluating your business from the perspective of patient need, the strengths you bring, and how you differ from the competition, you will be able to align your efforts on initiatives that drive your business's success.

Key Questions

- What are the economic and social trends occurring in the healthcare market, especially your practice area?
- What is going on in the healthcare industry that will positively and negatively affect your practice?
- What social, technical, environmental, regulatory, or economic changes are taking place within the market and how will they affect your ability to attract patients from this market?
- What external factors are affecting the decisions of your potential patients to choose your practice?
- What are your challenges in reaching your target audience?

Look around your environment and determine what may be impacting your practice that you have not noticed. Is there a new free clinic opening close by? Do you have a large concentration of other practitioners located within a 5 to 10 mile radius? How is the Health Insurance Portability and Accountability Act (HIPAA) affecting your practice? Is there an economic downturn that is resulting in higher unemployment rates and therefore fewer people with insurance or money to pay for services? These are the types of questions to ponder. The more you know about your environment, the better you can react to its effect on your business.

Competitive Review: Understanding Your Competition

Before you can fully analyze your practice's strengths and weaknesses, you need to understand your competition. A competitive analysis helps you understand what your competitors are doing from both a business and a marketing perspective. Knowing who your competitors are and what they offer can help you determine what you need to do to make your services and marketing stand out. Understanding your competition and how you are different from them enables you to develop a plan that differentiates you in a way that gets you visibility with your target audience.

Your competition is any other physician's practice that competes for the same dollars that you are trying to acquire. If you have an orthopedic practice, your competition is other orthopedic practices, chiropractors, sports physicians, and physical therapists. In other words, you compete with any business that is going after the dollars, both insurance and personal, of the patient requiring the service. Competition could also involve other services that target your market, such as drugs for arthritis or nerve blocks for pain.

Understanding the overall market for the types of competition is a good start. Next you should research a couple of specific, direct competitors, and learn as much about how they market their practice as you can. Use the Internet to see where their name appears—whether in press releases, articles, or other media—to see how they are using public relations to gain and maintain visibility. Information gleaned from similar practices can be used to get ideas on how to improve or better market your practice. Look at what any physician does to market her practice, both good and bad, and learn from it.

Depending on your practice, you may want to understand your competitors' service offerings and how they price, market, and sell them. Knowing how they speak to their patients through their Web site, literature, or marketing campaigns can help you determine if you need to make adjustments to your own messages and marketing activities. Try to find out how they treat their patients. Ask people you know who have gone to them not only what was bad but also what was good about the level of service your competitors offered. Learning about your competitors' positive qualities may be far more useful than only hearing the negative.

What Do You Do with All This Information?

The value of having competitive information is that it gives you insight into what you need to do in your practice to better position yourself against your closest competitor, establish your unique selling proposition (USP), and develop marketing activities that help you stand out. Learn as much as you can from them and use this information to determine where you need to improve.

Watching the competitive landscape can give you valuable information on how you can better reach your patients, improve your image, update your messages, and gain an advantage. The competitive landscape is always changing. It is important to keep your ears and eyes continually open to what has changed, what is working and what is not. Keeping your analysis up to date ensures that you can make adjustments in your business that will gain you the visibility and additional income that can help your practice flourish.

Key Questions

- Who is your competition?
- What are their strengths?
- How do you compare?

- How are they marketing themselves, that is, what are their key messages and what tactics are they using to build awareness in the market?
- What are their strengths and weaknesses?
- What could they do that would make it difficult for you to practice and compete?

Look closely at the competition and be objective in your analysis. Get someone not close to your practice to help bring an objective eye to the task. Knowing you are better than your competition is irrelevant at this point if your competitors are doing better than you. Why do people think they are better? What do they offer that you do not? How are they perceived in the community? Perception is reality. It makes no sense to argue with people about their perspectives, only to adapt to a dynamically changing marketplace.

Practice Review

Objectively analyzing your practice from both an internal and external point of view can help you better define what you are trying to accomplish. To conduct this analysis, you need to assess your practice from different perspectives using a SWOT analysis, as described in the next paragraph.

SWOT stands for strengths, weaknesses, opportunities, and threats. Strengths and weaknesses are internal factors. Opportunities and threats are external factors. A SWOT analysis provides a snapshot of your business position at a point in time and will change as the business evolves. The point of the SWOT analysis is to assess where your strengths are today and align them with new opportunities you see coming in the market you serve. It also will help you avoid areas where your strengths are lacking. The analysis should be short, to the point, and realistic about the strengths and weaknesses in relation to your competition. A SWOT analysis can provide you with new insights about your practice that will help you guide your business into new, profitable markets and avoid high-risk situations.

A SWOT analysis can help you understand the characteristics of your practice and the environment around it that can affect its overall success. It allows you to uncover opportunities that you are well placed to target and manage or eliminate threats that could otherwise catch you off guard. It is also a tool for assessing your business against your competition.

Strengths and Weaknesses

Strengths are the positive, internal characteristics of your practice with respect to your competition. Identifying strengths can help set you apart from the competition. Do not underestimate any quality when determining your strengths because what may seem insignificant to you just may be an interesting quality that will attract new patients and help you retain established patients. Think about your expertise, your people's strengths, your contacts, any distinctive services you offer, the location of your business, any processes that are unique or that could simplify your patient's visits, affiliations and alliances, or any other aspect of your business that adds value to what you offer your patients.

Weaknesses are factors internal to your business that detract from your ability to maintain a competitive advantage. Although it is good to be candid, it is not necessary to attack your practice. The point of understanding your weaknesses is to help you correct them or market around them. By identifying your weaknesses, you have the potential of converting them into strengths. Think about areas that need improvement, such as a lack of experience in certain markets, limited resources, a poor location for your business, critical dependencies that would hurt your business if they disappeared, or other factors that are under your control but are difficult to improve in the short term.

Key Questions

Strengths

- What is it about your business that sets you apart?
- What advantages do you have over your competition, such as breadth of services, outcomes, accessibility, and service to patients?
- What is your key to success?
- Does your staff bring anything different or special to the practice?
- Does the market know about your strengths?

Weaknesses

- In what areas can your practice improve?
- What should be avoided?
- What do your competitors do better than you?

Opportunities and Threats

Opportunities are external factors that are attractive to the business and represent areas that if approached properly can increase revenue, market share, and net income. You want to find opportunities that you can exploit with your strengths. For example, you may meet someone who has skills that complement your businesses and by collaborating, you can open new markets for your company and offer more in-depth services to your customers.

Threats are external factors beyond your control that could place your marketing strategy, or the business itself, at risk. Identifying threats allows you to take actions and have contingency plans in place to address these factors, should they arise, before they can negatively affect your business. These challenges are unfavorable economic trends that could lead to reduced revenues and profits. Competition, whether existing or potential, is always a threat. Your existing competitors can make moves that can undermine your practice. Other threats could be government regulations, changes in patient behavior, and new technology that reduces the demand for your current services. Make sure you address your worst fears during this part of the exercise. It is better to be prepared than blindsided.

Once you have your SWOT analysis information, you can then use it to form a strategy to capitalize on your strengths, minimize your weaknesses, exploit opportunities, and deal with threats. The strategy should align with your practice's objectives and goals, but you may want to determine if you need to shift the business model to accommodate new, more profitable opportunities or deal with an established or potential threat.

Opportunities

- What untapped or undeveloped opportunities exist?
- Are there new market segments you could effectively target?
- Are there new trends coming that you could use to your advantage?
- Do you have special expertise that competitors are lacking?

Threats/Challenges

- What moves could competitors make that would put your practice in an unfavorable situation?
- What factors could most hurt your practice now and in the future?
- What would happen to your practice if regulations became more burdensome?
- What new technology could undermine your practice?

Look for ways to capitalize on your opportunities that play to your practice's strengths and pursue a strategy that will get you into that space, especially if it enables you to leave an area that threatens your business. In addition, assess your weaknesses and determine which ones you can address now and which will take time to correct.

TARGET MARKET AND SEGMENTATION

"Pin the tail on the donkey" is a blindfolded game that may be fun for children, but when it comes to your practice, you need to approach your business with your eyes wide open. Unfortunately, many owners seem to be playing this game with their business, meandering "blindfolded" through the market and trying to land patients without knowing who the most appropriate audience would be.

A target market is the group (of people or of businesses) that has a need, is aware of the need, and is willing to spend money now to satisfy that need. It helps if your target market includes people whom you enjoy serving by virtue of shared values or interest in improving their condition(s). Selecting an appropriate target market for your practice is the most important but also the most difficult part of the marketing plan. You must sacrifice some markets to be successful in others. This is the hardest concept for many business owners to accept because by narrowing the market, they will leave money on the table.

Every business owner goes through this thought process until you realize that targeting enables you to target a more lucrative audience and develop messages with greater precision. Then a counterintuitive phenomenon happens—your clarity about what you offer makes other prospects, even outside of your target, more likely to call you. If you narrowly define your niche market, your messages are clear, your offerings are precise, and your marketing efforts are more effective, even to those not within your target market.

To be direct, we call this group of people or businesses you want to do business with a target market because that is the market at which you aim all your marketing efforts. Being focused on one particular market enables you to make choices that are difficult if you trying to market to a broad array of candidates. For example:

- You can select publications that your target market reads and advertise or work with the editors to get coverage through a public relations strategy.
- You can select networking functions that only target your market.
- You can direct your messages to your market's key need, focusing on what is important to that audience using the language they understand.

By selecting a target market, you can focus and be really clear about why your target should be interested in your services. It is not necessarily a restriction on what types of patients you may attract or wish to work with. That is a business choice. Those are decisions you can make as the opportunities arise.

In most physician practices, selecting a target market will most likely include two groups of patients:

- Existing patients. Proactively staying in touch with your current patients is crucial. Offering them useful information on new treatments, new discoveries, healthy ideas, or the latest in research can ensure that they continue to be your patients.
- New patients. Whether building a new practice or managing an existing one, you need to constantly attract new patients. In order to focus your practice on delivering the care you most enjoy to the patients you want to see requires that you target those patients specifically.

Another target audience that may be beneficial to identify are your referral sources. Depending on your practice, referral sources may include general physicians, acupuncturists, massage therapists, chiropractors, physical therapists, sports trainers, athletic directors and coaches, or any other group of professionals that have the same target market but do not compete with you directly. Marketing your services to a referral source can help you reach more patients more easily.

Key Questions

- What is the market for your product or service—that is, your ideal target market?
- What do they need and what are they lacking?
- What are the characteristics of your ideal customer?
- Why do they want to do business with you?
- What do you offer them that others do not?

Knowledge of your target market enables you to make better decisions about your practice, including pricing and services that you may want to offer. Understanding how you can service your target market helps you focus your practice and serve the appropriate audience more effectively.

Market Segmentation

Once you have defined a target market, you may want to divide the market into smaller segments to address the more specific market needs, media, pricing patterns, and decision criteria for each of the different market segments. Segments may be based on age, gender, health needs, location, or any criteria that enable you to determine how your services apply to different segments of the market—how they vary in the perceived benefits they bring to that segment and the messages needed to address that segment. Segmenting enables you to target specific people with specific messages, focusing on their specific needs. Marketing opportunities become more evident when you are able to analyze a group of prospects that have similar wants and needs. For example, you may want to segment your current patients by their health needs and offer them advice and information to help them manage their specific health issues. Market segmentation allows you to determine:

- the services required to satisfy that market segment that you may not already offer
- whether a segment is worth addressing based on your resources and skills
- whether some of your services are not worth offering to particular segments

Segmenting the target market also helps you gain insight into which patients your practice can be more successful caring for and what you may need to do within your practice to expand your services to other groups. Likewise, analyzing a particular segment may provide insight into a segment that is losing money or one that you are not capable of servicing effectively. You may determine that one particular segment is so lucrative that you only want to work with that segment.

For example, if you are an orthopedic surgeon, you may want to segment the market into groups based on the type of condition you are treating in order to target the messages accordingly. If one of your target segments is athletes, you may want to break that segment by gender and age, as the needs of athletes differ based on these two demographics. Once you have identified these segments, you are now ready to address their needs with specific messages. It is also easier to identify marketing activities that can reach these segments more effectively. You may want to post your brochure at health clubs or run seminars on injury prevention at these facilities. If you run seminars in the mornings, you may want to discuss sports injuries in women or senior citizens. If you run them in the evening, you may want to discuss injury prevention for weekend athletes.

Key Questions

- Which segment of the market is the most attractive in terms of future growth potential, ease of entry, competition, profit potential, and overall risk?
- Why are you focusing on a specific target market?
- What makes a particular segment more interesting than others?
- What characteristics of this segment are important?

In summary, market segmentation is another way to more precisely focus your efforts. Although you may think that all athletes are your target segment, by looking more closely at this group of potential patients, you can identify which segment within that market that would be best served by your practice and how you can reach patients in that segment.

POSITIONING, DIFFERENTIATION, AND MESSAGES

Positioning is how you want your practice to be viewed in the minds of your patients relative to the competition. It is how you differentiate your practice from your competition and explains to your patients what makes you the best choice for them. It is not enough to be different, but your target market must feel that the difference offers a benefit substantial enough for you to stand out in their minds.

Differentiation is the uniqueness you offer your target prospect that sets you apart from your competition. It must be meaningful, measurable, and defensible. Most likely, your differentiation is a combination of your credentials and a business practice that makes you stand out.

To identify your unique differentiation, view your practice from the patient's perspective and ask, "What's in it for me and why do I care?" Ask yourself why you can promise and deliver a benefit better than the competition. Begin with a statement that describes the benefit, and then explain how you uniquely achieve that benefit. If you cannot do this, then it is probably not your differentiator. Your benefit must be measurably better than your competition or unique to your practice.

Be creative and look at your business from a new set of criteria such as more convenient hours, easier access, and a more welcoming experience. Expand the breadth of services to your patients outside of your specialty but in a way that relates to your practice. For example, orthopedic surgeons may wish to add a massage therapist, a personal trainer, or a chiropractor to the practice to offer related services that encourage patients to come in more frequently. A trend in women's health centers is to offer spa treatments—facials, chemical peels, laser hair removal, and other "med-spa" type offerings. Someone who comes for a spa treatment, but is not currently a patient, may later have need of your services, and will be much more likely to book an appointment in a familiar place where he or she already feels comfortable and confident.

The positioning statement verbalizes how you differentiate your practice from your competition, describing the single most important aspect of your practice that you wish to instill in your patient's mind. Your positioning statement takes your key strength and communicates this compelling advantage to your target market, creating clarity and consistency in the way you speak to your market.

The following template was adapted from one authored by Geoffrey Moore[1] to help high-technology companies develop a positioning statement, but it can be used by businesses from any discipline. The model helps you create a two-sentence positioning statement that tells prospective patients what you offer, how they will benefit, and why your practice is different from others.

For <target patient> who <statement of problem>, our product/service is a <describe the solution> that provides <key benefit>. Unlike <primary competitive alternative>, our solution <describe your key differentiator>.

For example, "For athletes who need quick resolution of pain, the XYZ Orthopedic Group offers same-day diagnosis and innovative treatment of orthopedic conditions that gets to the source of your injury. Our practice offers quality patient care, plus complementary treatments such as massage therapy and chiropractic care, convenient hours, and easy-to-schedule appointments."

Once you have your positioning statement created, you can develop key, supporting messages targeted at your specific target segments. Your messages should focus on educating and informing, explaining the benefits of your services, and creating an image. They must be crystal-clear and must speak to the needs of your prospective patients. They should make patients want to find out more, examine your Web site, and call for an appointment.

Unlike the positioning statement, developing your key messages is more of an art than a science. There is no precise formula that can be used to clearly develop these messages. You should take the key points from your positioning statement and provide supporting evidence for those points. From there, those secondary differentiators and other messages you collected during the positioning process can be explored and expanded. Keep in mind the following points:

- Be honest and credible in your messages. Tell people who you really are and what you really do.
- Be clear and concise with what you offer. Make it easy for the reader of your message to know what you are promising.
- Test your message. Try your message out and measure the results you are getting to ensure the message is clear.
- Know your audience. Send your message to the right audience to ensure the best use of your marketing resources.

When you have developed a set of messages that speak to the needs of your target market, you need to use them consistently and repetitively in all of your marketing efforts.

VISION, MISSION, AND GOALS

Does your practice need mission and vision statements? And if so, what is the difference? There is value in creating these two components of the marketing plan. Developing a vision and mission statement is a way of articulating what your practice is about and why you started it in the first place.

A vision statement is a statement about what you want your business to be. It is your dream of the future without respect to current resources. It inspires you, gives you direction, and keeps you on course. For an orthopedic practice, a vision statement could read:

> The XYZ Orthopedic Group strives to become the premier orthopedic practice for athletes, baby boomers needing joint replacements, and women facing the challenges of osteoporosis. We will offer highly innovative treatment of orthopedic conditions while educating our patients on preventive measures.

A mission statement is a concise statement of the fundamental purpose of your practice as viewed from the perspective of the patient. Although it supports the vision, the mission statement is firmly grounded in today's reality. It should be brief, explain the connection between your practice and your target market, suggest action yet couch this in nonspecific terms, and have a geographic or demographic dimension. A mission for our orthopedic practice could be:

> The XYZ Orthopedic Group is an eastern Massachusetts private practice that takes pride in providing high-quality, cost-effective treatment and education services to all of our patients regardless of their challenges. We are leaders in the innovative treatment of orthopedic conditions while remaining compassionate in our dealings with patients.

The key here is to be honest about what you really want from your practice. If you really want to run a major health clinic, then use that vision. But if your dream is to have a small, lucrative practice that you can handle without a large business structure or high overhead, then express that in your vision and mission statements. Doing what you think you should do rather than what really inspires your passion will only frustrate you and limit your success.

Marketing Goals

When writing your marketing plan, it is valuable to identify your goals and how you plan to achieve them. Your marketing goals are the quantifiable, measurable targets that are being aimed for by your practice, such as number of new patients, percentage of patients that remain loyal to your practice, or total revenue for the practice.

A common approach to developing your marketing goals is to use the acronym S.M.A.R.T. for the five characteristics of well-developed goals. There are many variations of this model and all are effective. The following can be used as a guide:

- Specific—Who is involved? What do I want to accomplish? Where will it happen? In what timeframe? What is the purpose or benefit of accomplishing the goal? The more specific you can be, the more likely the goal will be accomplished.
- Measurable—You need to be able to measure your progress toward achieving your goals. If the goals are measurable, you can answer the questions "How much?" "How many?" and "By when?"
- Attainable—Goals need to be realistic and attainable based on the resources you have or can acquire to achieve them. The best goals should encourage your practice to reach beyond its immediate comfort zone, but not so far as to involve unavailable resources or unrealistic expectations.
- Relevant—Goals should help you reach your vision. Setting goals that do not align themselves with your ultimate outcome will divert your attention from those that help you get where you want to go.
- Timely—Goals need to have deadlines. Without having specific timeframes associated with each goal, you most likely will not achieve them because the day-to-day interruptions will take over.

Using the vision for the orthopedic practice—to become the "the premier orthopedic practice for athletes, baby boomers needing joint replacements, and women facing the challenges of osteoporosis"—some of our goals could be:

- Grow the patient base by 30 percent in the next 12 months. This growth will be made up of professional athletes (5 percent), college athletes (10 percent), and recreational athletes (15 percent).
- Over the next 12 months, generate 50 percent of our gross revenue from current patients, developing an ongoing relationship that promotes wellness and loyalty.

- In the next 18 months, derive 20 percent of gross revenue from related, alternative services such as personal training, massage therapy, and chiropractic care. These services will bring current patients back more often and attract new patients to the practice that may not need orthopedic services at this time.

Once you have your goals, prioritize them in order of importance to furthering the mission and realizing the vision. Setting your specific goals for your business allows you to measure and gauge the success of your marketing activities. Without them, how can you tell if you are accomplishing what you initially set out to do?

MARKETING STRATEGY

The marketing strategy outlines your plan of action and allocation of resources needed to achieve your marketing goals, utilizing the seven types of marketing promotion at the top of the visual marketing plan diagram. If one of your marketing goals is to generate 50 percent of your revenue from current patients, what activities will you use to ensure that this market segment continues to come for treatment, in what timeframe, and with what budget? Think through each of your marketing goals and identify the key activities that will help you achieve success. You most likely will not utilize all types of marketing, but will select from those that make the most sense for your practice.

To develop the most effective marketing strategy, you will need to determine the marketing mix based on market segment. The strategy to reach one target audience will differ from the strategy to reach another. For example, marketing to athletes will be different from the strategy used for marketing to women with osteoporosis because their needs and requirements differ (which should have been identified as part of your market segmentation exercise). You have opportunities to reach athletes through sports newsletters, seminars, and other activities catering to the athlete. In contrast, reaching women with osteoporosis would be through publications, organizations, seminars, or other venues that attract older women. By looking at the segments, you can uncover opportunities you may not realize are there otherwise.

Understanding the Marketing Mix

The marketing mix is sometimes referred to as the four P's of marketing—*product*, *price*, *promotion*, and *place*. For your healthcare practice, it is still important to look at these four areas and understand for each market segment the benefits you offer your patients, any special pricing or packaging of services that may benefit certain types of patients that you can control, and your promotional activities. Of the following categories, select those that you are comfortable using for your practice:

- *Events*—Gain visibility by offering seminars, participating in health fairs, and taking part in civic gatherings such as the Chamber of Commerce, charity walks, and other networking opportunities.

- *Advertising*—Build awareness through ads in magazines, journals, billboards, television, and radio spots to reach your target audience.
- *Direct marketing*—Send information or special offers directly to your target market including letters, postcards, gifts, and telemarketing.
- *Internet marketing*—Generate visibility using online venues such as banner or pay-per-click advertising, newsletters, e-mail marketing, and acquiring links from other reputable web sites.
- *Public relations*—Build awareness with the media by writing guest columns or becoming an expert interview source.
- *Word of mouth*—Network to build and foster relationships and generate referrals within your community.
- *Strategic alliances and joint ventures*—Develop relationships that help expand your business by adding value to your offerings.

To develop the marketing strategy for your practice, you want to consider the different types of activities you have the time, resources, and budget to put into action. You may want to send your patients a newsletter, discussing new services or an educated opinion about the merits of a new procedure in the news.

The marketing strategy for an orthopedic practice could contain the following:

- Educate and inform current patients using a combination of direct and Internet marketing.
- Attract athletes by sponsoring sporting events, offering talks to team coaches, and placing selected advertising in local sports programs. Develop one relationship with a local health club per quarter that results in referrals of members to the practice.
- Develop relationships with other physicians, personal trainers, chiropractors, massage therapists, physical therapists, and other noncompeting related professions.

For each of the strategies that you identify, you will need to develop a set of tactics and a timeline to accomplish them. For example, if an orthopedic practice wants to educate and inform their current patients using direct and Internet marketing, the activities could include a quarterly newsletter that discusses new techniques in your practice area, articles from your chiropractic, massage, and personal trainer alliances, and other articles that help your patients become and stay healthy. You may want to develop a blog for your Web site, posting information for your patients and links to other blogs of interest. If you collect patient e-mail addresses and you receive their permission to send them information, you could segment patients by what they were treated for or by area of interest and send brief, informative e-mails to them on their particular issue and how to alleviate it. Online newsletters, blogs, and other types of knowledge increase your visibility, enhance your credibility, and improve your competitive advantage.

In summary, remember that strategies are not tactics. Strategies are the route you will take to make your goals a reality. Tactics are specific actions needed to accomplish each strategy. Each strategy can have many possible tactics. Keeping strategies and tactics separate helps you evaluate the success of your marketing plan. If you try one tactic and fail, that does not mean your strategy is at fault. But, if you try many tactics for the same strategy and all of them fail, you need to adjust your strategy. Perhaps the needs of your market have changed or there are new competitive forces in the dynamically changing marketplace.

BRAND IMAGE AND IDENTITY

Developing Your Brand

Your brand is the image you wish to portray to the world and is one of your practice's most valuable assets. A strong brand is more than your logo or what appears in your advertising and marketing campaigns. It is everything you are and the value you deliver. It includes the total patient experience from when they make an appointment through when they leave your office and pay the bill. It communicates the personality of your practice clearly and visually, and promotes credibility. It shapes patients' perceptions of who you are and conveys the expectations and promises that you extend to your patients in terms of quality, service, reliability, and trustworthiness. A strong brand helps the audience differentiate you from your competitors and can positively influence their decision to come to your practice, directly impacting your profitability.

To develop your brand, identify what you want your brand to do for your practice and what you want patients to think, feel, and say about it. What are the adjectives that best describe your business? How do you want that description communicated to your patients? What images would you like people to associate with you? Conversely, what qualities and messages are not associated with your practice? Every image you project, including your logo, location of your practice, office furnishings, and the way your staff answers the phone, needs to reflect the personality of your business.

Building a strong brand for your healthcare practice depends on the positive, consistent experiences patients receive when they come in contact with you, your materials, your staff, your office, and all aspects of your image that might be visible to the community. Once you have developed your image, use it consistently in everything that you do.

SALES TOOLS

Historically, marketing your practice was frowned upon because it was not seen as professional for doctors to advertise. Today's competitive marketplace has made marketing an important component of your overall business plan. If you think of marketing as an educational resource for your patients, you can increase your visibility and build relationships that will benefit your practice.

Sales tools provide valuable information to current and prospective patients and the medical community.

Sales tools are your Web site, business cards, letterhead, newsletters, brochures, and other materials needed to fulfill the call to action of your marketing programs. Developing your sales tools is the last activity you should undertake before you execute your marketing tactics. Until you know what types of marketing you will do, you cannot know which tools you will need to support them. Using your brand identity and messages, combine them to create the sales tools that help you communicate with your target audience. A good first impression is important for your practice, and a consistent set of materials with a strong identity and a compelling, powerful, and enduring message gets you noticed and remembered.

Why Develop a Web Site for Your Practice?

Many physicians may not believe that a Web site will benefit their practice, that no one finds a doctor by surfing the Web. In today's competitive marketplace, your Web site can provide many benefits. Your Web site can reduce the number of calls to your office by enabling patients to schedule appointments, request prescription refills, provide patient information through secure forms, or pay bills online. Your business is really no different than others, and with many consumers wanting the convenience of online purchasing, scheduling, and education, you may sell your practice short if you do not provide automated appointments and electronic prescription refills at the minimum.

As an information source, you can educate your patients with targeted articles and question and answer forums. You can opt to answer specific questions and provide follow-up information through a secure e-mail correspondence system. New services can be announced, new research can be discussed, and innovative services, products, and equipment can be introduced. Remember, your current patients are your best "new customers" and your most powerful marketing assets. Offering them a valuable online service will keep you visible to them, ensuring they continue to come to your for their health needs. Providing answers to questions they may be too intimidated to ask or too nervous to remember, or that require more than a quick consultation, makes their total experience with your practice much more useful. In addition, satisfied patients are more likely to refer you to their friends and colleagues, turning your current patients into a powerful source of referral business.

Prospective patients may turn to your Web site to learn more about you, your skills, and how you can help them. Your Web site can provide answers to questions they have about their condition, enabling them to know that you can help them, and encouraging them to make that difficult first appointment with you. Getting to know you and your practice before a new patient comes in for an appointment can help reduce the anxiety of that first visit and make the experience much less stressful.

Remember that your Web site is your major fulfillment piece for all marketing activities. If you send a direct mail piece, the call to action should send prospective patients to your Web site. If you meet someone and hand them a business card, your Web site will offer them an anonymous way to find out more about you. People today are more accustomed to researching service providers on the Internet and are more apt to call and book an appointment with someone they feel they know through a Web site. Hire a professional Web developer and designer to build your site, and make sure you are working with someone who understands the marketing aspects of Web site creation in terms of ease of use, navigation, search engine optimization, and the type of content that attracts and retains prospects.

Getting Found on the Internet

Having a quality, informative Web site is just the first step. Making sure your prospective patients find it is a critical requirement. Search engines and directories generate the majority of Web traffic by users who are trying to search the Web for information and services. Search engine optimization is the act of developing your Web site to make it easier for search engines to review the content on your site and decide where to place it in the search results based on certain keyword terms. When you have your Web site developed, make sure you work with someone who understands search engine optimization and can incorporate the basic techniques during the development process.

Before you can begin search engine optimization techniques, you need to define your keyword list based on how your target market would search for your services on the Internet. The keyword can be one word or a phrase. Keyword phrases are more likely to narrow the search and get a better quality list of results. For example, the keyword "orthopedic" returns 15 million pages. The keyword phrase "orthopedic surgeon Boston" returns 700,000. A more specific phrase like "sports related orthopedic injury Boston" returns about 200,000. If one of your pages discusses treatments for sports-related injuries and you incorporate the techniques using that phrase that we discuss below, in time your page will rise in the ranks and you will increase your odds of being found by a prospective patient.

Search engines use different indexing algorithms to review Web sites, making it difficult to stay current with what works and what does not. Because of the rapidly changing environment, the best way to stay current is to read online forums from reputable search engine companies. However, the basic search engine optimization techniques listed below will remain important, regardless of what the search engines do to their products.

- The page titles of your Web site are among of the most important parts of your page as far as search engines are concerned. The title tag has to contain your major keyword, which describes the page and which should be between 60 to 80 characters in length including spaces. Tightly focused titles with your important keyword at the beginning perform best with Google and help with many other engines.

- Use text links that incorporate your keywords to enable the search engine robot to quickly identify what is on the page. Image links, although they may look interesting, are less effective. A good Web developer can make text links look interesting, giving you the best of both worlds.
- Make sure your content contains your keywords and try to put them in your headers and bold them when possible.
- The page description meta-tag is the content displayed under the title in the search engine results. If you don't have one written, the search engine will use content from the page. Take advantage of this tag and define it wisely for each page in the site, ensuring it describes the page using keywords. Some search engines compare the page descriptions, titles, and keywords to see if the content on the page matches.
- If your site has many pages within different areas (such as a resource area that contains articles, information, and links), you need a site map. A site map links to every page on the site. This will help the search engine robots find every page with just two clicks. For small sites, a well-defined navigation scheme will perform just as well.
- Make your site popular. Get links to your site from other sites that add value to yours. Buy links from reputable sites to help, but work out exchanges with people who have the same type of clients but do not directly compete with you. The quality of links is important—pick your links as you would pick your friends.
- If your site has a consistent theme throughout, that will help you in the rankings. The spiders. are looking for consistent, valuable, and fresh content to serve up. Make sure your site provides the value they are looking for. (Web spiders or Web crawlers are automated programs that are used by the search engines to index the pages to provide fast searches. The better the content they see when crawling the pages, the better the ranking in search engine results.)

In summary, making sure your Web site can be found is important to marketing your business. Using these search engine optimization techniques can help improve your rankings and drive business to your practice.

MARKETING BUDGET

The marketing budget needs to include everything that goes towards marketing your practice. If you need consulting help with the marketing plan, be sure your overall budget earmarks consulting funds for marketing purposes. The cost of the marketing plan will be well worth it if it focuses your efforts and ensures that you spend only on the activities that make sense for your practice. Too many times small businesses work without a plan and needlessly spend money on "marketing" efforts that have absolutely no return on investment. A simple marketing plan can identify where you should spend based on an analysis of the market and your competition.

To get a quality marketing plan that fits within your budget, you might want to consider working with a marketing coach who guides you and helps you complete the process. Instead of paying for the consultant to research and write your marketing plan, you pay him or her to work with you a couple of hours a week. Depending on how you structure the coaching effort, the cost of developing the plan yourself with guidance could be 30–50 percent of the cost of a marketing plan done by the marketing consultant directly. You need to add the cost of your time into the equation to determine if developing the plan with guidance is the best use of your time, but in many cases, working with a coach is a way to get a quality plan for a lot less money.

If you are starting a new practice, you need to invest in brand development. Developing your brand image is more than just getting a logo, but a quality logo done by a skilled designer is an important centerpiece for your branding efforts. Your brand image needs to be aligned with your practice's brand identity so that everything you do projects a consistent message to your patients, including how you answer the phone, how your office looks, and how your Web site and sales tools appear to your patients.

If your budget cannot support the cost of having a custom logo, then check out some online companies that offer logos for a small price. One important benefit of these services is that you get a quality image in all the formats needed for Web and print media. The downside is that the logo is not unique. If you are going to spend the time marketing your company to establish a brand identity, be sure that you can live with the logo you select for some time.

Another area of the budget that can be controlled is your sales tools. To control your costs, limit what you create rather than cutting corners on the design or quality of the tools. Cutting corners on your sales tools will make you look inexperienced and send a negative message to your patients and families. Business cards and a Web site are a necessity and should be developed first. If you have limited written correspondence, you can have a letterhead template created in Microsoft Word that can be printed using 28-pound letterhead paper on a color printer. Office supply stores carry a large selection of paper in weights and colors that will go with your brand. Printing the envelopes yourself is not as easy. Given the amount you need, you may want to invest in professionally printed envelopes.

Most businesses benefit from a highly professional, quality Web site. Depending on your business, you can select a template-based Web site or a custom-designed Web site. The option you choose is based on what appeals to your target audience. Be sure you understand the importance of your Web site to your business and the impact it can have on your revenue before you determine the budget you need to spend on your site. If your primary marketing effort will be Internet marketing based, you need to invest in your Web site and have it developed correctly. You will also need to implement search engine optimization for your site so that the search engines can find you. When you get prices for Web sites from different sources, make sure you understand exactly what you get. You may think you are getting a $500 site, but if the firm requires you to use their hosting company, and charges extra for pages over a set number, for forms, and for search engine optimization, you can spend a lot more than you may have budgeted.

Each activity you want to execute needs to be accounted for in your budget. Your most cost-effective activities include networking, Internet marketing, health fairs, and public relations. The activities that can be expensive are direct marketing, advertising, and events that you host such as seminars, although there are less expensive activities in each of these categories as well.

Keep in mind that you do not need to do all the activities at once. Plan them out over the year so that you can budget for them and measure their effectiveness. If you have too many activities going on at once, it gets difficult to track and measure your results so that you understand what activities optimize your investments. Understanding the return on investment of a marketing activity enables you to determine whether to continue it or stop and try something else.

Establishing a marketing budget helps you identify the amount of money you want to spend on marketing activities over the year and to set a schedule for executing the plan. If a program is not giving you an appropriate return on investment, then you can take the money and invest it in some other marketing activity. Setting a marketing budget gives you the flexibility to move funds around for additional marketing opportunities that arise throughout the year. Without a budget, you may not know if you have the funds to take advantage of the opportunity or you may find that you spent a lot more on marketing at the end of the year than you had planned. Managed appropriately, your marketing budget can be the best investment you make in your practice. If you wisely invest your marketing dollars, you can keep your costs down and obtain a sufficient return on your investment.

CONCLUSION: BUILDING UPON THE FOUNDATION

Once you have a road map for your practice, a budget for your activities, and an understanding about how you will reach your prospective patients, you are ready to execute the plan. By building your foundation first, your programs will be consistent, targeted, and more likely to succeed. You can be assured that no matter what type of programs you choose, you will consistently communicate your value to your prospects, increasing your ability to increase awareness, attract ideal prospects, and increase profitability.

Key Concepts

- Every business benefits from having a well-defined marketing strategy. A marketing plan provides you with a roadmap for how you will communicate with your target audience and for how much. Trying to market without a plan can result in wasted marketing dollars and disappointing results. Your marketing plan should answer the following questions:

  - Who are your patients and what type of services do they need?
  - Why should patients come to your practice?

- How are you different from your competition?
- How are you communicating your services to your target audience?
- What is the budget required to successfully execute this plan?

- The marketing strategy section of your plan outlines your game plan to achieve your marketing goals and should include information about how you package, price, and promote your practice's services. Promotional activities will come from the following categories: events, advertising, direct marketing, Internet marketing, public relations, word of mouth, and strategic alliances and joint ventures. Select the types of marketing activities that make the most sense for your practice.
- Sales tools including your Web site, business cards, letterhead, newsletters, brochures, and other materials needed to fulfill the call to action of your marketing programs should be the last activity you undertake before you execute your marketing tactics. Until you know what types of marketing you will do, you cannot know which tools you will need to support them. Using your brand identity and messages, combine them to create the sales tools that help you communicate with your target audience, projecting a good first impression that gets you noticed and remembered.

REFERENCES

1.   Moore, G. A. 1999. *Crossing the Chasm: Marketing and Selling High-Tech Products to Mainstream Customers*. New York: Harper Business.

2.   Molpus, J., B. Cain, and P. Betbeze. 2006. "What's Your Best Specialty?" *HealthLeaders Magazine* (March 16). Available at: http://www.healthleadersmedia.com/view_feature.cfm?content_id=77932. Accessed November 7, 2006.

ADDITIONAL READING

Kennedy, D. S. 2000. *The Ultimate Marketing Plan*. Avon, MA: Adams Media Corporation.

Stevens, M. 2003. *Your Marketing Sucks*. New York: Crown Business.

Trout, J. 2000. *Differentiate or Die: Survival in Our Era of Killer Competition*. New York: John Wiley.

Trout, J. 2000. *Positioning: The Battle for Your Mind*. New York: McGraw-Hill.

APPENDIX: SAMPLE MARKETING PLAN

The following marketing plan is a brief example of one that could be developed by an orthopedic group that wanted to grow their practice over the next 12 months.

MARKETING PLAN

Executive Summary

XYZ Orthopedic Group is a physician-owned group of skilled, board-certified orthopedic surgeons. Since inception, our goal has been to provide exceptional care to our orthopedic patients. Our practice is dedicated to caring for injured athletes, individuals of all ages with an active lifestyle, and patients with injuries to the shoulder, elbow, and knee, as well as many general orthopedic problems. The focus of the practice is sports medicine and joint reconstruction.

Our goal for the practice is to double our patient traffic in 12 months, from 80 patients per week to approximately 160. We also need to ensure that everyone views our practice as the most efficient and patient-friendly orthopedic practice in the area. To achieve this goal, we will undertake new marketing activities that increase the awareness of our practice throughout the surrounding communities.

SITUATION ANALYSIS

Market Summary

The subspecialty of sports medicine continues to emerge as one of the major components of orthopedic surgery due to the continuing rise of professional and amateur athletes in our country. According to an article by Molpus, Cain, and Betbeze (2006) in *HealthLeaders* Magazine,[2] the orthopedic service line is a highly profitable area in which to practice. Active baby boomers are entering their sixties in the next few years and will need knee or hip replacements or other treatments so they can continue their active lifestyle. The article cites statistics provided by the American Academy of Orthopedic Surgeons in Rosemont, Illinois, projecting that the total number of hip replacements will grow from 156,400 in 2000 to more than 272,000 by 2030, and the number of knee replacements will rise from 257,795 to more than 457,000 in the same time period. In terms of revenue, a 2004 survey by Irving, Texas-based Merritt, Hawkins & Associates found that net inpatient/outpatient revenue in orthopedics grew 61 percent from 2002 to 2004, 20 points higher than cardiology.[2]

For the geographic location where XYZ Orthopedic Group exists, we have an abundance of athletes. There are three health clubs, four professional sports teams, 10 colleges, and many high schools all offering a myriad of team sports to the students.

Competition

The competitive environment for the XYZ Orthopedic Group includes three other practices within the 25-mile radius of our ideal target market. These practices have the following characteristics:

- Practice One has 3 surgeons located 10 miles from our practice. They offer minimal ancillary services, but offer sports medicine services. One of the surgeons is affiliated with the town's high school athletic program and serves as the team doctor.

- Practice Two has 5 surgeons located 30 miles from our practice. They offer general orthopedic services and do not specialize in sports medicine.

Company Analysis

Strengths

- The location of the practice is ideal since it is conveniently located in an easy-to-reach business district with easy access to free parking. Also, it is in close proximity to the hospital used for surgery.
- We are located close to many educational environments that offer team sports.
- We currently offer ancillary services to our patients, such as occupational and physical therapists, a chiropractor, and a massage therapist.
- We offer specialized services for female athletes, mature athletes, and growing athletes.

Weaknesses

- We have not gained visibility in the community. Our practice is relatively young, and we have not done any marketing to build the awareness in the community.
- Our cash flow is relatively weak; we need to spend wisely on our marketing activities.

Opportunities and Threats

Currently, XYZ Orthopedic Group is the primary center for orthopedic care in a 25-mile radius and provides orthopedic services to the local hospital. Our opportunity is to continue to build our relationship with the hospital and ensure they are serviced appropriately. A threat to our practice would be that if we could not service the hospital's needs, the hospital would recruit its own team of orthopedists to challenge our services and compete against us.

TARGET MARKET AND SEGMENTATION

The target market for our practice is athletes of all types, such as individuals of all ages with an active lifestyle, professional athletes, and high school and college athletes.

Our target segments include:

- Female athletes
- Mature athletes
- Growing athletes

POSITIONING, DIFFERENTIATION, AND MESSAGES

Positioning Statement

- For athletes who need quick resolution of pain, the XYZ Orthopedic Group offers same-day diagnosis and innovative treatment of orthopedic conditions that gets to the source of your injury. Our practice offers quality patient care, complementary treatments such as massage therapy and chiropractic care, convenient hours, and easy-to-schedule appointments.

Differentiation

- XYZ Orthopedic Group helps patients of all ages and activity levels reach their fitness goals through comprehensive orthopedic care. In addition to providing expert medical treatment for the full range of orthopedic medicine, we partner with athletic trainers to assist our orthopedic and primary-care sports-medicine physicians in the clinic extending the traditional on-the-field athletic training room model to the sports-medicine orthopedic clinic.

Messages

- XYZ Orthopedic Group has the experience to know which types of treatments will be most successful based on the specific requirements of each individual patient. We are committed to finding a solution that is best for you, whether you need conservative care and medical treatment, or complete joint replacement surgery.

VISION, MISSION, AND MARKETING GOALS

Vision

The XYZ Orthopedic Group strives to become the premier orthopedic practice for athletes. We are committed to state-of-the-art orthopedic service, defined by excellence in patient care, a highly qualified medical staff, employee dedication, and strong community relations. We will build a community of services that cater to the athlete regardless of ability or age.

Mission

The XYZ Orthopedic Group takes pride in helping people from every age and skill level regain and maintain a healthy and active lifestyle. We encourage physical activity for our patients in order to live a healthy lifestyle and we promote safety in sport participation as a crucial element in preventing further injury. We strive to educate the public about the importance of treating sports injuries as early as possible to achieve the best possible recovery and avoid the potential of developing a chronic condition.

Goals

- Double the volume of patients seen over the next 12 months by effectively building awareness of the practice at schools, universities, and health clubs.
- Develop strategic relationships with supporting services to increase the number of patients we get through referrals.
- Institute new marketing programs that keep all current patients educated about the latest orthopedic treatments for sports injuries, ensuring that they remain patients with our practice and obtain services from our partners.

MARKETING STRATEGY

The marketing strategy for XYZ Orthopedic Group will include a combination of events, advertising, public relations, word-of-mouth marketing, strategic relationships, and Internet marketing programs. The types of activities we will invest in include:

- Public education programs about injury prevention in athletes that will be part of an overall community outreach plan offered at health clubs, schools, and colleges.
- Public visibility and promotions including sponsorship of sports teams, banners at athletics functions, and other activities that connect our practice name with athletics.
- Internet marketing activities that enable local athletes to find our Web site and get critical information about injury prevention and resolution. These would include developing local pay-per-click advertising and placing a sponsorship link to our site from an athletic event.
- Public relations activities that establish our practice as experts in our field. These will include writing and placing articles about sports medicine and becoming an expert resource for editors to call.
- Advertising in targeted publications for the local athlete such as supporting the school or university newspapers; programs for the professional athletic events; buying a banner ad on the appropriate web sites that target our market.
- Strategic relationships with supporting services such as chiropractic massage therapy and personal trainers, and developing referral-based marketing programs with these partners.

BRAND IDENTITY

We will develop a new brand identity that associates us with athletes and use it consistently in all of our materials including our Web site, business cards, brochures, signage, banners, and other promotional items we decide to use. We will invest in a new logo that projects the brand we want to be associated with.

REQUIRED SALES TOOLS

To support the marketing activities outlined above, we will invest in the following sales tools:

- Web site
- Business cards
- Tri-fold brochure

MARKETING BUDGET

The estimated market budget for our activities is $25,000 to be spent over the next 12 months. The logo and sales tools need to be developed initially in order to support the activities.

Table 7.1
Marketing Plan Budget Summary

Strategy	Goal	Tactics	Budget
Public education programs	Build awareness with athletes	Seminar with high school athletes regarding injury prevention	$1,000.00
Public visibility and promotions	Build awareness with athletes	Sponsor local sporting events	$1,000.00
Internet marketing	Drive the appropriate patients to our practice by finding us on the Web	Localized pay-per-click advertising Sponsorship link from an event to our practice	$1,000.00
Strategic partnerships	Word of mouth	Develop relationships with supporting services Cross-link Web sites Develop a referral rewards program	$1,000.00
Advertising	Awareness	Advertise in select publications	$3,000.00
Public relations	Build credibility in community	Write articles to be published Engage a PR specialist for 6 months for coverage and article placement	$6,000.00
Sales tool development		Logo design: $1,500.00 Web site: $5,000.00 Business card design: $300.00 Brochure design: $700.00	$7,500.00
		Print costs (estimates)	$4,500.00
Total			$25,000.00

CHAPTER 8

Revenue Cycle Management

Brian K. Morton

A thriving medical practice can gauge its success through a number of methods—high patient satisfaction, quality awards, employee surveys, and other subjective measurements that indicate a practice's performance. Ultimately, however, simple economics prevail: The practice must have enough incoming cash to pay the bills.

Without sufficient cash, high levels of patient and employee satisfaction are inadequate to stave off creditors. In an ideal situation, a practice generates enough incoming cash to pay competitive staff wages and provide for physician bonuses at year-end. The most critical aspect of ensuring an appropriate cash flow is revenue cycle management (RCM).

Revenue cycle management involves multiple activities such as payer contracting, patient registration, charge capture and coding, patient flow, claim processing, and payment posting. Each of these activities is crucial to the process. As such, the practice must ensure that each activity is performed and completed with a high level of accuracy. Failure in the simplest of these activities oftentimes accounts for increased days in collections, extensive amounts of resubmissions, multiple phone calls to patients, and oftentimes nonpayment of claims that have been filed late.

In this chapter we will summarize the most important aspects of revenue cycle management. We will review the ideal RCM process and examine insights into necessary critical decisions, policies, controls, and metrics. Some of the information covered may inspire further questions and research on the part of the reader. Ultimately, a practice needs either to have a staff expert to handle these issues, or to know someone who is available to answer questions as they arise.

THIRD-PARTY PAYERS

Before any patient is seen or a claim submitted, the physician must decide which payers the practice will accept. While it is completely legal and ethical to have a cash-based practice whereby patients pay for services upon receipt, it is not a feasible reality in most markets. Most patients will see only those physicians who are credentialed for their insurance, whether it is Medicare, Medicaid, or a commercial payer. In order to be paid by any of the these groups, the practice must be a participating provider—meaning that the physician will accept the payer's approved charge limits as the total payment for the service provided. It does not mean the payer will pay 100 percent of the approved charges, only that the approved charges are the maximum the physician will receive. Some payers cover a percentage (usually 80 percent) of the total, leaving the patient responsible for the remainder, while others require the patient to supply a copayment at the time of service.

The first decision for most physicians is whether to participate in Medicare. If the physician chooses not to participate, federal law still imposes fee limits when service is provided to a Medicare beneficiary. Based on the fee limits mandated by Medicare for nonparticipating physicians, it is oftentimes best to participate with Medicare, thus ensuring that the practice will receive at least the 80 percent portion of the approved fees. Exceptions to this practice would be those specialties that have minimal Medicare patients (such as pediatrics).

The next major decision will be whether to accept Medicaid as a reimbursement source. Medicaid typically pays the least for services provided and often creates cash flow problems depending on the state's budget cycle. Some practices choose to participate on a limited basis with a predefined panel; others elect to participate only to the extent possible in order to collect the 20 percent portion of services for patients who have Medicare as their primary insurance.

After decisions have been reached on Medicare and Medicaid, the practice must decide which commercial payers to pursue for contracts. These decisions are highly dependent upon local market conditions: For example, who are the major employers, what plans do they offer, which plans are perceived by patients as "good"? The practice must research the local market to make data-driven determinations on which plans to pursue in order to ensure patients. A good source of payer information in a local market is oftentimes the medical staff office at the hospital. That office can usually place the physician in contact with the appropriate person who manages payer contracts for the hospital. While the hospital staff cannot contract with the insurance plan for the physician, they can provide the names and contact numbers for the predominate plans in the market. In addition, almost every state has an insurance commission, and contact information can often be found on the respective state's Web site. (Most state government Web sites follow a format of www.STATENAME.gov.) Once on the Web site, enter "Insurance Commission" or "Insurance" in the search box usually visible on the home page of the state's Web site. There should then be several references to the individual state's insurance commission.

Insurance plans generally create economic incentives for patients to utilize contracted providers. These incentives are usually in the form of lowered copayments for the patient as well as payment of a higher percentage of covered services. Most plans will allow an out-of-network physician to treat under some circumstances; however, the patient will be required to pay a higher level of copayment and co-insurance for the services rendered.

Once the plans have been identified, the practice must be credentialed and contracted with these plans. The contracting process involves a legally binding document that details requirements for credentialing, claim submission, payment, and appeals. The credentialing process ensures that the physician meets the plan's quality requirements, is licensed to provide the services, and has the appropriate processes in place to service the patient. To assist physicians with credentialing, several state medical societies provide referrals to a centralized credentialing service. These services allow the physician to submit credentials to a single entity, which then provides the information to the various payers as requested. While this service helps lessen the burden of credentialing, it does not absolve the practice from having to negotiate a contract with each payer.

FEE SCHEDULE

Concurrently, the practice should be establishing its initial fee schedule. Several resources exist to help determine the codes to use and the amount to charge. An Internet search using the term "physician fee schedules" will identify different options should the practice wish to purchase a fee schedule template. If the practice does not wish to purchase a schedule, it is relatively easy to obtain a starting point by downloading fee data from Medicare. At a minimum, the practice should obtain a utilization report from Medicare, which shows the codes billed in the past year by practice specialty. Medicare via its Web portal provides extensive information that can be used to help the practice create an initial fee schedule. This data is free of charge and available at www.cms.gov.

The following calculation shows how Medicare determines the fee for each service (for 2007):

2007 Nonfacility Pricing Amount =
((Work RVU × Budget Neutrality Adjustor (0.8994)) (round product to two decimal places) × Work GPCI +
(Transitioned Nonfacility PE RVU × PE GPCI) +
(MP RVU × MP GPCI)] × Conversion Factor

Source: http://www.cms.hhs.gov/PhysicianFeeSched/.

As shown above, there are multiple components to the creation of the fee. The primary components of fee creation are the Relative Value Units (RVUs). RVUs were developed to provide a basis for equity among different physician services. The values of RVUs increase based on the complexity of a given service. The following list (from http://www.cms.hhs.gov/apps/ama/license.asp?file=/pf slookup/02_PFSsearch.asp) shows the Work RVU values for office visit codes for an established patient based on the January 2007 table from Medicare:

2007 Work RVU Values for Medicare Office Visit Codes

CPT Code	Total RVUs
99211	0.55
99212	1.02
99213	1.66
99214	2.52
99215	3.42

In effect, Medicare estimates that a level 3 visit (99213) requires three times the work and complexity as a Level 1 visit (99211), and half the work and complexity of a Level 5 visit (99215).

There are three different RVUs that are included in the Total RVUs associated with any particular code:

- Work RVU, or WRVU. The WRVU is indicative of the amount of work, time, and complexity involved by the physician or other healthcare provider in the service.
- Practice Expense or PE RVU. This PE RVU is indicative of the amount of practice expense resources needed to perform the procedure. These resources include rent, utilities, supplies, and other items associated with running a practice
- Malpractice Expense or MP WRVU. This component accounts for the cost of malpractice insurance for the individual code.

In addition to the RVUs, there are three other terms in the formula:

- Geographic Practice Cost Index (GPCI). The GPCI is used to provide a market-based index to Medicare fees. GPCIs have been established for every potential area within the United States. In addition to the GPCI for an individual state, there are also oftentimes GPCIs established for the major metropolitan regions within a state. These tables can also be accessed at www.Medicare.gov.
- Budget Neutrality Factor. The Budget Neutrality Factor is a multiplier established to ensure that Medicare expenditures fall within the budgetary requirements established by Medicare. This factor changes on at least

an annual basis. As of January 2007, the factor has been established at .8994.

- Conversion Factor. The Conversion Factor provides the actual amount of revenue for a given code. This factor also changes on at least an annual basis. As of January 2007, a Conversion Factor of $37.8975 was in effect for Medicare payments for code 99213.

All of these factors can be computed for each service in a simple worksheet as follows:

	Code	99213
A	Budget Neutrality Factor	0.8994
B	Conversion Factor	37.8975
C	Work RVU	0.92
D	GPCI	1.003
E	Total Work RVU (A*B*C*D)	$ 31.45
F	Practice Expense RVU	0.71
G	GPCI	0.942
H	Total PE RVU (B*F*G)	$ 25.35
I	Malpractice RVU	0.03
J	GPCI	0.569
K	Total MP RVU (B*I*J)	$ 0.65
L	Total Medicare Payment (E + H + K)	$ 57.45

Therefore, based on the above example the practice must charge a minimum of $57.45 to receive the fully allowed payment from Medicare. As most insurance contracts are established as a percentage of Medicare for allowed payments, it is highly recommended that the practice adopt a pricing strategy that assures fees are consistently set higher than the highest allowable. Therefore, if the managed care contract pays 118 percent of Medicare, it is recommended that the practice utilize an additional factor of at least 118 percent of the above-calculated amount ($57.45 x 1.18 = $67.79) to determine the fee. Oftentimes, rates are rounded to the nearest amount close to the fee to make loading the fee schedules easier. Therefore, a computed fee of $67.79 would be raised to $68 or $70.

DEVELOPING RCM PROCESSES

Now that the practice has decided on its payers, the next step involves establishing processes that will ensure the practice maintains a focused revenue cycle. This phase details what is needed in terms of systems, people, forms, policies, and processes. The work performed in this phase will establish the practice's culture of accountability, as well as train the patient base for what is expected of them. As discussed briefly in the introduction to this chapter, it is imperative that these processes be established immediately after deciding which payers to accept, and consistently enforced with all members of the practice. The establishment of accountability for information gathered, accuracy, and consistency in policy at this stage significantly decreases the potential of poor collections and helps ensure that the practice will receive payment for the services it provides, thus ensuring cash flow for continued practice operations.

Small practices have the ability to use manual processes for billing. While this option is available, the complexity of billing, along with reporting needs and forms creation, all but mandate the need for a computerized billing system. Several options exist—from a scheduling/billing platform to a fully integrated practice management system that includes electronic medical records. There are many reputable software vendors in the marketplace as well as those that do not deliver what was promised. It is highly recommended that practices be extremely diligent in the selection of the vendor. Practices should not only utilize ratings and surveys that show vendor performance, but also interact with current users of the system, schedule site visits, and review reports generated from the system. Surveys of vendors are available from both MGMA (www.MGMA.org) and KLAS (https:// www.healthcomputing.com/).

Computerized billing systems have become so costly that application service providers (ASPs) are now becoming common. ASPs allow practices to use a higher-end program for a monthly fee or on a percentage-of-collection basis. These services allow the practice access to the vendors' data services. These vendors also have differing levels of services at different price points. Another benefit of an ASP is access to up-to-date technology. The vendor is responsible for software upgrades, maintaining services, maintaining redundant data repositories, and oftentimes for the performance of several billing office functions such as cash posting, claim follow-up, and denial tracking. Two of the industry leaders at the time of this chapter offering an ASP product are AthenaHealth (www.athena-health.com) and Med3000 (www.med3000.com).

Regardless of option, the system should include—as a minimum—forms generation, line item posting, reporting, and integration with scheduling. Regardless of the software vendor, all systems are dependent upon obtaining the correct information, entering the information accurately, and enforcing the accountability of staff involved in the process. Without strong accountability, all systems are destined for failure.

FRONT DESK STAFF

Consider that the front desk person is the face of the practice to the public. This person must be highly engaged and accountable for the duties performed. This person often is the one who obtains personal information from the patient that is necessary to process the bill. The front desk staff member also asks for any old balances as well as copayments that are due and enters the insurance information into the billing system. Therefore, he or she must be detail-oriented and highly accurate. The person must be able to perform task-based duties while functioning in an environment that may be fraught with multiple interruptions. When hiring for this position, practices should carefully screen their candidates to ensure they have the traits that will enable them to perform such duties in a manner that enhances customer service.

PATIENT REGISTRATION

Now that the contracts, system, and staff are in place, the real work of revenue cycle begins. The first step is the patient registration process. Registration provides the opportunity to capture all the information necessary to submit a claim for service, as well as to send statements to the patient for any remaining balance. The minimum information required during registration includes:

- Patient name
- Current address
- Phone number (or alternative)
- Birth date
- Guarantor name, address, phone number (if different from patient)
- Employer name (often used for insurance verification)
- Insurance information (a copy of the insurance card provides a reference if information is entered wrong in the system; in addition, the card often includes phone numbers for obtaining preauthorization when needed and to check on member eligibility)
- Social security number (though not required for billing, the patient's social security number must be included if the practice needs to report bad debt to credit reporting agencies).

Some practices choose to obtain this information by phone when the patient calls to schedule a visit; other practices gather the information when the patient presents for services. Either way, federal law mandates that the patient receive a copy of the practice's privacy policy before services are provided to ensure compliance with the Health Insurance Portability and Accountability Act (HIPAA).

BENEFITS VERIFICATION

The practice now has the necessary information to verify benefits before any service is provided. In fact, the practice should create and enforce a policy that ensures benefits are verified prior to the provision of services. Most payers offer some type of Internet-based verification process. Several practice management systems also provide a mechanism for electronic verification. If neither electronic option is available, the practice can contact the insurance company to verify benefits. If the payer reports that the patient is not eligible for benefits or that the benefits cannot be verified, the patient should be informed that full payment must be rendered at the time of service. The practice may establish a process whereby the claim is held for a finite timeframe (usually less than one week) to allow the patient time to supply updated information. By ensuring the verification process prior to providing the service, the practice can set the expectation that the patient is responsible for payment in advance. Of course, benefits verification does not guarantee that the patient is eligible. It is possible the patient has changed employers or benefit levels and that the payer system is out of date. Nor does the verification ensure that the services are medically necessary or approved for payment.

In addition to the eligibility check, the registration process should follow a policy that requires staff to ask patients for payment on balances along with the necessary coinsurance for the day's visit. It is best to remind patients (at the time their appointment is being made) to bring the balance due with them, and then ask for the balance when they present at the front desk.

In terms of any copayment and/or coinsurance for the current visit, the practice can seek these funds before or after the physician sees the patient. If the patient is on a percentage basis for the coinsurance (e.g., Medicare), it will be more effective to ask for this payment after the physician has indicated the services provided. This way, the front desk can quickly calculate the expected payment from the patient for the day's services.

DOCUMENTING SERVICE

Now that the registration information is complete and benefits are verified, the physician can provide services to the patient. Revenue cycle management relies on the physician's knowledge of coding in terms of services and diseases. Services for the day are documented on an encounter form, which also goes by other names such as charge ticket, fee slip, and visit summary. Regardless of the name, the form contains the basic information necessary for the physician to document the services provided along with the diagnosis necessary to support those services. These forms usually contain a list of the most common procedures performed by the practice. The list is categorized by service type and offers the physician the option to indicate procedures not included. In addition to documenting the service and diagnosis codes, the physician should link the service to the diagnosis.

To ensure accurate reimbursement, the physician should attend in-depth training on appropriate evaluation and management coding. The E/M codes account for the majority of services provided by the primary care physician. Most payers compare the physician's own coding levels to averages by specialty to determine if physicians are overcoding their services. If the payer believes the physician is overcoding, it will ask for clinical notes to prove the service level billed. If the payer determines that the notes do not support the service, the payer can retract the billing and ask for repayment from the physician. If the payer is Medicare or another government agency, it can also apply a percentage of error to all billed services and ask for a payback of this percentage to the practice's complete billings to the payer over a period of time. Obviously, the documentation of coding levels is critical, and physicians should seek all training available to ensure accuracy.

Once the physician completes the encounter form, the form and the patient are walked to the front desk for processing. The ideal process at this time involves entering the charges into the system, collecting any coinsurance/copayments, and providing the patient with a summary of the day's services including the total amount charged. When charge entry occurs as the patient is leaving, any missing information can be easily obtained from either the patient or the physician. Depending upon the system used, feedback in this manner helps avoid potential errors on the claim.

SUBMITTING THE CLAIM

The charges are now ready for submission to the insurance carrier. To begin, most payer systems perform an initial review of the claim using what is commonly referred to as "claim scrubbing." The claim scrubbing process ensures that all information is in the correct blocks, ID numbers are in the appropriate format, and the claim appears "clean" from a submission standpoint. If potential problems are found, the claim is returned to the practice for editing and resubmission. If the claim is clean, it moves on to the next step for processing. At this point, the practice may receive verification that the claim has been successfully submitted.

Prior to payment, however, the payer again edits the claim for completeness. If errors are found, the payer will either return the claim electronically or deny it based on the errors. If the claim passes the edit process, it will be accepted for payment. Depending upon the contract and state regulations, the practice will receive payment within 14 to 30 days after approval of the claim.

CLAIM PAYMENT

Claims are paid to the practice via a remittance advice, commonly referred to as a remit. The remittance advice lists the practice's claims that were processed in the current payment cycle. It also includes a list of claims that were denied and the reason for each denial. Most remits will provide the information needed for posting the payments on the account, as well as any contractual allowances (which are the differences between the payer's approved fee schedule and the amount billed by the practice). Remits also list amounts that are due from the patient or that should be submitted to a secondary insurance carrier. Many Medicare patients have supplemental insurance to pay the 20 percent portion that Medicare deems is the patient's responsibility. In addition, some patients have multiple policies that can pay the claim depending upon the patient's coverage, their spouse's coverage, or a multitude of other options in which they have arranged for complete coverage for medical services.

Many payers prefer that the remittance and the payment for services occur through electronic means rather than paper remits sent via the mail. Several practice management systems can accept these files from the payer and automatically post the remits into the system. If the system does not support this functionality, the remits must be printed and then manually posted, along with the paper remits received in the mail. To post a remit, the practice must follow the process documented within its practice management system. Most systems use a process whereby the payments are applied to the individual line item and then any remaining balances are either "dropped" to the patient or submitted to the secondary insurance.

During remit posting, it is recommended that the denials also be processed. Often, these denials can be reversed by correcting some part of the demographic information, providing additional documentation, or rebilling under a code that more accurately describes the service provided. By working the denials at this point, the practice can prevent backlogs as well as help build efficiencies by handling one piece of paper one time only.

CONTROL POLICIES

Revenue management as described here would seem to be a fairly straightforward process. In its purest form, it is. However, every step does not always go according to plan. To help maintain an efficient revenue management program, a practice must implement effective controls, policies, processes, and measurement metrics to ensure that the systems function as designed.

Control policies are a central principle in a well-designed revenue management system. Control policies minimize the risk of staff impropriety as well as providing guidelines for all involved. Control policies should be followed by all practice personnel, including the physician, and should be designed to facilitate productivity while ensuring full compliance.

Cash Control

One of the most essential control policies is cash control. Cash in the medical practice is no different than cash in any retail establishment. In the event of a robbery, offices often have cash stolen along with drugs and computer equipment. In addition, without strong cash controls, it is extremely easy for a front desk staff member to pocket copayments from the patient and not show the payment in the system.

The first aspect of a cash control policy is physical control over the cash box. The box needs to be secured in a locking desk drawer or other area not easily accessed by the patient. Office personnel should be trained to not leave cash lying out where a patient or other visitor could easily take it without being noticed. In addition, the cash control policy should clearly state that all patients are to receive a receipt when the cash transaction occurs. Receipts should be provided on a prenumbered receipt pad if a manual process is used or by a system-generated receipt pad if the process is automated. For system-generated receipts, the practice needs to ensure that a clear audit trail exists if the transaction is subsequently voided or changed.

Daily Cash Reconciliation

A daily cash reconciliation process should exist as well. This process should include the following items:

1. A verification of the total cash received for the day, including a breakdown of cash, checks, and credit card payments.

2. A verification of any missing receipts if the process is manual. All receipts should be accounted for, including voided transactions.
3. A verification of cash against the system-generated report if the process is automated. Discrepancies should be researched and corrected.
4. A verification of the change funds remaining at the end of the day. The amount noted here should match the funds that were in place at the end of the prior day. Discrepancies should be researched and noted.

Upon completion of the daily cash reconciliation process, the daily deposit ticket should be completed with a list of all cash and checks received. The daily credit card submission should also be recorded. The deposit is then ready to be taken to the bank. As a final step, the deposit slip from the bank should be given to the office manager or practice accountant, who will be responsible for verifying the deposits with the monthly bank reconciliation.

In addition to posting cash to the receivables system, zero pays are also extremely important to the cash control process. Most payers will indicate denials as a zero payment. These zero pays should be posted at the same time as the remit. Denial codes and write-off adjustments should have very clear codes so that they can be differentiated from contract allowances, which are also posted at this time. If the practice were to use a global contractual allowance code for all noncash credits to the patient's account, it would lose the ability to later analyze and trend denials. By tracking these codes every month, the practice can readily analyze root causes and thus prevent recurrences of the same denial.

Charge Capture

Charge capture is another process that requires strict control measures. Charge capture helps ensure that the practice captures all charges for services performed. For most offices, the encounter form provides the basis of this process. If the encounter forms are system generated, a report can easily show which are outstanding. For offices that do not use system-generated reports, a process should be established as part of the daily closing procedure, whereby all encounter forms are compared against the daily schedule. Daily accounting of the encounter forms will ensure that every patient who presented in the office has a bill for the day's services.

It is harder to ensure that all charges are captured for services performed outside the office. Services performed outside the office include hospital rounding, nursing home visits, and service provision at other sites. Due to daily changes in patient status, prearranged schedules do not usually take place for these services. The physician will often receive a rounding list for the hospital or nursing home; other times, the physician's office might provide a notice that a new patient is being treated in a facility. To help ensure the capture of external services, many practices use a rounding slip. This slip contains abbreviated information such as the patient's name and a short list of the most common procedure codes for external visits. The physician should complete one slip for each patient. Some practices choose to use one slip per patient admission; others use a slip for every day of service.

Regardless of whether slips are generated daily or based on the complete admission, the billing should include services related to admission, discharge, and daily consults as needed. Most hospitals and nursing homes will provide the practice with a list of patients who have been admitted under the physician for the time frame indicated. This report then becomes the control mechanism for these services. The practice should compare the report against the charge slips turned in by the physician.

Another aspect of charge capture that cannot be overlooked is the assurance that oral orders are documented on the encounter form prior to charge entry. Physicians often give an oral order to a clinical assistant to provide a treatment, give an injection, or draw some type of lab sample. When these orders occur, the clinical assistant needs to be trained to document the procedure both in the medical chart and on the encounter form. By having the physician *and* the clinical assistant document on the form, the practice will minimize the possibility of lost revenue from missed procedures. Several of these procedures and injections may involve costly drugs. Therefore, if a procedure is missed, not only is revenue lost but (depending on the cost of the vaccine or drug) the practice could in theory be paying a vendor for the visit. A recent example of this problem has been for the human papillomavirus vaccine (HPV). As HPV is a relatively new vaccine, several payers have not yet established a reimbursement amount for its administration. In addition, access to the vaccine has been somewhat limited, driving the acquisition cost higher than what the few payers have allowed for reimbursement. Early adopters of this vaccine oftentimes lost money on every vaccine administered. As market forces allow for greater distribution and the payers update their schedules, this issue should resolve itself.

CONTROLS AND GROWTH

It is essential that cash and charge control measures be developed at the onset of the practice start-up. The measures will be simple at first. However, as the practice grows in patient volume, physicians, and staff, these controls will form the basis for further expansion. For example, a small practice has only a few employees. But as the practice grows, its processes should change to allow for double checks. That is, the person who checks the patient in should be different than the person who checks the patient out. The person who takes the cash should be different than the person who deposits the cash.

FINANCIAL POLICIES

Along with implementation of control measures, the practice must also develop fairly rigid financial policies. These policies enable front desk personnel to effectively manage communication regarding the patient's responsibility to pay and provide guidance for difficult decisions.

Credit Extension

The first policy that should be addressed is a credit extension or self-pay policy. This policy would cover both the true self-pay patient (no insurance) as well as the patient who has copayment and out-of-pocket requirements. Ideally, this policy would be written so that the expectation to pay any balance is firmly set when the patient first registers. In addition to stating the fee schedule, points that should be addressed in the policy include:

- Patients are expected to bring their copayments with them for all visits. Copayments will be collected at the time of service.
- After the insurance company pays, patients are expected to pay any balance remaining on the account within 15 days of being sent a statement.
- Follow-up appointments may be withheld for patients with outstanding self-pay balances. In addition, failure to pay the balance in full will result in discharge from the practice.

Some practices choose to include these statements within their assignment of benefit forms. Some practices will post these policies at the front window. Regardless of how they are communicated, policies are ineffective unless the physician is willing to enforce them. In addition, it is a violation of law to not collect a Medicare coinsurance amount, and managed care plans have been known to revoke physician contracts for failure to collect copayments.

For the true self-pay patient, practices have options. True self-pays are patients who either by choice or by circumstance do not have insurance coverage, yet may have the ability to pay directly for services. Some practices use their standard fee schedule or provide a percentage off for self-pay patients. Others have a fee schedule that is an aggregation of the different payer rates or equivalent to the highest or lowest contract. Regardless of which option is preferred by the practice, it is advisable that with any discount from the normal fee schedule, the patient sign a contract that stipulates the discount as well as the expected payment terms.

To help ensure tight cash control, all staff must be trained regarding the importance of cash to the practice. It should be required that staff tell patients about their outstanding balances when they make appointments. In addition, patients should be asked to pay the balances when they present for payment of the day's services. By having all staff aware of the importance of cash collections and providing consistent information to patients, the practice will ultimately minimize the risk of poor collections.

Understandably, some physicians have difficulty with these policy points, especially the one regarding the discharge of a patient. Physicians feel they have a duty to treat their patients regardless of the patients' compliance with payment. While there is a duty to treat, the practice cannot exist without cash flow. In addition, the community learns quickly who will enforce financial policies and who will not. Therefore, the practice could very quickly have a large base of patients who do not pay their bills. Discharging a patient is a last resort only and must be accompanied by a notice to the patient. It is recommended that the physician check with the appropriate state medical board to determine the notification period necessary to discharge a patient from care for nonpayment. Most states require a 30-day period, but it varies by state.

A final point of consideration for the credit extension or self-pay policy regards accounts that have been submitted to collections. Some practices will allow a predetermined percentage "discount" to be applied if the patient is willing to make immediate payment. Regardless of the discount used, this policy should allow any staff member involved in billing to implement the policy when needed. By doing so, the person on the phone with the delinquent patient will be able to work with the patient without adding additional delay to the process.

Noncovered Services

The next financial policy deals with noncovered services. Government payers such as Medicare and most third-party carriers will allow a physician to directly bill a patient for a noncovered item. However, to do so, the patient must sign a document called an "Advanced Beneficiary Notice" (ABN) detailing why the service is not covered, as well as the expected charge for the item. Common items that are often not covered include preventive services, some lab testing, some vaccines, sports physicals, and school physicals. Different payers, however, have different rules for each of these services, and it is imperative the practice have a thorough understanding of the payer-specific rules.

In order to ensure payment for these services, the front desk staff must know the specifics of each major carrier. Ideally, the staff will have called and verified the coverage of a specific code prior to the service being provided. The reality, however, is that a patient will ask for or need a specific service at the visit that will likely not be covered. To prevent this situation the physician, as well as the back-office staff, will need to be trained on completing an ABN prior to actually performing the service.

Under Medicare law, a patient can ask that the service be billed to Medicare, even knowing it will be denied. These are called demand denials and can easily be processed with a modifier indicating that it is being billed at the patient's request and that an ABN is in place. Without the ABN, the practice has little opportunity to recoup payment from the patient.

MEASUREMENT METRICS

The final aspect of the revenue cycle is that of measurement metrics. Ultimately, the only "real" metric is cash in the bank and all else is management process. The other metrics, however, allow for predictive models for cash flow and provide indicators of how well the practice is managing receivables and, thus, cash flow. The metrics also provide a comparison for the practice to benchmark against other practices to determine if the revenue cycle metrics are in line with the industry.

These metrics are published in annual surveys from various trade organizations, the prevalent one being the Medical Group Management Association (MGMA).

A/R Days

The first metric that is usually looked at is the Days of Sales Outstanding (DSO); also referred to as the number of Days in Accounts Receivable (A/R), or A/R Days. This standard is computed by dividing the total accounts receivable by the average amount of charges in a given day. The average amount of charges can be for a week, month, quarter, six-month period, or even a year. The purpose of using a longer period for comparison is to remove any seasonality from the equation.

This metric tells the practice, on average, how long it takes to collect on the services generated. Therefore, if a patient is seen today and the DSO is at 28 days, the practice should expect to collect on this account 28 days from the current date, if not sooner. Some practices choose to further refine this metric and track it by different payers. Government payers such as Medicare usually pay within 14 days, while other government agencies will pay within 30 days or even up to 180 days for workers compensation, Black Lung benefits, or Champus. Commercial payers have different payment cycles as well. Oftentimes these are agreed upon in the contract signed by the payer and the practice. Commonly, the contract with the payer stipulates that they will pay a clean claim within 30 days of receipt.

Breaking this metric down to a payer level also provides information for the practice in states that have a clean claim submission law. Ohio is currently a state with this type of law. Within Ohio, the payer must pay a clean claim within 30 days. If the claim is not paid, the carrier must also pay interest to the provider at the Federal Reserve Rate for all days beyond the 30-day period. A report that shows the A/R days by payer gives the practice a bargaining tool, as well as a tool to help predict interest payments or show missing interest payments.

Typically, A/R days are measured monthly and trended against prior months. The trending is important to explain variances. An increase in days can be related to several different factors, the first of which is that the practice is growing. As revenues grow and more physicians are hired, A/R days tend to increase. However, even in growth modes, significant increases could indicate problems in the revenue cycle process.

When the A/R days grow, a root cause analysis should be performed to look at the underlying issue. A root cause analysis involves six basic steps:

1. Define the problem.

   - What has occurred?
   - Why is it a problem?
   - What will happen if the problem or situation continues?

2. Gather data/evidence.

- Gather reports
- Graph the change in values over multiple periods of time
- Depending on the problem, look for evidence of changes in claim submission rules, deposit histories, remits, and so forth.

3. Identify issues that contribute to the problem.

- Are there new staff or temps in the process?
- Audit the accuracy of information capture at the front desk
- Is the billing system printing outdated forms or using outdated claim submission rules?

4. Find the root cause.

- Use the 80/20 rule in looking at the data. Group the issues into like causes (e.g., registration, claims processing, denial management). Focus on the causative factors that would contribute to 80 percent of the problems.

5. Develop solution recommendations.

- Do staff need additional training?
- Would a software update solve the problem?
- Would a meeting with a payer solve the problem?
- Do forms need updating?
- Do all staff have access to the appropriate tools to perform their job?

6. Implement the solution.

- Fix whatever was identified in the above steps, focusing on the 80/20 rules

7. Reevaluate the effectiveness of the solution. If necessary repeat steps 2 through 6.

180-Day Claims

The next metric that should be examined within the aging report are the claims aged beyond 180 days. Most aging reports break the outstanding claims into categories of 30 days. These reports often lump all the claims over 180 days into one final category. What is important in this report is the percentage of claims that are aged over 90 days and again over 180 days. It becomes increasingly difficult to collect a claim that has aged beyond 90 days. Most payers have timely filing requirements established within their contracts. The timely filing clauses state that a claim must be submitted by the practice within a certain number of days from the date of service. The practice must be able to prove that the payer had received the claim within the set time limit of the contract. If the practice can prove the submission, the claim will usually be adjudicated and paid. If the practice cannot prove the submission, the practice might or might not be able to bill the patient (depending upon language of the contract). In addition, self-pay balances become harder to collect as they age out. If the visit was a one-time visit and the patient does not maintain an ongoing relationship with the practice, there is little incentive for the patient to pay, beyond the fear of collection agencies and credit reporting. The medical practice needs to make a determination of when these accounts reach a bad debt status and are written off the receivable report.

Depending upon the judgment of the practice's accounting staff and whether the practice uses accrual-based accounting, reserves may be established based on the age of the receivables. Some practices reserve 50 percent of value over 120 days, while others reserve 100 percent of the claims aged beyond 180 days. Regardless of which system is used, the aged accounts have a negative effect on the practice's fiscal performance. If the practice maintains a cash-based accounting methodology, revenue recognition is based on the cash received.

It is extremely important to review the aging based on the date of service rather than the date filed. Several computer systems provide the report using both criteria. Running the report based on the claim submission date shows the efficiency of that individual payer, but it can mask the actual performance of the billing process. Since many payer contracts as well as Medicare and Medicaid have limits on timely filing, it is extremely important to closely manage the aging of accounts. The practice needs to ensure that all claims are submitted to the payer within the appropriate time-filing limits or the claim will not be paid, and the practice is contractually obligated to not bill the patient.

Net Revenue versus Gross Revenue

The next metric is net revenue (or cash collections) compared to gross revenue. While this measurement is very helpful to predict future cash flows, it should be realized that there is a great deal of variability when comparing rates to other practices and even national standards. The greatest factor in the variability is the fee schedule compared to managed-care rates. Often, fees are established that ensure that the practice bills more than their highest contracted fee schedule from managed care companies, while other practices simply establish their fees based on Medicare reimbursement. While two practices could each be paid $85 for an office visit, the first practice might charge $85 for the visit, and the other practice could charge $100. Thus the net-to-gross revenue rate for the first practice is 100 percent and the other practice is 85 percent.

Some practices choose to use a revenue realization metric rather than a collection percentage. Revenue realization removes the variability of fee schedules and provides an effective review of billing efficiencies. In its simplest form, a revenue realization report will total all the charges for a specific month and then apply all payments and adjustments received on those charges. Revenue realization can take place only when there are a sufficient number of months of accounts receivable data. Ideally, the revenue realization report will show that 100 percent of a given month's charges has been fully adjudicated through payments and adjustments. Any amounts remaining are indicative of money that is still owed the practice.

CONCLUSION

While there are several other processes, policies, control measures, and metrics used in revenue cycle management, the ones mentioned here, along with the ideal RCM process first explained in this chapter, will help to ensure that the practice has a comprehensive approach. As the practice continues to expand, additional control measures and practices will need to be established. However, it is highly advisable to establish policies that are communicated to all staff and enforced without exception. Every exception to policy and control process creates an additional opportunity for lost revenue and decreased collections. By having clear policies and processes and establishing clear expectations for performance with staff and patients from their very first encounter, the revenue cycle will function well from the beginning.

FURTHER READING

Henry, T. C. 2000. *Looking for the Cash Cow.* Englewood, CO: Medical Group Management Association's Center for Research.

Medical Group Management Association. www.MGMA.com. Publications include prewritten policies, billing system vendor surveys, collection agency surveys, and a listserve to answer questions.

CHAPTER 9

The Future of the Physician Practice

Severine Brocki and Kathleen Henrichs

The turbulence and uncertainty that physicians have experienced in the last 20 years in adapting to the multiple forces transforming the delivery of healthcare will continue and likely increase. Cost pressures, quality issues, increasing competition, and burgeoning scientific and technological innovations are challenging the way healthcare is delivered. Confronting these issues will result in a major redirection and realignment in physician practices across the delivery spectrum, including the types of services provided and the ways they are delivered, practice organization, and provider and patient relationships.

This chapter reviews the current status and trends in the practice of medicine and discusses future directions for physician practice, both obvious and not so obvious, as the medical profession advances to the next generation of practice. The forecasts, while potentially disruptive in the shorter and even longer run, do not consign the medical profession to a bleak future in terms of professional satisfaction and stature. In fact, medical practitioners who are able to adjust to these changes by actively advancing their stake in the continuing evolution of healthcare will survive and even prosper. With change comes opportunity, including the prospect of new tools and systems that, while fundamentally changing physician practice in many ways, will advance the quality of care that the medical profession can provide.

The authors are grateful to Bruce E. Balfe, Vice President of Strategic Planning, the American Medical Association, for his insightful and visionary guidance and first-rate scholarship.

CURRENT STATE OF MEDICAL PRACTICE

This section profiles some fundamental features of medical practice as it currently stands. These practice characteristics constitute a platform from which many future practice patterns will emanate. They also identify some of the ways physicians are adapting to today's healthcare market and how changes in the personal values of physicians themselves are influencing practice patterns.

Practice Groups: Growth in Number and Size

Group practices are on the rise, both in number and size, necessitated by the high costs of maintaining competitive solo and small practices. The number of group practices increased from 16,500 in 1990 to more than 37,000 in 2003.[1] Data from the American Medical Association (AMA) show that from 177,000 to 185,000 physicians in the United States are practicing in groups.[2] (The AMA considers a practice a group if it has 3 or more physicians.) Excluding physicians who practice in institutional settings, only 33 percent of physicians were in solo practices in 2001. The remaining 67 percent of office-based physicians worked in practices with two or more physicians, an increase from 54 percent in 1991.[3] In 2001 (the latest year for which AMA data are available), the distribution of physicians by practice size was solo practices (33 percent), 2-physician practices (11 percent), 3 physicians (9 percent), 4 to 8 physicians (22 percent), and practices of 8 or more physicians (25 percent).[4]

Employment as an Emerging Phenomenon

Physicians are increasingly becoming employees. They are working as salaried providers of services in group practices, hospitals, health maintenance organizations, and other delivery systems and facilities. More physicians are seeking employment with hospitals and large group practices for the financial stability they afford as well as their ability to provide physicians with the state-of-the-art resources, including advanced health information technology systems.[5]

Lifestyle Factors and Their Impact

Younger physicians express a greater interest in balancing their personal and professional lives than previous generations of medical practitioners, looking to allocate more time for their families and recreational pursuits.[6] Lifestyle considerations such as predictability of working hours and some control over the total number of hours worked are not only major factors in a physician's decision to become an employee but also affect specialty choice.[7] The effects of lifestyle preferences on physicians' practices are due in large part to the "feminization" of medicine. Presently, almost 27 percent of physicians in this country are female and this percentage is growing steadily.[8] In 2006, over 17,000 students enrolled in United States medical schools and 48.6 percent of these first-year enrollees were women.[9] Women tend to approach their careers differently than men, focusing more attention on the personal components of their lives. Survey data showed that child-rearing causes 25 percent of female physicians to work fewer than 40 hours per week compared to 12 percent of male physicians who do so.[10] However, this phenomenon is not exclusive to women physicians. Male physicians are also increasingly looking for more balance between their professional and personal lives.

Student Debt Impacting Career Decisions

Over 80 percent of medical school graduates carry educational debt.[11] In 2003, the median debt for graduates from public medical schools was $100,000 and for private medical schools, $135,000.[12] In constant dollars, medical school debt has risen more than 150 percent since 1984.[13] While the relationship between debt and specialty choice has been debated, many believe that a considerable number of medical students consider their amount of debt as a factor in making career decisions. In a 2002 survey by the Association of American Medical Colleges (AAMC), 32 percent of medical students responded that their debt level influenced their choice of specialties.[14] The AAMC believes that large debt is partly responsible for the decrease in students who elect to enter the primary care specialties. The American College of Physicians (ACP) has also expressed concern that students will avoid primary care practices because of lower reimbursements coupled with high student debt.[15]

Supply for 24/7 Services Not Meeting Demand

While there has been a rapid growth of patients making Emergency Department (ED) visits, this has been occurring as the number of the facilities offering these services has been declining. Between 1993 and 2003, the number of hospitals in the United States decreased by 703 and the number of American EDs fell by 425.[16] Yet in 2003, there were almost 114 million ED visits; compare this to the figure of over 90 million visits 10 years earlier.[17] The Institute of Medicine's (IOM) Committee on the Future of Emergency Care in the U.S. Health System (2006) reports that ED overcrowding leads to problems such as boarding patients in the ED (sometimes in hallways) until inpatient beds become available and ambulance diversions from an ED that is full to a more distant one that is not.[18] Factors contributing to the inadequacy of "24/7" services include the difficulty in finding specialists who want to be on-call, lack of reimbursement because many emergency patients are uninsured, and higher liability payments for specialists who work in EDs because of the riskier procedures.

The Healthcare Team: Need for a Game Plan

Chronic disease management is driving healthcare expenditures and with the aging baby boomers, costs will escalate dramatically. The scale of team care needed by chronically ill patients is staggering when one looks at the statistics for this population. Current estimates are that almost 100 million Americans have some type of chronic disease. Of Medicare beneficiaries, 78 percent have at least one chronic condition while two-thirds have two chronic conditions or more.[19] Of those with two chronic conditions or more, almost one-third (or 20 percent of the total Medicare population) has five more chronic conditions or comorbidities. A Medicare beneficiary with two chronic conditions averages over 11 doctor visits per year and sees more than five different physicians annually.

One outcome of these numbers is that except for those who specialize in pediatrics, physicians who are currently in training will spend half of their future practice time treating patients who are over 65 years of age, the large majority of whom will have multiple chronic illnesses.[20] Well-coordinated healthcare teams are critical in the management of chronic disease, but the current insufficiency of care coordination is well acknowledged. The "silos" of care that the Institute of Medicine described produce treatment that is fragmented because of inadequate communication among providers and across delivery sites.[21] The problem is exacerbated by a deficiency of provider incentives for coordinating care because many of these services go unreimbursed.

Continued Pressure on Practice Income with Detriments to Healthcare Access

Reimbursement constraints and escalating costs are exerting downward pressure on practice income and these strains on physician income will undoubtedly increase, at least for the next decade. Between 1995 and 2003, the average net income from the practice of medicine declined about 7 percent after adjusting for inflation.[22] Research by the Center for Studying Health System Change shows that after inflation adjustment, the average net income for primary care physicians declined 10 percent from 1995 to 2003, to $121,000, while physician specialists experienced a 2 percent drop to $175,000 in the same period.[23] Declining and flat fees from both public and private payers are primarily responsible for this squeeze on practice income, a situation spurred by the soaring costs of healthcare, which are projected to exceed $2 trillion in 2006, equivalent to 16 percent of the gross domestic product (GDP).[24]

The future for physician income looks just as bleak since the federal government proposes to decrease Medicare payments to physicians by 37 percent over the next 9 years while the cost of providing patient care is expected to rise 22 percent or greater.[25] Reimbursement cuts may also affect physicians' service populations. An AMA survey indicated that if Medicare reimbursements continue to decrease, 38 percent of the physician respondents said that they would be forced to decrease the number of new Medicare patients they accept.[26]

FUTURE DIRECTIONS: THE OBVIOUS

The following are practice patterns that have gained momentum in the last 10 to 20 years and represent trends that are reasonably well entrenched. They are anticipated to continue in the future, with some of them increasing in intensity.

Impending (and in Some Cases Current) Shortages of Healthcare Practitioners

The shortages of physicians, nurses, and other healthcare professionals are real concerns for the delivery of quality care. The Council on Graduate Medical Education (COGME) predicts that if present trends continue, physician demand will outweigh supply substantially by the year 2020 with a shortage of 85,000 physicians.[27] Federal projections estimate that nurses will also be in short supply by 2020, although the gap may be narrowing by the increase of people choosing to assume nursing careers in their late 20s and early 30s.[28] Ultimately, the market will help calibrate and adjust for this, but the lag times in the health professions education system are considerable and there will be substantial discontinuities as we go forward. These are real or unavoidable problems in the short term and will exert impact on which physician practice specialties and nonphysician providers the market ends up rewarding. These shortages will also be a factor in the "negotiations" that physicians and other health professionals have with their "employers" over wages and working conditions.

Increased Separation of Business and Clinical Decision Processes

The larger the group practice, the greater the separation of elements involved in decision making, and the smaller the practice, the more integrated these elements are. Given the growth in number and size of medical practice groups, the following will characterize their business and clinical decision making as the business side becomes more complex:

- If efforts to increase market competition are successful (even moderately so), the level of business and marketing sophistication it will take to run a practice from a business perspective will increase dramatically and physician group management will grow in size and stature as a profession to the point where it rivals what hospital administration has become.
- As the business side of a practice "professionalizes" there is the real prospect that some of the tensions between the business and clinical sides of practices will increase. A "we-they" syndrome may well develop, especially in groups where there are both equity and nonequity partners. Organizing clinical staff in a manner similar to the way hospital medical staffs are organized (with bylaws, officers, and so forth) may well become a common pattern. It is also possible that this organizing could occur through unions, which will be discussed further in this chapter.

More Employment and Fewer Independent Practices

As noted previously, employment is increasingly becoming the choice of physicians and will continue to be so. For many physicians, spending more time on patient care in larger practices where administrative support and information technologies insulate them from the day-to-day business decisions is an attractive practice feature.[29] There is evidence that doctors are beginning to hire agents to help them locate employment and negotiate contracts with insurance and health plans.[30] While this activity is in its embryonic stage at this point, it is yet another symptom of physicians acting more like employees and seeking career assistance rather than practice management support.

A Mix of Equity Partners and Physician Employees, Including the Law-Firm Model

The Medical Group Management Association (MGMA) estimates that the capital required to develop and support the type of physician organization capable of competing in the marketplace can run from several hundred thousand dollars to millions.[31] Partnering with hospitals, health plans, and venture capitalists are some alternatives that practices are exploring to raise this capital. With the escalation of physician group practices, a growing option for equity financing is the classic law firm model. Typically this model is organized around partners who jointly own the firm and share in its profits and losses and associates who are employed by the firm, in some instances having the opportunity to one day become partners. This type of practice arrangement will present some interesting directions related to workforce supply, attitudes toward scope of practice issues, and physicians' expectations from their practice.

- The law firm model and younger physicians' attitudes toward a more balanced lifestyle will be in conflict, particularly as more group practices have both equity and nonequity partners. The dominant pattern now is that nonequity partners are junior partners or associates who expect to become full partners with a real stake in the practice. However, some younger physicians are joining practices as employees who do not expect to become partners, or who expect it but will not necessarily achieve it. A major factor in the potential discord of these practices will be whether the senior physicians emulate law firm partners who expect junior members to work 80 hours per week for lower compensation while the senior partners get the lucrative cases and earn the large incomes. Presently, there is not enough evidence to predict a pattern on this.
- The lifestyle preferences of younger physicians and the more ambitious business goals will be in some conflict. Physicians in specialties where there is a shortage will have some leverage in determining their working conditions and the overall impact of this across the system will be less workforce (in terms of full-time-equivalents (FTEs) for purposes of meeting patient demand). This will set up negotiations between physician employees and their employers, and open up an opportunity for agents who negotiate employment terms for physicians.

- Physicians in "law firm model" practices will be looking to their medical societies for counseling on career development and climbing the corporate ladder instead of learning skills in practice management.

The Procedural versus Cognitive Differential: Likely to Continue

The procedural versus cognitive differential in payment remains resilient to change, and practices in cognitive specialties such as internal medicine, cardiology, and pediatrics are continuing to expand their in-office diagnostic procedures to improve their bottom lines. This differential will persist, at least until the growth of health information technology (HIT) enables the quality movement to mature and there is real outcomes data that can be brought to bear on this issue. If improved outcome measures demonstrate that medical interventions are equal to or more effective than procedural interventions, the cognitive-procedural differential will probably be reduced. However, outcomes-based adjustments are probable in both the procedural and cognitive arenas, and there will likely be a lasting tendency to invest "actually doing something" with a higher value than "just knowing something."

Automated Offices Become the Norm

Computerized provider order entry (CPOE) has been around for over 30 years and yet CPOE is used by only 5.7 percent of nongovernmental U.S. hospitals.[32] Yet broader use of HIT in clinical situations is inevitable, receiving assistance from the Department of Health and Human Services (DHHS) funded Health Information Technology Standards Panel, which reported on its first set of standardized clinical vocabulary in late 2006. While patient health records are now largely paper and scattered among caregivers and across delivery sites, electronic records will be self-contained and accessible from almost anywhere by patients as well as providers. Although there is significant movement in implementing this technology, there is still a long way to go before the healthcare industry has an electronic and interoperable system of patient records.

- Cost is a major barrier, and an alignment problem between payers and providers about who should bear the burden of the investment will occur in the short run. In the end, it is reasonable to expect that this technology will be subsidized by the government and the creative capitalization efforts of both payers and providers.
- To compete successfully, physicians will ultimately need to obtain and use digital applications, regardless of their practice size and setting. Automation in records and practice administration will permit easier measurement development for quality and efficiency analysis as well as more timely and effective treatment. Examples of benefits include the better

management of medical prescriptions, projected to be 4 billion in 2006, up from 3.4 billion in 2003.[33] Evidence-based protocols can also be delivered right to physicians' desks. Such an instantaneous dissemination of information may help bring more state-of-the-art medicine to remote geographical areas. There are concerns that automation will make it easier to sort out the patient types who are less desirable for practices and payers. Taking lessons from the continued advancement of security measures being implemented today in e-commerce, physician practices and the healthcare industry as a whole must develop and adhere to technologies and protocols that protect the privacy of patients' electronic records.

Bioethics: A Continued Struggle

In today's world, societal values change at a much slower pace than technology and this lag will likely continue. Stem cell research and its application, organ transplantation, end-of-life care, and genetic engineering are just some of the areas that will remain bioethical issues. Physicians will continue to be confronted with making judgments on behalf of or in conjunction with their patients for which current ethical thinking does not provide ready or clear answers. This same issue will play out on a societal level. The question of universal coverage is ultimately a societal value related to using technology that is available. Outcomes information from the quality movement will help inform this quandary but it will not answer the fundamental question of how much is enough and whether the health of people and thus healthcare is a societal asset in which to invest or a commodity to be bought and sold. Medical practices will continue to be at the center of this conundrum both as partial drivers of the calculus itself and as a key component of the system that is affected by it.

Marketing of Medical Practices Becomes Essential

To become or remain competitive, medical practices need to market themselves the same way that other successful businesses do. The realities of the healthcare environment, both now and in the future, require physicians to promote the advantages of their practices over those of their competitors. To attract patients, acquire capital, and develop strategic partnerships, it is important for a practice to develop a presence in the market, by raising its profile and identity in its service area. Since consumers are becoming more reliant on the Internet for obtaining information about businesses, practice Web sites are progressively essential for success as Internet competition for patients continues to intensify. Solo and small practices are no exceptions since larger group practices have the resources to market themselves more extensively and many do a very effective job. Reliance on word of mouth is no longer sufficient to grow a practice and all physician practices will have to make efforts to understand the dynamics of their service areas and develop strategies to compete successfully.

FUTURE DIRECTIONS: THE NOT SO OBVIOUS

Many future implications for the practice of medicine are not very obvious, resulting from the complex interaction of events and conditions that will emanate from the healthcare marketplace.

How the "Quality Agenda" Will Play Out with the Help of Health Information Technology

In their publication, *Redefining Health Care,* Porter and Teisberg make a compelling argument for how value-based competition (the best outcome per unit cost) is the only solution to the country's healthcare problems of uneven quality, limited access, and high cost.[34] They contend that many pay-for-performance proposals and experiments will reward compliance with a process rather than with quality outcomes and thus confuse cost-savings with quality. The authors reject the assumption that quality means higher cost by maintaining that good quality should cost less. While Porter and Teisberg's argument has intuitive appeal, it appears that the whole structure of healthcare must change to realize a situation close to the one they propose. Yet maybe this is beginning to happen already organically.

- Private groups such as the Integrated Healthcare Association (IHA), the Leapfrog Group, and the Quality Forum have developed their own programs to influence the use of data to measure quality and to make the reporting of quality results a standard at healthcare facilities.
- In the area of information technology, concern about the level of investment needed to establish HIT systems and the issues of who has to invest (providers) and who reaps the benefits (payers) will arise in the short term in what the HIT world refers to as the "alignment problem." However, a look at how technology has evolved in other industries can be used as a reference point. Initially, there are many vendors in a field, but eventually, a dominant player starts to prevail (although there is no guarantee it will be the technically superior one). The overwhelming need for standardization will drive the market to one system or several with high degrees of compatibility (as in the VCR, ATM, and software industries).
- As healthcare providers start using whatever system emerges, will the efficiency of healthcare delivery improve dramatically? Will unit cost go down or increase at a slower rate? Will data to support quality assessment and assurance become readily available? As in other fields, the answers to these questions will derive more from other phenomena than from what is going on in the HIT sector per se. Fifteen years ago, the big push in business consulting was that the Internet would change everything and any company that did not redefine itself via the Internet would be out of business within the decade. The reality is that while the Internet did dramatically affect many things, most industries are not in a different business because of it. They just have a new tool, a very significant one in many instances, to use in their enterprises. Other than those involved

in running the Internet itself such as Google, only a small number of businesses were created by the Internet, like eBay, Amazon.com, and Match.com. A similar fate will happen to HIT. When it comes into its own, it will be analogous to a utility that enables many activities but does not constitute a redefinition of the industry.

- The dimensions of medical practice and healthcare that will be substantially enabled by HIT will be quality of care measurement and related quality assurance activities. The availability of data enabled by HIT will make it possible for the outcomes dimension of quality assurance to fully develop. When that happens, the economic and scientific dynamics of healthcare will change forever. Value-based assessment of outcomes will inform and educate patients and drive major change in how medical education is taught. Purchasers and payers will be able to assess the cost-benefit of different clinical and delivery approaches and tailor coverage options accordingly. In short, the existence of value-based outcome measures will demystify medical care to the point where rational decision-making about healthcare options will be much more feasible.

- Outcomes measurement will happen in two stages. First will be applying HIT to current systems and processes of organizing and delivering care (a duration of possibly 4 to 8 years). Second will be when those systems and processes for organizing and delivering care are redesigned by people who think about them in a nontraditional context (mostly from the "digital generation"), such as critical enablers of quality care (another 8 to 15 years).

The "Art" of Medicine Gives Way to the "Science"

The question of what will happen to the mix and balance of art versus science as the various forces for quality measurement play out is one that comes to the fore. The prominence of HIT and the call for more quality information (particularly outcomes data) will accentuate the science dimension. The art component of medicine may well become completely lost in the shuffle and possibly even become looked down upon as lore of a bygone era when art was all physicians really had to offer. However, if outcomes data on the application of the same technology vary significantly and it turns out that the "art" involved in knowing when and how to apply the technology is the primary differentiating factor in the outcomes, the opposite is likely.

The Healthcare Team's Scope of Practice Distinctions May Start to Shift

- The aging population and corresponding increase in chronic care is going to change how the various health professions interact, and what the healthcare team ultimately looks like. The issue is whether this just "happens" in response to changing conditions or if it is so apparent and urgent a need that formal team models are consciously developed and tested, leading to a dominant model that can be demonstrated to work the best. For the short term, the former scenario will prevail. However, the increased professionalization of practice management and the resulting pursuit of successful business models will combine with pressures from payers to find more cost-effective ways to deliver care and will accelerate the development of a healthcare team model that is truly effective. This will almost certainly involve a different mix of physician and nonphysician professionals who will be interacting in different ways than they do today. The pressures driving the system in this direction, together with the decreased leverage that physicians may have as employees, will make the existence of the de facto healthcare team more short term.

- While a tried and true health team model is not yet a part of current healthcare delivery, there is ample evidence that nonphysician providers will play increasingly prominent roles in physician practices. Collaboration between physicians and nonphysician providers (NPPs) is increasing and the scope of practice for NPPs is expanding.[35] An impetus for this trend is the belief that NPPs can deliver some physician services at the same quality level with lower cost, a phenomenon that will likely decrease many routine services that physicians currently provide. Payers will not reimburse physicians more for performing the same services as NPPs unless there is some demonstrated advantage of having physicians do so. Increased use of NPPs such as physician assistants, nurses, technologists, and other physician extenders will add value to practices by increasing patient oversight, communication, and coordination of care. "Scope of practice" for all members of the health team will be in flux for a time while new patient care roles are established.

- New types of health professionals may arise to fill any perceived needs to maximize the team's effectiveness, as seen with the increased introduction of hospitalists, who see only inpatients, and surgicalists, hospitalists who do surgery. With regard to physicians, the increase in outcomes data will help define what their distinctive contribution is to the healthcare team, with their specific roles evolving to optimize their unique input to the quality of care. This could lead to a significant change in the skill set that the physician is viewed to need and could be reflected ultimately in medical training. While it is probably assumed that as the healthcare team evolves, physicians will become the team managers, this may not be the case, at least on all types of teams. Some physicians may become high-end technicians on the team instead of the directors of this enterprise.

- If the Porter and Tiesberg model has any validity and begins to emerge, healthcare teams may well form around medical conditions. If this happens and if they can demonstrate better outcomes, it could be the stimulus for broader reshaping of the entire healthcare delivery system. As noted above, some of this clustering is already beginning to happen.

- To increase the potential for coordinating care along the entire health-care spectrum, large group practices will have an advantage of having a considerable variety of specialties and services under one roof. Multispe-cialty groups, however, will be obliged to manage the clinical boundaries between specialties and subspecialties.

The Doctor-Patient Relationship Continues to Evolve

Within the next 20 years, there will be a surge in chronic disease due to the aging of the baby boomer cohort. Success in managing chronic conditions de-pends heavily upon vigilant personal management and the prudent use of commu-nity resources. Might a decrease in face-to-face interaction between the physicians and patients change the substance of the traditional doctor-patient covenant? Some argue that certain types of managed care systems and the increase in phy-sicians becoming employees have already weakened the bonds of this link. It is plausible that another healthcare practitioner could surface from the chronic care team to be the primary interface with the patient and assume significant compo-nents of the role that physicians now play vis-à-vis their patients. Also affecting the doctor-patient relationship is the growth of both number and size of medical practice groups. With the inevitable division between business and clinical deci-sion making in larger practice groups, which was addressed earlier in the chapter, the physician-patient relationship could become enhanced because clinicians will be able to focus strictly on clinical work. However, if groups turn out to be unsat-isfactory employers and physician employees become dissatisfied, there is strong potential for physicians to become less invested in the practice and develop a poor service ethic.

The Potential for Collective Bargaining Moves Closer to the Table

Physician unions in this country have existed since 1957 and they represent mostly physicians and medical residents employed in public settings.[36] An es-timate of the total number of members in these unions is between 14,000 and 20,000.[37] Historically, the medical profession has viewed the union as an unsuit-able organization for physicians because of a variety of reasons, including its threat to the physician's clinical and practice autonomy and to the physician's ability to keep the patient's best interests at the center of all practice matters. Changes in the healthcare market, however, could make unions a realistic option for practicing physicians in the future.

The potential for collective bargaining by physicians has probably been made more viable by the high growth in the number of physicians who are choosing to become employees. As employees they are moving closer to the nonsupervisory status that exempts them from antitrust laws and allows them to engage in collec-tive bargaining with employers in matters involving the terms and conditions of employment. Yet even without formal management positions, physicians who are employees are often designated as managers because they direct other members of the healthcare team. As courts are asked to revisit the "physician employee" concept and as healthcare teams may evolve in a way which makes it more difficult to characterize the physician's role as supervisory, the union option may gain momentum.

Collective bargaining may have appeal to a segment of the physician population as a response to a perceived need for a more effective, structured way of negotiating with employers because of current and projected practice situations, including a continued downward pressure on physician income and a desire among younger physicians for balance between their personal and professional lives. Too, these younger physicians have demonstrated by their practice choices that they are not as tied to the traditional concept of what a doctor should and should not be. There are some difficult questions that arise over the prospect of physician unions. How might the public's image of physicians change if they became union members? How would unions affect the cost, quality, and delivery of care?

The New Consumerism: Mixed Participation

- Calls for new ways to repair the "broken" healthcare system, such as the IOM's *Crossing the Quality Chasm* report and the American Academy of Family Physicians' *New Model of Care,* focus on the importance of including consumers in treatment decisions.[38,39] While many or even most patients will be more than willing to take on this role, some will be reluctant to do so. Regardless, physicians will promote consumer involvement in healthcare decision making as it becomes a standardized expectation for the delivery of quality care.
- Informed consumers will become a reality, but the vision of patients searching the Internet for hours to download research results that they will discuss with their caregivers (and possibly use to challenge the caregivers' recommendations) will not be nearly as common as some seem to suggest. Many consumers will view the study of healthcare literature as not only too labor intensive but also as somewhat futile given their lack of experience to interpret it correctly.
- As the HIT-enabled quality movement begins to generate outcomes data that really mean something, consumers will become more informed and savvy as this information emerges and sources such as the general media and health education programs in schools interpret this data to the public. Given the wealth and variety of performance information, they may also need to rely on various consumer groups or even healthcare "brokers" to help them understand provider performance data. This will likely increase the number and aggressive marketing of consumer-report types of services to help consumers choose their care more wisely.
- While it is assumed that more transparency, especially in pricing, will help patients make more cost-effective treatment decisions, the extent to which this will occur and the rate at which it will occur remains unclear.

While in theory, quality care is cost-effective, the links between outcomes data and pricing may not be readily apparent to the average consumer. If the price-outcome value relationship is not clearly manifest, patients will rely more on outcomes data than price data in their decision making, especially for less routine and more invasive procedures.

- Consumers who are dissatisfied with the state of their healthcare will have the opportunity to share their complaints with a larger audience than just their family and friends. They, and many others like them, can exercise their blogging skills on the World Wide Web to affect public opinion on the delivery of care, which could well influence the actual delivery of care. Patients already compare disease symptoms and the success of various treatments with each other on Internet sites designed for this purpose. As "digital generations" eventually comprise the vast majority of the patient population, global patient constituencies will develop to share information on a more structured, consistent, and broad scale.

A New Taxonomy for the Sites of Care

- Embedded mindsets still tend to think of the health delivery system as divided into inpatient and outpatient. But this dichotomy is changing quickly and will continue to do so in ways that are not even envisioned now. Practices are increasingly doing their own imaging and many other procedures previously performed in the hospital (particularly in cardiology and orthopedics). The number of for-profit specialty hospitals is growing at a tremendous rate, contributing to the deteriorating financial viability of general acute care hospitals. These patterns suggest a system that is quickly evolving into a continuum of delivery sites that range from high-tech acute care institutions requiring sophisticated capital equipment and super-specialized providers (usually in teams) to low-tech, decentralized management of chronic conditions at home and other settings that are not traditionally considered health delivery sites. There will also be many delivery points along the continuum, not just a few.
- The implications of an increased continuum of delivery sites for care are many and some are questions that cannot currently be answered. For example, will this result in lower or higher overall cost? Will quality of care be enhanced by specialized sites for various conditions, or deteriorated by more fragmented and reduced continuity of care? And, how will this affect what is defined as "a medical practice"? However, increased continuum of delivery sites is another trend that could open the way for the Porter and Tiesberg model of value-based competition, discussed previously in this chapter. The big question about their model is how the structural change necessary to implement their approach could ever be achieved in an industry with so many entrenched

patterns of behavior and traditional mindsets. Perhaps the market is driving it that way in spite of these institutional impediments.

Healthcare Goes Retail: Big Box and Boutique

- Catering to consumers' quests for convenience and affordability, there are hundreds of store-based clinics, mostly operating in the Midwest and South in retail chains such as Wal-Mart, CVS, Target, and Kroger. Estimates are that number will expand to several thousand in the next few years.[40] Some practices in the vicinity of store-based clinics are concerned that such clinics will disrupt the loyalty of their patient base and cull out the more routine ailments, leaving them with the more costly, time-consuming ones, in which margins may not compensate for the loss in procedure volume. Even though much of the care performed by the store-based clinics is low margin, or even net loss service, for regular practices, those practices will be reticent to lose patients to the clinics for fear of the patients leaving the practice altogether. Loss of patients to these clinics may turn out to be the case in various localities. The American Academy of Pediatrics has spoken out against retail-based clinics on the basis that they make the continuity of care more difficult by spreading care over multiple providers. These clinics typically operate by leasing space from a retailer like Wal-Mart for a flat fee and strictly limiting the types of treatment they provide (immunizations, strep, sinus infections). With no appointments necessary, they charge patients an up-front fee ($45 at Wal-Mart), an attractive price for many patients without insurance. The extent to which this phenomenon flourishes will be mostly dependent on profitability, which could be affected by factors such as professional liability, for both the clinics themselves and their big box landlords.
- Boutique medicine, also called concierge practice, is a small but growing trend that presently appears to be limited in its overall appeal, although its patients currently have a high rate of renewal. For an annual fee, patients receive highly personalized services including guaranteed same-day appointments, routine checkups that may not be covered by insurance, and home visits. Presently, the number of these practices is not tracked because boutique medicine is relatively new and still too small to have an impact on the healthcare system. In 2004, a U.S. Government Accountability Office (GAO) report found that there were just 146 physicians practicing medicine in this manner, mostly located in the Northeast, Northwest, and Florida.[41] Patients pay annual retainers from a low of $1,500 per individual to $24,000 for a family of four.[42] In 2003, AMA agreed that this concept was ethical if it followed certain guidelines. There are bills in Congress to prohibit concierge practice physicians from charging retainer fees to Medicare patients or at least to preclude them from billing Medicare for two years if they charged such

fees. Depending upon patient satisfaction and profitability for providers, this niche market may grow more than current trends indicate.

- Although the concept of overt differentiation for those who can pay for extra service is an offensive idea to some, Tufts-New England Medical Center, one of a significant number of teaching hospitals with fiscal problems, is experimenting with the boutique concept to develop a primary care practice that provides amenities such as private waiting areas and longer appointments for an annual retainer fee.[43] In these instances, such services are viewed as a way to help subsidize nonprofit hospitals that treat underinsured patients. If the difficulties of gaining access to primary care in a timely manner continue or become worse for some patient markets, this type of practice may prove to be a profitable enterprise.

Lifestyle Choice May Eventually Bend to Help Meet Patient Demand

- The advent of store based-clinics and the professionalization of practice management are phenomena that might become countervailing forces to the lifestyle tradeoff discussed earlier in the chapter. In spite of younger physicians wanting to work fewer hours, the demands of competition from convenience clinics and practice group managers who will be acutely aware of market share may end up putting sufficient pressure on the physicians to increase their practice time. While physicians may push back and end up generating a whole different kind of rotational coverage system, traditional practices may well start to have evening and weekend hours. If the law firm model discussed earlier grows significantly in medicine, younger physicians for whom lifestyle issues are more important will be the ones expected to assume relatively more of the additional burden of extended hours of service availability.

Physician Income Will Reconverge toward That of the Average Worker

The widening gap between physicians' incomes and those of the average workers' began to accelerate around 1950 as a result of advances in medical technology and the growth of health insurance coverage, and has reached its widest point during the last 20 years or so. Market conditions have already worked to flatten and decrease physicians' incomes and bring them closer to the level of advantage they had over the average workers' incomes in the pre–World War II period. As noted previously, between 1995 and 2003, the average net income from the practice of medicine declined about 7 percent after adjusting for inflation, while income for nonphysician professionals increased 7 percent in that period.[44] While physicians will continue to be compensated substantially above the level of the average worker, the differential that existed for much of the last half of the twentieth century will be hard to sustain in the face of current and predicted market forces.[45]

Medical Technology, an Increasingly Crucial Catalyst for Affecting the Delivery of Healthcare across Its Entire Spectrum

- The mapping of the human genome, now completed, will profoundly alter the delivery of healthcare. Within the next generation, genetic tests and the ability to manipulate the activity of genes that are responsible for a variety of diseases will become standard procedures. Knowing genetic proclivities toward illnesses, preventive care will have a vital tool for improving patient outcomes and could catapult preventive medicine to a status that may well rival the management of chronic diseases in the investment of healthcare practice time. The advancement of gene therapy has the prospect of both enabling the pharmaceutical industry to customize drugs for patients according to their specific genetic profile and expanding the scientific platform for more breakthroughs by the research of data gathered from genetic maps.[46] Aside from the obvious patient benefits, gene mapping and manipulation will give physicians the tools to be more effective medical practitioners, thus providing them with greater personal and professional satisfaction from their enhanced abilities to prevent and treat diseases such as various types of cancer, for which current prognoses are overwhelmingly dire. There will be issues to tackle with gene mapping, including who will perform the gene maps, physicians or competing business ventures directed to this purpose or both. The development of processes to prevent adverse selection will also be germane to the incorporation of this technology into healthcare practices. Concerns that payers and employers will use genetic information to exclude high-risk individuals from insurance and employment pools are very real.
- Telemedicine is the remote communication between physicians as well as between physicians and patients that transmits two-way audio and video in addition to medical information. While telemedicine will not replace human contact, it has the potential to enable doctors and patients in different locations to interact in real time and transfer medical imagery. With the use of other technology such as electronic stethoscopes, telemedicine can even help monitor patients by listening to their heartbeats.[47] Such a capacity will facilitate the management of chronically ill patients with complex treatments and multiple providers. The University of California—Davis School of Medicine has a multimillion dollar grant to establish the school as a statewide center for medical telecommunications to help improve healthcare for patients living in the remote areas of the state, including linking primary care providers in small counties to specialists for consultations.[48] Lack of access to healthcare in rural areas has been a long-standing problem. While not the optimal solution to the lack of care in remote areas, telemedicine will become an important step toward expanding access to care.

- The use of HIT systems gives solo and small physician practices an opportunity to establish "virtual group practices" to better compete with "actual group practices." Providers as well as patients will have access to their medical and healthcare records through their cell phones or new, similar platforms. While HIT systems have already given rise to issues such as the outsourcing of diagnostic services currently performed domestically, the digital revolution will continue to become one of the most historically significant factors in directing the course of healthcare delivery.

CONCLUSION

The current challenges to successful physician practices are daunting and will remain so for years to come. To help determine the future of healthcare delivery and their stake in it, physicians need to exercise proactive and innovative efforts to maximize their professional positions in the present environment. The destabilization of a healthcare system that is not operating at peak performance and requires an infusion of new ideas to achieve its goals can force that system into a situation where the experimentation with solutions can ultimately increase its efficiency. There is no reason to believe that this will not happen in the case of medical practice. With the assistance of health information technologies that may finally enable real progress in addressing quality issues, the future medical practice model will look much different from that of today but may well be more personally and professionally rewarding.

REFERENCES

1. Medical Group Management Association (MGMA). *Group Practice Fast Facts*. Available at: http://www.mgma.com/print.aspx?id=1434. Accessed February 10, 2007.

2. American Medical Association. 2000. *AMA Physician Marketplace Report: The Practice Arrangements of Patient Care Physicians1999*. Physician Characteristics and Distribution in the United States, 353.

3. MGMA, *Group Practice Fast Facts*.

4. Wassenarr, J., and S. Thran. 2003. *Physician Socioeconomic Statistics 2003*. Chicago: American Medical Association Center for Health Policy Research, 91.

5. "Physicians Venture Out." 2006. *Modern Healthcare* (August 7): 76.

6. Abdo, W., and M. Broxterman. 2004. "Physician Employment Trends." *Physician's News Digest* (June): 4.

7. Dorsey, E. R., D. Jarjoura, and G. W. Rutecki. 2003. "Influence of Controllable Lifestyle on Recent Trends in Specialty Choice by Students." *Journal of the American Medical Association* 290:1173–1178.

8. American Medical Association, Women Physicians Congress. 2006. *Table 1: Physicians by Gender (Excludes Students)*. Available at: http://www.ama.assn.org/ama/pub/category/12912.html. Accessed February 9, 2007.

9. Association of American Medical Colleges. 2006. *Facts: Applicants, Matriculants and Graduates. Table 4: Applicants and Matriculants by School and Sex*. Available

at: http://www.aamc.org/data/facts/2006/2006school.htm. Accessed February 9, 2007.

10. Steinhauer, J. 1999. "For Women in Medicine, a Road to Compromise, Not Perks." *New York Times* (March 1): Health Section.

11. Jolly, P. 2004. *Medical School Tuition and Young Physician Indebtedness.* Washington, D.C.: Association of American Medical Colleges, March 23, p. 2.

12. Ibid.

13. Ibid., 6.

14. Zeltser, M. 2007. *Reclaiming Professionalism; Revolutionizing Medical Education!* Reston, VA: American Medical Student Association. Available at: http://www. amsa.org/meded/studentdebt.cfm. Accessed February 7, 2007.

15. American College of Physicians. 2007. *Student Loan Debt Relief.* Philadelphia, PA: American College of Physicians. Available at: http://www.acponline.org/hpp/ advocacy/leadday05/debt_relief.pdf. Accessed February 6, 2007.

16. Institute of Medicine of the National Academies. 2006 (June). *The Future of Emergency Care in the United States Health System.* Washington, D.C.: Institute of Medicine of the National Academies. Available at: http://www.iom.edu/CMS/3809/16107. aspx. Accessed February 2, 2007.

17. Ibid.

18. Ibid.

19. Berenson, R. A., and J. Horvath. 2002. "The Clinical Characteristics of Medicare Beneficiaries and Implications for Medicare Reform." Paper presented at the Conference on Medicare Coordinated Care, Washington, D.C., March 2002.

20. Council on Long Range Planning and Development, American Medical Association. 2006. *Health Care Trends Report* (June): 5. Available at: http://www.ama-assn. org/ama/pub/category/4266.html. Accessed August 2, 2007.

21. Committee on Quality Health Care in America, Institute of Medicine. 2001. *Crossing the Quality Chasm: A New Health System for the 21st Century.* Washington, D.C.: National Academy Press.

22. Tu, H. T., and P. Ginsberg. 2006. *Losing Ground: Physician Income, 1995–2003.* Center for Studying Health Systems Change, Tracking Report No. 15, June 2006. Available at: http://www.hschange.org/CONTENT/851/. Accessed February 2, 2007.

23. Ibid.

24. National Health Statistics Group. 2006 (January). *National Health Care Expenditures Projections: 2005–2015.* Baltimore, MD: Centers for Medicare and Medicaid Services. Available at http://www.cms.hhs.gov/NationalHealthExpendData/downloads/proj2006.pdf. Accessed August 2, 2007.

25. American Medical Association. 2006. "Busy Week for Medicare Physician Payment on Capitol Hill." *eVoice®* (July 27). Available at: http://www.ama-assn.org/ ama/pub/category/16621.html. Accessed November 3, 2006.

26. American Medical Association. 2005. "AMA Survey Shops Steep Medicare Payment Cuts Will Hurt Access to Care for America's Seniors." News release of April 5, 2005. Available at: http://www.ama-assn.org/ama/pub/category/14924.html. Accessed January 4, 2007.

27. Council on Graduate Medical Education (COGME). 2005. *Physician Workforce Policy Guidelines for the United States, 2000–2020.* Sixteenth Report (January). Rockville, MD: Department of Health and Human Services, Health Resources and Services Administration. Available at: http://www.cogme.gov/16.pdf. Accessed August 2, 2007.

28. Evans, M. 2007. "Following the Money to Nursing." *Modern Healthcare* (January 15): 10.

29. "Physicians Venture Out." 2006. *Modern Healthcare* (August 7): 76.

30. Bethely, J. G. 2007. "Talk to My Agent: Some Physicians Let Others Arrange the Job." *Amednews* (January 22): Business section. Available at http://www.ama-assn.org/amednews/2007/01/22/bisa0122.htm. Accessed August 2, 2007.

31. Wiberg, C. 2007. Senior Knowledge Manager, MGMA Information Center. Personal communication with author, March 7, 2007.

32. Doolan, D. F., and D. W. Bates. 2002. "Computerized Physician Order Entry Systems in Hospitals: Mandates and Incentives." *Health Affairs* 21 (4): 180–88.

33. Hanson, R. S., and D. P. Feeney. 2004. "Future Physicians Can Play Key Role in Driving New Technology Adoption." *American Physician and Scientist* (February). Available at: http://www.acphysci.com/aps/resources/PDFs/Feb04_web.pdf. Accessed November 15, 2006.

34. Porter, M. E., and E. Olmsted Teisberg. 2006. *Redefining Health Care: Creating Value-Based Competition on Results*. Boston: Harvard Business School Press.

35. Cooper, R. A., P. Laud, and C. L. Dietrich. 1998. "Current and Projected Workforce of Nonphysician Clinicians." *Journal of the American Medical Association* 280 (9): 788–94.

36. Smith, D. H. 1998. "Wishful Thinking About Unions." *Physician's News Digest* (October). Available at: http://www.physiciannews.com/discussion/smith.html. Accessed February 13, 2007.

37. Ibid.

38. Committee on Quality Health Care in America, Institute of Medicine. 2001. *Crossing the Quality Chasm: A New Health System for the 21st Century*. Washington, DC: National Academy Press.

39. Future of Family Medicine Project Leadership Committee. 2004. "The Future of Family Medicine: A Collaborative Project of the Family Medicine Community." *Annals of Family Medicine* (March): S3–S32.

40. Moran, T., and C. Herman. 2006. "Future of Health Care or Quick Fix?" *ABC News* (October 17). Available at: http://abcnews.go.com/Nightline/print?id=2577785. Accessed November 11, 2006.

41. Williams, D. E. 2006. "Boutique Medicine: When Wealth Buys Health." *CNN.com* (December 19). Available at: http://edition.cnn.com/2006/US/10/19.bil.healthy.wealthy/index.html. Accessed December 7, 2006.

42. Ibid.

43. Smith, S. 2003. "The Boutique Medicine Boom: Perspectives on the Growth of a Controversial Trend." *Practice Builders* 2 (9): 1–2.

44. Tu and Ginsberg, *Losing Ground*. See reference 22.

45. Friedman, M. 1991. "Gammon's Law Points to Health-Care Solution." *Wall Street Journal* (November 12): A20.

46. Nwanguma, B. C. "The Human Genome Project and the Future of Medical Practice." *African Journal of Biotechnology* 2 (12): 649–56.

47. "Could Telemedicine's Impact on Health Care Cause Investors to Take Notice?" 2006. *PRWeb®* (December 5). Available at: http://prweb.com/releases/2006/12/prweb487323.htm. Accessed February 15, 2007.

48. UC Davis Health System. 2006. *More Doctors and Better Health Care.* Available at: http://www.ucdmc.ucdavis.edu/welcome/features/20061213_doctors_ruralprime/index.html. Accessed December 8, 2006.

CHAPTER 10

Can Pay-for-Performance Really Pay for Performance?

Douglas E. Hough

The concept of "pay-for-performance" has become one of the most hotly debated topics in health policy, including proposals by think tanks,[1] demonstration projects by payers,[2] resolutions by professional associations,[3] and federal legislation.[4] The challenge is whether this concept will succeed—or follow the path of many other proposals to improve performance or contain costs that did little to add value but instead added to the rise in healthcare spending. To consider this prospect, one must consider both the theoretical and pragmatic consequences of the pay-for-performance initiative. In this chapter, we will:

- Describe the issue, the reasons for the growing interest, and the perspectives of the various stakeholders.
- Summarize the current pay-for-performance initiatives that are being undertaken.
- Present the evidence of the effectiveness of pay-for-performance to date.
- Articulate the challenges that may inhibit widespread adoption of pay-for-performance plans.
- Speculate on the long-term prospects for pay-for-performance initiatives in healthcare.

WHAT IS THE ISSUE?

Pay-for-performance can be defined as any formal effort to reward those providers who deliver "better" care, whether defined as lower cost, higher quality (either service or technical), or greater access. In some sense, this approach is patently obvious; after all, consumers usually pay more for better goods and services, be they hotels or restaurants or universities. However, in healthcare it is a revolutionary concept; for the most part, physicians, hospitals, and other providers of healthcare in the United States that generate superior outcomes, easier access, or lower cost are paid the same as lower performing providers. This system has prevailed for at least a century.[5]

The concept of paying better-performing providers is generating discussion now for two reasons. First, over the past decade healthcare reform has evolved from top-down, structural transformation (as exemplified by the Clinton healthcare plan) to a more bottom-up approach that focuses on effecting change at the organizational level. For example, a 2005 survey by the Commonwealth Fund found that 57 percent of 289 healthcare opinion leaders rated "rewarding more efficient and high-quality medical care" as their top choice for lowering healthcare spending.[6] Second, the patient safety initiative (sparked by the Institute of Medicine studies and the work of the Institute for Healthcare Improvement) motivated thousands of hospitals to analyze and improve their safety practices, and pay-for-performance is one of the policy levers that leaders of this movement have advocated to reward providers who are dedicated to improving patient safety.[1,7]

Pay-for-performance has promise primarily because healthcare currently offers few, if any, financial rewards for performance.[8] Physicians are paid the same amount for the same service to Medicare patients (based on the Resource-Based Relative Value Scale) regardless of the quality or outcome of care. In some instances, better-performing providers are penalized for more efficient care. According to the Centers for Medicare and Medicaid Services (CMS), "[W]hen physicians and hospitals take proven steps to improve quality and lower costs, their reward is often getting paid less"[9] (because they provide fewer services, shorten length of stay, or keep patients out of hospitals). In a remarkable admission, CMS further states that, "If we just keep paying the bills the same old way, we will not get higher quality, more efficient care." As a result, one of CMS's five strategies in its Quality Improvement Roadmap is to "pay in a way that reinforces our commitment to quality, and that helps providers and patients take steps to improve health and avoid unnecessary costs." The U.S. Congress expressed its support for this initiative by adopting the Deficit Reduction Act of 2005, which requires CMS to develop plans for "value based purchasing" for hospitals by 2009.[4]

Given these foundations, policy wonks are beginning to articulate the preferred details of pay-for-performance plans. John Rowe, a physician and former CEO of Aetna, is advocating that plans reward the level of performance as well as sustained improvement, based on quality measures that are "evidence-based; based on reliable, aggregated, observable performance information; transparent; and clinically important."[10] Arnold Epstein has enunciated key features needed for a pay-for-performance program: widespread public reporting of care quality; extension beyond narrowly defined quality indicators (including efficiency); and limited expansion of budgets for physician services.[11]

Healthcare organizations have weighed in, as well. The Joint Commission on Accreditation of Healthcare Organizations issued a set of 10 "Principles for the Construct of Pay-for-Performance Programs," including incentives that are a mix of financial and nonfinancial (such as lessened administrative oversight for high-performing providers), incentive programs that support team-based care and are aligned with professional responsibility and control, and rewards for accreditation.[12] Many physician associations—such as the American Medical Association, the American Academy of Family Physicians, the American College of Physicians, the American College of Cardiology, the Society of Thoracic Surgeons, and the Alliance of Specialty Medicine—have given general support for pay-for-performance programs, as long as they involve rewards, not penalties; measure outcomes rather than process; measure excellence as well as improvement; and provide additional funds for physician services.[13]

On the other hand, consumers/patients present a contrary view toward pay-for-performance. A 2004 survey of 1,223 adults with health insurance conducted for American Healthways found that although 81 percent believed that bonus pay for meeting goals or doing superior work is a good idea in general, only 51 percent agreed that bonuses should be given to physicians (compared to 84 percent for teachers and 87 percent for retail sales clerks).[14] When asked why they opposed physician bonuses, those responding said most frequently that physicians should always do their best, that physicians already make a lot of money, and that physician behavior should be governed by their professional ethics.

A *Wall Street Journal*/Harris Interactive Poll conducted of 2,123 adults in 2006 found that 33 percent favored health insurance plans paying more to hospitals and medical groups that provide better care and paying less to those that do not (with 13 percent opposing and 54 percent not sure). However, only 19 percent thought that it would be fair for patients to pay more to be treated by medical groups or hospitals that provide better care (with 57 percent opposing and 24 percent not sure); likewise, only 14 percent would be willing to pay a significantly higher premium for a health insurance plan that covered hospitals and medical groups that provided superior care (with 55 percent opposing and 31 percent not sure).[15]

WHAT IS BEING TRIED?

Pay-for-performance initiatives are growing rapidly. A 2004 publication identified a total of 78 demonstration projects or operational pay-for-performance programs in the United States.[2] A survey of 252 health maintenance organizations (HMOs) conducted in the last half of 2005 found that 126 (52 percent) used some form of pay-for-performance in their provider contracts.[16] These 126 HMOs represent 81 percent of those enrolled in the 252 plans. Of the HMOs with pay-for-performance programs, 48 (38 percent) had programs for hospitals and 113 (90 percent) had programs for physicians. Of the physician-targeted programs, only 15 (13 percent) measured and rewarded the individual physician, whereas 64 (57 percent) measured and rewarded the medical group, and 26 (23 percent) did both. All of the 51 capitated plans with pay-for-performance programs targeted to physicians measured clinical quality, 80 percent measured information technology uptake, and 69 percent measured patient satisfaction. The 62 non-capitated plans with pay-for-performance programs targeted to physicians were more diverse in how they measured performance: clinical quality (79 percent), information technology (45 percent), patient satisfaction (50 percent), and cost (42 percent). In terms of bonus structure in the 113 physician-related pay-for-performance programs, 36 (32 percent) gave rewards only to the top performers, 70 (62 percent) based the rewards on attainment of predetermined performance thresholds, 23 (20 percent) based the rewards on improvement of performance, and 16 (14 percent) rewarded both attainment and improvement.

A survey conducted by the Commonwealth Fund in 2006 found that 28 of the 50 state Medicaid programs were operating a total of 35 pay-for-performance programs for physicians, and 15 additional states expected to have such plans in operation within five years.[17] Twenty-five of the 35 Medicaid pay-for-performance plans operate in managed care or primary care case management environments. Some of the programs include only one or two performance measures, while others include 10 or more. The most commonly used measures (69 percent) are from the Health Plan Employer Data and Information Set (HEDIS) created by the National Committee for Quality Assurance (such as childhood immunization rates, diabetes care measures, and various types of cancer screening); 60 percent of the Medicaid pay-for-performance programs use structural measures, such as accreditation, health information technology adoption, and time required to get an appointment. Eighty-five percent of Medicaid pay-for-performance plans reward physicians based on a predetermined target level of performance; 33 percent reward based on performance improvement; and 21 percent reward based on peer comparisons. The plans use diverse financial incentives: 69 percent use bonuses; 34 percent use penalties; 31 percent use differential reimbursement (i.e., ongoing payments rather than one-time increases), and 9 percent reduce withholds. When asked the characteristics of a good pay-for-performance program, the surveyed state Medicaid medical directors responded that the following were most important:

- Incorporates scientifically sound measures (78 percent rated as "very important")
- Uses measures that are feasible to collect (73 percent)
- Uses measures that are regularly reviewed and updated (70 percent)
- Promotes continuous quality improvement, not just attainment of a target (62 percent)
- Developed in coordination with providers and purchasers (61 percent).

When asked what factors would be detrimental to a pay-for-performance program, the two most cited were "It penalizes providers" (69 percent) and "It could result in greater spending" (57 percent).

There are a number of demonstration projects and organizational initiatives on pay-for-performance that merit discussion. First, CMS and Premier, Inc. (a healthcare alliance of over 200 not-for-profit hospitals and health systems) partnered to create the Hospital Quality Incentive Demonstration Project (HQID).[18,19] This three-year project was launched in October 2003, with approximately 250 hospitals participating in 38 states. The participating hospitals are collecting and submitting to CMS patient-level data and hospital-level quality data for all discharges, using 34 standard quality metrics for five key clinical areas:

- Acute myocardial infarction (9 measures, such as aspirin given at arrival to the hospital and inpatient mortality rate [all measures are listed in the Appendix])
- Coronary artery bypass graft (8 measures, such as aspirin prescribed at discharge and postoperative physiologic and metabolic derangement)
- Heart failure (4 measures, including left ventricular function assessment and adult smoking cessation advice/counseling)
- Community acquired pneumonia (7 measures, including percentage of patients who received an oxygenation assessment within 24 hours before or after hospital arrival)
- Hip and knee replacement (6 measures, including prophylactic antibiotic received within one hour prior to surgical incision and number of readmissions 30 days postdischarge)

The top-performing decile of participating hospitals receives a 2 percent bonus; the second decile receives a 1 percent bonus; beginning in year 3, the lowest two deciles receive up to a 2 percent penalty. Results from the first two years of the demonstration project have been analyzed, and will be discussed in the section below.

CMS has also launched a physician-oriented pay-for-performance demonstration project: the Medicare Physician Group Practice Demonstration.[20] The three-year project began in April 2005 with 10 large multispecialty physician groups—Billings Clinic (MT), Dartmouth-Hitchcock Clinic (NH), Everett Clinic (WA), Forsyth Medical Group (NC), Geisinger Health System (PA), Marshfield Clinic (WI), Middlesex Health System (CT), Park Nicollet Health Services (MN), St. John's Health System (MO), and University of Michigan Faculty Group Practice. The incentive methodology is based on both cost and quality performance. Figure 10.1 shows the bonus payment algorithm, which is explained in a 248-page report written by the company contracted by Medicare to administer the program.[21] First, a participating group receives a bonus only if the group generates savings to Medicare of at least 2 percent (compared to what Medicare would have paid the group on a standard fee-for-service basis). If so, Medicare takes 20 percent of the savings above the 2 percent threshold, and the group receives the remaining 80 percent. The group's bonus is divided into two parts—cost and quality—with that split varying from 70/30 in year 1 to 60/40 in year 2 and 50/50 in year 3. The cost performance incentive goes directly to the group. The actual size of the quality payout depends on the performance of the group on 32 quality measures (listed in the Appendix) for five clinical areas (phased in over the three years of the demonstration):

- Diabetes mellitus (10 measures, with a "weight" of 22)
- Congestive heart failure (10 measures, with a weight of 13)
- Coronary heart disease (7 measures, with a weight of 10)

- Hypertension (3 measures, with a weight of 3)
- Preventive care (2 measures, with a weight of 5)

To be eligible for each of the 32 quality measures, the group must satisfy at least one of three targets:

- The higher of 75 percent compliance with the measure or the mean value of the equivalent Medicare HEDIS measure
- The 70th percentile Medicare HEDIS level
- A 10 percent or greater reduction in the gap between the level achieved by the group in the base year and 100 percent compliance with the measure in the performance year

Results from the first year of the project have been released, and will be discussed in the section below.

There are three major private sector pay-for-performance initiatives currently under way. The first was organized by the Integrated Healthcare Association (IHA), a California-based, not-for-profit organization of 30 payers, providers, consultants, and the government. In 2000 the leaders of several large physician groups approached IHA with the idea of developing a uniform program of quality incentives for physicians. After a detailed consensus process of developing and piloting measures, the pay-for-performance program was launched in 2003 with seven of the largest health plans in the state (Aetna, Blue Cross, Blue Shield, CIGNA, Health Net, PacifiCare, and Western Health Advantage). The 225 participating physician organizations (representing 35,000 physicians) are now being assessed along 10 clinical measures (childhood immunizations, cervical cancer screening, breast cancer screening, asthma management, HbA1c screening, HbA1c control, LDL screening, LDL control [less than 130], chlamydia screening, and appropriate treatment for children with upper respiratory infection, for a total weight of 50 percent), five patient experience measures (specialty care, timely access to care, doctor-patient communication, overall ratings of care, and care coordination, for a total weight of 30 percent), and two information technology investment measures (population management and clinical decision support, for a total weight of 20 percent).[22]

The second private sector initiative is being led by the Leapfrog Group, an organization with over 170 Fortune 500 company members founded in 2000 by the Business Roundtable, to initiate breakthrough improvements in healthcare safety, quality, and cost. In 2005 the Leapfrog Group developed a performance measurement and management tool called Hospital Insights Program, which is the basis for the group's Hospital Rewards Program. Hospital Insights ranks hospitals in five clinical areas—coronary artery bypass graft, percutaneous coronary intervention, acute myocardial infarction, community acquired pneumonia, and deliveries/newborn care—along two dimensions (quality and resource efficiency).[23] The Leapfrog Group is working with several payers—for example, Horizon Blue

Figure 10.1 Process for Calculating Bonus Payments in the PGP Demonstration

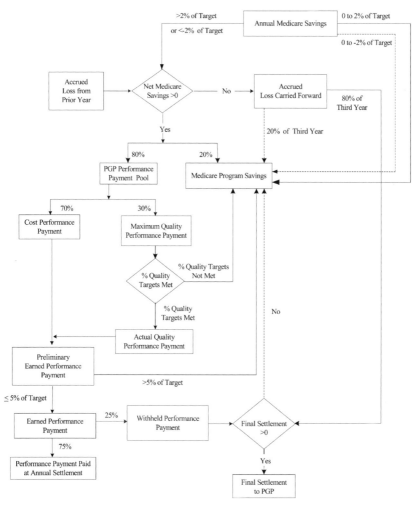

Note: Dotted lines represent negative contribution to Medicare program savings.

[1]Annual Medicare Savings between –2% and 2% of target expenditures are not included in bonus computations because they may result from random fluctuations. They are included in Medicare Program Savings.

[2]In Performance Year 1, the cost bonus and maximum quality bonus shares of the PGP bonus pool are 70 percent and 30 percent, respectively. In performance year 2, the shares are 60 percent and 40 percent, respectively, and in Performance Year 3, the shares are 50 percent and 50 percent, respectively.

[3]For the calculation of the percentage of quality targets met in a performance year, claims-based quality targets will be weighted four times as much as chart-based and hybrid quality targets.

Source: RTI International

Cross Blue Shield of Massachusetts and Horizon Blue Cross Blue Shield of New Jersey—to apply this methodology in their payment schemes for hospitals.

The third private sector pay-for-performance initiative is "Bridges to Excellence," a loose organization of employers, physicians, and health plans. Its goal is to "encourage physicians and physician practices to deliver safer, more effective and efficient care by giving them financial and other incentives to do so."[24] Similar to the approach of the Leapfrog Group, Bridges to Excellence has developed four methodologies—Physician Office Link, Diabetes Care Link, Cardiac Care Link, and Spine Care Link—and works with health plans to implement pay-for-performance plans with physician practices. The efforts as of March 2007 have been modest, with programs in 18 states recognizing 3,025 physicians in 275 practices.

Finally, the National Health Service (NHS) in the United Kingdom initiated a pay-for-performance program for family practitioners in 2004, which has received widespread attention. The NHS committed £1.8 billion ($3.2 billion) over three years to fund the pay-for-performance program.[25] Family practitioners could earn bonuses of up to 25 percent, based on their performance on 146 quality indicators[26] related to:

- Ten "clinical domains"

  - Coronary heart disease (15 measures)
  - Transient ischemic attacks (10 measures)
  - Hypertension (5 measures)
  - Diabetes (18 measures)
  - Chronic obstructive pulmonary disease (8 measures)
  - Epilepsy (4 measures)
  - Hypothyroidism (2 measures)
  - Cancer (2 measures)
  - Mental health (5 measures)
  - Asthma (7 measures)

- Five organization of care components

  - Records and information about patients (19 measures)
  - Patient communication (8 measures)
  - Education and training (9 measures)
  - Practice management (10 measures)
  - Medicines management (10 measures)

- Four patient experience measures

- Four additional services

  - Cervical screening (6 measures)
  - Child health surveillance (1 measure)

- Maternity services (1 measure)
- Contraceptive services (2 measures).

Each measure was assigned a number of points, with a total of 1,050 points; family practitioners earn points largely by having the percentage of their patients exceed a preestablished threshold for a quality indicator. For the most part, the thresholds were established at what was predicted to be the 75th percentile of family practitioners. For the 2004–2005 fiscal year, payment was set at £76 ($133) per point; in 2005–2006 forward, payment was £125 ($218). Thus, the maximum bonuses were £79,800 ($139,400) in 2004–2005 and £131,250 ($228,900). The first-year results of this program will be discussed in the section below.

WHAT IS THE EVIDENCE?

Given all the interest in pay-for-performance in healthcare, one would expect to see a multitude of studies evaluating demonstration projects of the concept. The evidence for pay-for-performance—albeit preliminary and contradictory—is only beginning to arrive. Rosenthal and Frank undertook the first review of the evidence on pay-for-performance.[27] In 2004 they scoured the peer-reviewed, empirical literature related to payment for higher quality; they found only seven such studies in healthcare. Only two of the seven studies demonstrated statistically—and clinically—significant improvements in measured quality. The authors then searched outside the healthcare sector for evidence of pay-for-performance: executive compensation (minimal effects found), teacher and school performance (null or mixed effects found), and job training (a combination of real effects and "cream-skimming" by job training programs).

The authors also examined the literature in experimental psychology. They found that financial incentives improved performance for those tasks for which increased effort (i.e., quantity) was strongly related to performance, such as production or clerical tasks. However, "incentives appear not to matter" for those tasks for which quality determines performance, such as problem solving or reasoning. Given that much of healthcare delivery involves the latter more than the former, the experimental psychology literature suggests that financial incentives may not be relevant in improving the performance of health professionals. Finally, psychological research has repeatedly demonstrated the tendency of people to consider themselves to be above average—and thus overconfident in their ability to perform tasks. Rosenthal and Frank conclude that, "[I]f physicians are overconfident, they will tend to believe that their usual practice will yield rewardable performance. The end result would be weak response to pay-for-performance schemes."

Not long after Rosenthal and Frank's review was published, Petersen and others did a more comprehensive review of the pay-for-performance literature in healthcare.[28] Using a somewhat more systematic review methodology, they searched PubMed for articles related to quality of care and payment from 1980 through 2005. From their initial identification of 3,256 articles, Petersen and others selected 33 articles that were original reports providing empirical results assessing the relationship between financial incentives and at least one quantitative measure of healthcare quality. Of these, they excluded 16 studies that had no comparison group or baseline measure of the quality indicator(s). (Five of the studies reviewed by Rosenthal and Frank were in the 17 included studies, and two were in the 16 excluded studies.) Petersen and others reported their assessment of the 17 studies as follows:

- Two studies examined financial incentives provided at the payment system level; of these, one showed a large and statistically significant impact of financial incentives on quality; the other did not.
- Nine studies assessed the use of financial incentives at the provider group level; of these, 7 found partial or positive effects of financial incentives — but most of the effect sizes were small.
- Six studies addressed financial incentives directed to individual physicians; 5 of these found partial or positive effects.
- Four studies used an absolute target to measure performance, two used relative performance targets, and three used a combination. (The authors did not describe the targets for the other eight studies.)
- Four studies found evidence of unintended consequences of the incentive system, particularly providers "gaming the system" by excluding the most severely ill patients (if the providers were paid on absolute or relative performance) or improving documentation rather than quality of care.

Petersen and others concluded that "despite widespread implementation, we found few informative studies of explicit financial incentives for quality."

Since the publication of these two review articles, a number of assessments of large-scale pay-for-performance demonstration projects have begun to be released. Six of these will be reviewed here, two hospital-based and four physician-based assessments. First, the CMS/Premier Hospital Quality Incentive Demonstration Project has now collected data for two program years. The results are shown in Table 10–1.[19,29] Performance improved for all five clinical areas in each year: In the first year of the program, performance (as measured by composite quality scores) increased from 3.8 percent for acute myocardial infarction to 15.0 percent for heart failure; in the second year, the annual increase ranged from 3.7 percent for hip and knee replacement to 15.6 percent for community acquired pneumonia. In other words, over the first two years of the program performance increased the most for the two clinical areas that had the lowest base-year performance (heart failure [27.8 percent] and community acquired pneumonia [23.8 percent]), and the least for the three clinical areas for which base-year performance was already high (acute myocardial infarction [7.9 percent], coronary artery bypass graft [10.6 percent], and hip and knee replacement [10.4 percent]). These results are remarkable, given that bonuses are small (1–2 percent) and they are awarded to only the top 20 percent of participating hospitals. In fact, in the first year, bonuses averaged only $71,960, and ranged from $914 to $847,227.[30] Perhaps either the hospitals

Table 10.1

Composite Quality Scores for CMS/Premier Hospital Quality Incentive Demonstration Project

| | | Program Year | |
Clinical Focus Area	2003–2004	2004–2005	2005–2006
Acute myocardial infarction	87.5	90.8	94.4
Heart failure	64.5	74.2	82.4
Community acquired pneumonia	69.3	79.2	85.8
Coronary artery bypass graft	84.8	89.7	93.8
Hip and knee replacement	84.6	90.1	93.4

Sources: (1) Premier Inc. 2006. *Centers for Medicare and Medicaid Services (CMS)/Premier Hospital Quality Incentive Demonstration Project: Project Overview and Findings from Year One.* Charlotte, NC: Centers for Medicare and Medicaid Services. (2) "Groundbreaking Medicare Payment Demonstration Results in Substantial Improvement for Hospital Patient Care." Press Release, January 26, 2007. From http://www.cms.hhs.gov/apps/media/press/release. asp?Counter=2076. Accessed May 7, 2007.

that chose to participate in the program are already geared towards performance improvement, or the act of measurement is generating the intended response (cf. the "Hawthorne effect"[31]).

Lindenauer and others[30] deepened the analysis of the CMS/Premier Hospital Quality Incentive Demonstration Project (HQID) by comparing the participating hospitals with a natural control group. That is, they matched each HQID hospital with as many as two hospitals that were participating in the Hospital Quality Alliance (HQA), a national public-private collaboration to collect and report hospital data on quality of care. The HQA hospitals reported 10 of the 34 quality measures (which made up three of the five clinical areas) as the HQID hospitals, but were not given any financial incentives; thus, they act as a de facto control group. Lindenauer and others found that over the two-year study period both the HQID and HQA hospitals improved their performance in all 10 common performance measures; however, the HQID hospitals had a statistically significantly higher improvement than the HQA hospitals in 7 of the 10. The HQID hospitals performed better on the three clinical areas, with differences in composite quality scores ranging from 4.1 percent for community acquired pneumonia to 5.2 percent for heart failure.

Lindenauer and others then divided the HQID and HQA hospitals into baseline performance quintiles, and found a surprising result for both groups of hospitals: performance improved most for the lowest quintile, and least for the highest quintile. This finding is paradoxical for the HQID hospitals, because the lowest quintile participating hospitals were the least likely to be able to improve their performance to reach the highest quintile and earn the bonus payments. That the lowest quintiles of both HQID and HQA hospitals improved suggests that public reporting, peer comparisons, and/or Hawthorne effects might be more powerful in modifying behavior than simply financial incentives.[32]

Finally, after adjusting for baseline performance and matching the HQID hospitals with the HQA hospitals, Lindenauer and others found that the incremental effect of pay-for-performance for the HQID hospitals decreased to 2.6 percent in the composite quality score for acute myocardial infarction, 3.4 percent for community acquired pneumonia, and 4.1 percent for heart failure. This response may not seem material, but it should be remembered that the financial rewards were modest at best.

There are four pay-for-performance program targeted at physicians that have had enough experience to generate at least initial results. Since 1993, PacifiCare of California has been collecting information on clinical and patient-reported measures of quality for its affiliated medical groups. In 1998, it began to make these data public. In 2003, PacifiCare began paying bonuses of up to 5 percent of the capitation rate to the 163 affiliated physician groups in California that had at least 1,000 PacifiCare commercial patients. The performance targets were set at the 75th percentile of the 2002 performance by the participating groups on five ambulatory care quality indicators (cervical cancer screening, mammography, childhood immunizations, diabetic HbA1c testing, and screening of coronary artery disease patients for elevated LDL cholesterol), five patient satisfaction measures (medical group, primary care physician, referral process, specialist, and communications), and six measures of quality and patient safety for the hospital at which the group admitted the majority of its patients. In the first year of the program, PacifiCare paid $3.4 million in bonus payments (27 percent of the $12.9 million potential payout pool) to 129 of the participating practices, with a mean annual bonus of $26,560 and a maximum payment of $305,702.[33]

Rosenthal and others examined the first-year performance of the participating physician groups on the three measures of clinical quality for which complete pre- and postdata were available: cervical cancer screening, mammography, and diabetic HbA1c testing. They found statistically significant improvement for all three measures: rates of cervical cancer screening increased from 39.2 percent before the program to 44.5 percent at the end of the first year; rates of mammographies increased from 66.1 percent to 68.0 percent; and rates of HbA1c testing went from 62.0 percent to 64.1 percent. However, when compared to other practices in the Pacific Northwest that had capitation contracts with PacifiCare (but which did not have the pay-for-performance incentives), the quality improvement was statistically significant only for cervical cancer screening.

In addition, they examined the behavior of three sets of participating physician groups: Group 1 met or exceeded the 75th percentile threshold at baseline; Group 2 were within 10 percent of the threshold at baseline; and Group 3 were 10 percent or more below the threshold at baseline. Group 3 improved most on all three clinical quality scores, and Group 1 improved the least. Nevertheless, Group 1 received 75 percent of the total bonus payments. Rosenthal and others concluded from these results that "paying clinicians to reach a common, fixed performance target may produce little gain in quality for the money spent and will largely reward those with higher performance at baseline."

The pay-for-performance initiative by the Integrated Healthcare Association (IHA) described earlier has completed three program measurement years, with incentive payments of $37 million being made for the 2003 measurement year and $54 million for 2004, for an average of 1.5 percent of total physician compensation.[22] From year 1 to year 2, 87 percent of participating physician groups improved their overall clinical score, by an average of 5.3 percent; average improvements on individual clinical scores ranged from 1.1 percent for breast cancer screening to 10.2 percent for cholesterol screening for cardiac patients. During that same period, 66 percent of groups improved their overall patient experience performance, by an average of 1.2 percent; average improvements in individual patient experience categories ranged from 0.5 percent for rating of physician to 2.2 percent for problems with specialists. The largest improvement, however, was for adoption of information technology, with a 54 percent increase in the number of groups qualifying for at least partial credit for investment in healthcare IT. Although rigorous analysis was not performed on the IHA program as Rosenthal and others did for the PacifiCare initiative, the IHA report concluded that, "Payment incentives are indeed a powerful catalyst and motivator."

The Medicare Physician Group Practice Demonstration reached its two-year point in April 2007. Although quantitative results have not been reported, a conference of the 10 participating groups held after the first year yielded some interesting insights into how the groups are modifying their processes.[20,34] The participating groups have focused on reducing avoidable admissions and readmissions among congestive heart failure patients and increasing influenza and pneumovax vaccine rates. They also are focusing on the small number of patients that generate very high costs. Given that commonality, the groups are targeting different approaches: Everett Clinic, Middlesex Health System, and Marshfield Clinic are concentrating on improving cost efficiency; the University of Michigan Faculty Group Practice, Forsyth Medical Group, Park Nicollet Health Services, and Dartmouth-Hitchcock Clinic are emphasizing methods for care management and disease management; and Geisinger Health System, Billings Clinic, and St. John's Health System are targeting information technology applications for improving care. Finally, the leaders of the participating physician groups have indicated that they will use their incentive payments to invest in infrastructure rather than distribute them to individual physicians.

The fourth physician-based pay-for-performance program—and the one that has generated the most controversy—is the National Health Service initiative in the United Kingdom. Doran and others[25] analyzed the results for the 8,105 family practices in England that participated in the first year of the program (April 2004 through March 2005). They restricted their analysis to the 76 clinical quality indicators (which accounted for 550 of the 1,050 potential points that the practices could earn). The results were stunning. The median practice scored 1,003 points (95.5 percent), and 230 practices (2.8 percent) earned a perfect score. On the clinical indicators, the median practice scored 532 (96.7 percent), with 591 practices (7.3 percent) earning the maximum 550 points. (A recent conference presentation by Doran indicated that improvements have continued in the second year of the program.[35]) The practices "earned" an average of £76,200 ($133,200); however, because payouts were limited to 25 percent of practice income, the average bonus to the physicians was £23,000 ($40,200).

These surprising results generated two concerns. First, many questioned how the threshold could have been set so low; the measures were fairly standard, and surveys and data mining should have identified the 75th percentile of expected performance more accurately. (Doran and others report that for the 2006–2007 fiscal year, all minimum payment thresholds have been raised, 30 indicators have been dropped or modified, and 18 new indicators have been added.) Second, many were concerned that the family practitioners "gamed the system" by abusing their ability to exclude patients from inclusion in performance calculations for specific indicators (dubbed "exception reporting"). However, Doran and others found that the median physician excluded only 5.9 percent of patients, and concluded that "large-scale gaming was uncommon."

In anticipation of the next section of this chapter, it may be instructive to recount the lessons that Doran and others draw from the UK experience with pay-for-performance:

- Pay-for-performance can be expensive.
- Integrated information systems are required to monitor the program.
- A clear baseline is needed to avoid paying for improvements that have already occurred.
- Introducing pay-for-performance incrementally reduces risks for providers and payers.
- Payers should allow for the possibility of higher-than-expected achievement.
- The risk of inappropriate treatment can be decreased through exception reporting, but monitoring is required to prevent abuse.

WHAT ARE THE CHALLENGES WITH PAY-FOR-PERFORMANCE PROGRAMS?

These studies illustrate the conceptual and practical issues that must be addressed if pay-for-performance programs in healthcare are to succeed. The challenges can be categorized as: incentive structure, performance measures, and long-term viability.

Incentive Structure

It is clear from the pay-for-performance initiatives that have been undertaken so far that considerable attention must be paid to the structure of the incentives that participating providers are given. The major questions include:

- *Does the program pay for performance, for improvement, or for both?* If the program pays for performance, it may (as the PacifiCare and UK National

Health Service programs demonstrated) reward providers who were already high-quality (and willing to provide care at the prevailing rate). If it pays for improvement, the program may reward differentially those providers who were the poorest performers ex ante, and potentially pay these providers more than superior performers. To date, no program has paid for both performance and improvement, but there is no inherent reason that a dual system could not be developed.

- *If the program pays for performance, does it reward all who meet a minimum threshold or does it pay only a certain percentile of providers?* The former approach may be more appropriate if the payer can identify appropriate thresholds; however, as the NHS experience demonstrated, lack of solid benchmarks can engender financial risks. On the other hand, rewards to only the highest percentile of providers may discourage those who are close—but do not reach—the rewarded percentiles (although studies of the CMS/Premier and PacifiCare programs found that the lowest performing providers at baseline improved the most, even though they had little chance to earn the bonuses). These results speak to the importance of using pilot studies to assess the merits of alternative incentive schemes before implementing pay-for-performance on a widespread basis.

- *How large do the payment differentials need to be to change provider behavior?* The NHS program demonstrated that large incentives will generate large improvements in performance. However, as the CMS/Premier program illustrated, 1–2 percent bonuses—and given to only the top 20 percent of providers—also fostered significant improvements in performance in a short period of time. As a counter to that finding, though, modest rewards in the PacifiCare program barely generated performance that was better than control groups. These results raise the issue of whether pay-for-performance programs need to be tailored to an area's practice and professional culture, rather than designed on a "one-size-fits-all" basis.

  A related issue (more for the future than the present) is how providers will respond to multiple pay-for-performance programs. Glied and Zivin[36] found that physicians respond to multiple managed care plans by tailoring their behavior to the requirements of the dominant payer. If that finding can be generalized, the issue for pay-for-performance may not be just the size of the incentive per se, but the proportion of a provider's total revenue at stake.

- *Are the incentive payments timed to link to desired behavior?* Perhaps one factor that facilitated the performance of the family practitioners in the NHS was that the payments were made quarterly. Such reinforcement is unlikely with the Medicare Physician Group Practice Demonstration, in which payment is made six months after the end of each program year. (However, for this program it is unlikely that payment timing will affect behavior of individual physicians, since group leaders at the first-year review conference indicated that the groups were planning to spend any rewards on infrastructure rather than physician compensation.)

Performance Measures

The explosion of interest in measuring performance in healthcare delivery in general has raised a series of issues. Rodney Hayward has noted that, "Extensive work has shown how simplistic, all-or-nothing performance measurement can mislead providers into prioritizing low-value care and can create undue incentives for getting rid of 'bad' patients."[37] Among the specific issues that need to be addressed for pay-for-performance are:

- *Are the performance measures valid and reliable?* To be useful as policy tools, performance metrics need to be clinically relevant and have statistical power; this characteristic requires that each provider have a sufficient sample of patients for each measure to distinguish his or her performance from others in the payer's panel. Otherwise, Type I and II errors will abound, making it difficult to recognize true differences: truly superior providers may not be consistently recognized and rewarded, whereas truly mediocre or poor providers may be overpaid. For instance, Davidson and others analyzed data from the first year of the CMS/Premier Quality Incentive Demonstration project and found that small hospitals (defined as those that would have 20 or fewer patients in each of the five clinical areas) would experience between five and seven times more uncertainty about their true ranking (based on the size of the relevant confidence intervals) compared to large hospitals.[38]

  Such errors will be minimal for large payers such as Medicare or Medicaid; however, payers with smaller enrollments in a market could be unable to operate a valid and reliable pay-for-performance program, which might put them at a competitive disadvantage with their contracting providers.

- *To whom or what should provider performance be compared?* It is critical to determine the appropriate baseline: Is it other "similar" providers (and how is "similar" measured)? Or, is it the participating providers themselves in prior years (and how are individual providers within a practice or system to be measured)? To what extent should the providers be risk-adjusted based on their patient population and procedure mix? Should performance be normalized by the availability and quality of clinical or financial resources in a provider's organization or the community?
- *Should the performance measures be related to process or outcome?* Presumably, the ultimate indicators of performance are outcome of treatment and long-term satisfaction of patients. However, it may be difficult to measure these results directly (and thus reward providers in a timely way), so process measures may need to be used as proxies. Two recent

studies provide insight into the appropriateness of indirect measures. Werner and Bradlow[39] compared the performance of 3,657 hospitals as measured by the kinds of indicators used in the CMS/Premier Demonstration Project and other studies with those hospitals' condition-specific, risk-adjusted mortality rates. They found generally statistically significant—but numerically small—relationships between the two measures, and concluded that "the ability of performance measures to detect clinically meaningful differences in quality across hospitals is questionable." (This finding might be related to low in-hospital mortality rates for common medical conditions, and suggest a need to identify other outcome measures of hospital quality.)

On the other hand, Safran and others[40] surveyed over 44,000 patients regarding 11 measures of patient experience; they found that samples of just 45 patients were able to generate highly reliable measures of patient satisfaction. As a result, they concluded that such surveys are reliable methods of collecting performance metrics on individual physicians related to patient perception of care.

- *Is the appropriate unit of observation the individual physician or the practice—or both?* The 2004 study of HMO use of pay-for-performance cited above found that 80 percent of plans targeted the medical group, or both the group and the individual physician. The Medicare Physician Group Practice Demonstration clearly targeted the practice, not the individual physicians. A recent study by Pham and others[41] confirms the value of this approach. They examined the Medicare claims of 1.8 million Medicare beneficiaries who were treated by 8,600 physicians who participated in the Community Tracking Study Physician Survey in 2000 and 2001. By assigning each patient to the physician with whom the patient had had the most ambulatory care visits, they were able to determine that the median Medicare beneficiary saw two primary care physicians and five specialists working in four different practices in a single year. For the median patient, only 35 percent of visits each year were with "assigned" physicians, and the assigned physician changed from one year to the next for one-third of beneficiaries. Such dispersion and churning limit the ability of a single physician to manage the overall quality of care provided to any given patient, which highlights the importance of organizational as well as individual incentives to improve care.
- *How should the balance be set between the need for comprehensive measures and the burden of data collection?* Any pay-for-performance program needs to reward multiple measures, to encourage comprehensive care, and to minimize gaming by providers. At the same time, attention needs to be paid to the time and effort required by providers and program administrators in terms of collecting and analyzing data. The Medicare Physician Group Practice Demonstration is instructive in this regard. The methodology for defining and collecting data for the 32 quality measures is

specified in a 248-page report.[21] For example, the seventh measure for diabetes mellitus is "eye exam," defined as "Percentage of patients who received a dilated eye exam or seven standard field stereoscopic photos with interpretation by an optometrist or ophthalmologist or imaging validated to match diagnosis from these photos during the reporting year, or during the prior year if patient is at low risk for retinopathy." First, the numerator of that percentage needs to be calculated; this task would seem straightforward, but suppose the practice does not have an optometrist or ophthalmologist on staff. How does the practice ensure that the patient gets an eye exam, and how does the practice verify the exam from another practice's records (while adhering to HIPAA patient privacy regulations)? Second, the denominator needs to be calculated, which is "all patients with diabetes" in the practice between 18 and 75 years of age (as of the beginning of the performance year). How does the practice count a patient who came to the practice for the first three months of the year, but not afterwards, or the patient who joins the practice in the last three months of the year (and tells the practice that he had an eye exam "sometime in the past year")? The opportunities for inaccuracies and gaming are legion.

Long-Term Viability

Finally, one needs to consider how pay-for-performance initiatives will play out over the long term. The short-term performance of providers in pay-for-performance initiatives may not parallel their performance in the long term.

- *How can pay-for-performance programs avoid "bonus fatigue"?* Behavioral psychologists have demonstrated that people readily adapt to changing circumstances, and gradually shift their frame of reference.[42] As a result, they incorporate the change and come to expect it. This phenomenon implies that providers in a pay-for-performance program will, over time, build the bonus into their payment expectations. They will not respond as readily to the existing incentive structure, and suffer from what could be termed "bonus fatigue." Designers of pay-for-performance programs will need to modify the components of their incentives periodically to maintain the providers' engagement. One approach would be to use "virtual gainsharing" by directing the rewards to improve the practice environment (e.g., by renovating a patient care unit or investing in new equipment that will help practitioners care for patients) rather than increasing physicians' compensation directly.[43]
- *How should performance measures be adjusted over time?* As noted above, the NHS needed to modify its performance measures and thresholds even after the first year because so many family practitioners exceeded the targets. As quality of care improves, the expectations of payers will probably grow as well, and performance targets will most likely rise.

Payers need to be careful, however, not to frustrate providers, especially those who are seemingly "so close" to earning the bonuses only to see the targets moved further away.

• *Will the Hawthorne effects prevail over time?* Studies of the CMS/Premier and PacifiCare pay-for-performance programs found that the lowest performing providers made the largest improvements, even though they had the smallest chance of monetary reward. It will be interesting to see if these providers continue to improve (or even level out in performance) as they discern that they are not being rewarded for their performance — or whether intrinsic benefits of higher quality and patient satisfaction are sufficient to maintain involvement.

• *Will pay-for-performance programs over time shift from positive-sum to zero-sum, from new money to old money?* Almost all pay-for-performance initiatives to date have financed the plans through additional funds. If (as noted earlier) public resistance grows to increasing compensation to physicians for what they should already be doing, pressure will grow to redistribute existing budgets from low-performing providers to high performers. At that point, penalties will become as prevalent as rewards, and as Kahneman and Tversky[44] have shown, people value penalties/losses much higher than the same dollar amount of rewards/gains. The gaming behavior that worries policy analysts now will likely become more prevalent as penalties take hold.

WHAT ARE THE PROSPECTS FOR PAY-FOR-PERFORMANCE?

As these conceptual issues are debated, payers that seek to develop a pay-for-performance program face a daunting structural task. The measures need to be comprehensive, yet not so complex as to make the measurement process burdensome. The potential payouts to providers need to be of sufficient magnitude to affect behavior, yet not so large as to create politically indefensible rewards. The payouts need to be predictable and long-term, yet not so routine that providers consider them as an entitlement instead of a behavioral incentive.

These issues, as well as the debate over the appropriateness and merits of pay-for-performance, illustrate the complexity of the market for healthcare services. What are policy questions in healthcare are — in most other industries — worked out through the interplay of supply and demand. If consumers value a good or service that has a particular vector of attributes, they will bid up the price in the market for those products that offer that vector, which in turn induces more supply. It just happens, and does not require demonstration projects with elaborate structures and evaluation methodologies.

Why do most other markets (e.g., hotels, air travel) pay for performance without difficulty? There are at least four reasons. First, many non-healthcare goods and services have multiple and distinct levels of product attributes; hotels range from Holiday Inn Express to the Ritz-Carlton. Second, the product attributes are observable by the customer; for the most part, customers know what to expect from a Holiday Inn Express and from a Ritz-Carlton. Third, the differences in product attributes are transparent; customers can see and articulate the differences between a Holiday Inn Express and a Ritz-Carlton. Fourth, the consumer of the product is also the payer, so that the interests of the consumer and the payer are aligned.

For the most part, these characteristics of other markets are absent in healthcare. The American public and the medical profession have long resisted the implication that there are multiple tiers of healthcare quality. It is difficult for consumers/patients to perceive differences in clinical quality (which has, in part, generated the interest in developing and publishing distinct quality measures). Finally, with the prevalence of public and private health insurance, consumers/patients have been distanced from the direct purchase of care, and thus do not have much financial incentive to reward superior performance.

Based on issues presented in this chapter, the answer to the question posed in the title of this chapter ("Can pay-for-performance really pay for performance?") must be a resounding "maybe." The concept of pay-for-performance has considerable promise to reward providers who can improve quality and control cost. However, the logistics of developing and operating a sustainable pay-for-performance program are formidable. Ultimately, the detailed design and carefully measured clinical outcomes of the program will determine such a program's actual success. Theory suggests that a successful pay-for-performance program will have four characteristics: a large potential impact on provider revenue (to make behavioral change worth the provider's effort); a small number of metrics (to make a clear connection between behavior and reward); frequent payouts (to reinforce the preferred behavior); and a significant sustainable improvement in clinical outcomes (which is the intended goal). It will be intriguing to observe whether payers will be able to develop such programs.

REFERENCES

1. Institute of Medicine. 2001. *Crossing the Quality Chasm: A New Health System for the 21st Century.* Washington, DC: National Academy Press.

2. Healthcare Intelligence Network. 2004. *Case Studies in Pay-for-Performance Programs.* Manasquan, NJ: Healthcare Intelligence Network.

3. Glendinning, D. 2005. "AMA: Go Slow on Pay-for-Performance." *American Medical News* (October 17): 5.

4. Deficit Reduction Act of 2005. *S.* Vol 1932; 2005.

5. Starr, P. 1983. *The Social Transformation of American Medicine.* New York: Basic Books.

6. The Commonwealth Fund. 2005. *The Commonwealth Fund Health Care Opinion Leaders Survey.* New York: The Commonwealth Fund.

7. Berwick, D. M., N-A. DeParle, D. M. Eddy, P. M. Ellwood, A. C. Enthoven, G. C. Halvorson, K. W. Kizer, et al. 2003. "Paying for Performance: Medicare Should Lead." *Health Affairs* 22 (6): 8–10.

8. Robinson, J. C. 2001. "Theory and Practice in the Design of Physician Payment Incentives." *The Milbank Quarterly* 79 (2):149–77.

9. Centers for Medicare and Medicaid Services. 2005. *Quality Improvement Roadmap.* Baltimore, MD: Centers for Medicare and Medicaid Services.

10. Rowe, J. W. 2006. "Pay-for-Performance and Accountability: Related Themes in Improving Health Care." *Annals of Internal Medicine* 145 (9): 695–99.

11. Epstein, A. M. 2006. "Paying for Performance in the United States and Beyond." *New England Journal of Medicine* 355 (4): 406–8.

12. The Joint Commission on Accreditation of Healthcare Organizations. 2007. *Principles for the Construct of Pay-for-Performance Programs.* Available at: www.jointcommission.org/PublicPolicy/pay.htm. Accessed May 6, 2007.

13. Institute of Medicine. 2007. *Rewarding Provider Performance: Aligning Incentives in Medicare.* Washington, D.C.: National Academies Press.

14. American Healthways. 2004. *Consumers Doubt Bonus Pay Will Improve Physician Performance.* Available at: www.rewardingquality.com/perspectives.html. Accessed May 6, 2007.

15. "Few Americans Willing to Pay More for Better Health Care." 2006. *The Wall Street Journal Online* (March 28). Available at: http://online.wsj.com/article/PA2VJBNA4R/SB114346944251609001-search.html. Accessed May 6, 2007.

16. Rosenthal, M. B., B. E. Landon, S-L. T. Normand, R. G. Frank, and A. M. Epstein. 2006. "Pay For Performance in Commercial HMOs." *New England Journal of Medicine* 355 (18): 1895–1902.

17. Kuhmerket, K., and T. Hartman. 2007. *Pay-for-Performance in State Medicaid Programs: A Survey of State Medicaid Directors and Programs.* New York: The Commonwealth Fund.

18. Centers for Medicare and Medicaid Services. 2005. *Hospital Quality Initiative: Overview* Baltimore, MD: Centers for Medicare and Medicaid Services.

19. Premier Inc. 2006. *Centers for Medicare and Medicaid Services (CMS)/Premier Hospital Quality Incentive Demonstration Project: Project Overview and Findings from Year One.* Charlotte, NC: Premier Inc.

20. Trisolini, M., G. Pope, J. Kautter, and J. Aggarwal. 2006. *Medicare Physician Group Practices: Innovation in Quality and Efficiency.* New York: The Commonwealth Fund.

21. RTI International. 2005. *Physician Group Practice Demonstration Quality Measurement and Reporting Specifications, Version 2.* Waltham, MA: RTI International.

22. Integrated Healthcare Association. 2006. *Advancing Quality Through Collaboration: The California Pay for Performance Program: A Report on the First Five Years and a Strategic Plan for the Next Five Years.* Oakland, CA: Integrated Healthcare Association.

23. The Leapfrog Group. 2006. *Potential Benefits of National Implementation of Leapfrog Hospital Insights.* Washington, DC: The Leapfrog Group.

24. Bridges to Excellence. Available at: www.bridgestoexcellence.org. Accessed May 6, 2007.

25. Doran, T., C. Fullwood, H. Gravelle, D. Reeves, E. Kontopantelis, U. Hiroeh, and M. Roland. 2006. "Pay-for-Performance Programs in Family Practices in the United Kingdom." *New England Journal of Medicine* 355 (4): 375–84.

26. Department of Health, United Kingdom. 2006. *Annex A: Quality Indicators—Summary of Points.* Available at: http://content.nejm.org/cgi/data/355/4/375/DC1/1. Accessed May 6, 2007.

27. Rosenthal, M. B., and R. G. Frank. 2006. "What is the Empirical Basis for Paying for Quality in Health Care?" *Medical Care Research and Review* 63 (2): 135–57.

28. Petersen, L. A., D. W. LeChauncy, T. Urech, C. Daw, and S. Sookanan. 2006. "Does Pay-for-Performance Improve the Quality of Health Care?" *Annals of Internal Medicine* 145 (4): 265–72.

29. Centers for Medicare and Medicaid Services. 2007. *Groundbreaking Medicare Payment Demonstration Results in Substantial Improvement for Hospital Patient Care.* Available at: http://www.cms.hhs.gov/apps/media/press/release.asp?Counter= 2076. Accessed May 7, 2007.

30. Lindenauer, P. K., D. Remus, S. Roman, M. B. Rothberg, E. M. Benjamín, A. Ma, and D. W. Bratzler. 2007. "Public Reporting and Pay for Performance in Hospital Quality Improvement." *New England Journal of Medicine* 356 (5): 486–96.

31. Franke, R. H., and J. D. Kaul. 1978. "The Hawthorne Experiments: First Statistical Interpretation." *American Sociological Review* 43 (5): 623–43.

32. Epstein, A. M. 2007. "Pay for Performance at the Tipping Point." *New England Journal of Medicine* 356 (5): 515–17.

33. Rosenthal, M. B., R. G. Frank, Z. Li, and A. M. Epstein. 2005. "Early Experience With Pay-for-Performance: From Concept to Practice." *Journal of the American Medical Association* 294 (14): 1788–93.

34. Leavitt, M. O. 2006. *Report to Congress: Physician Group Practice Demonstration: First Evaluation Report.* Washington, D.C.: Department of Health and Human Services.

35. Doran, T. "Intended and Unintended Consequences in the UK's Pay-for-Performance Programme." Paper presented at the Policy Conference of the National Committee for Quality Assurance, Washington, D.C., December 1, 2006.

36. Glied, S., and J. G. Zivin. 2002. "How Do Doctors Behave When Some (But Not All) of Their Patients Are in Managed Care?" *Journal of Health Economics* 21: 337–53.

37. Hayward, R. A. "Performance Measurement in Search of a Path." 2007. *New England Journal of Medicine* 356 (9): 951–53.

38. Davidson, G., I. Moscovice, and D. Remus. 2007. *Hospital Size, Uncertainty and Pay-for-Performance.* Minneapolis, MN: Upper Midwest Rural Health Research Center.

39. Werner, R. M., and E. T. Bradlow. 2006. "Relationship Between Medicare's Hospital Compare Performance Measures and Mortality Rates." *Journal of the American Medical Association* 296 (22): 2694–2702.

40. Safran, D. G., M. Karp, K. Coltin, H. Chang, A. Li, J. Ogren, and W. H. Rogers. 2005. "Measuring Patients' Experience with Individual Primary Care Physicians." *Journal of General Internal Medicine* 21: 13–21.

41. Pham, H. H., D. Schrag, A. S. O'Malley, B. Wu, and P. B. Bach. 2007. "Care Patterns for Medicare and Their Implications for Pay for Performance." *New England Journal of Medicine* 356 (11): 1130–39.

42. Kahneman, D. 2003. "Maps of Bounded Rationality: Psychology for Behavioral Economics." *American Economic Review* (5): 1449–75.

43. Cohn, K. H., C. D. Dauner, and T. R. Allyn. 2006. "Socioeconomic Issues Affecting Healthcare Collaboration." In *Collaborate for Success: Breakthrough Strategies for Engaging Physicians, Nurses, and Hospital Executives,* ed. K. H. Cohn, 23–41. Chicago, IL: Health Administration Press.

44. Kahneman, D., and A. Tversky. 1979. "Prospect Theory: An Analysis of Decision Under Risk." *Econometrica* 47 (2): 263–91.

APPENDIX: PERFORMANCE MEASURES FOR PAY-FOR-PERFORMANCE PROGRAMS

CMS/PREMIER HOSPITAL QUALITY INCENTIVE DEMONSTRATION PROJECT

- Acute myocardial infarction (9 measures)

  - Aspirin given at arrival to hospital
  - Aspirin prescribed at discharge
  - Angiotension converting enzyme inhibitor for left ventricular systolic dysfunction
  - Adult smoking cessation advice/counseling
  - Beta blocker prescribed at discharge
  - Beta block at arrival to hospital
  - Thrombolytic agent received within 30 minutes of hospital arrival
  - Percutaneous coronary intervention received within 120 minutes of hospital arrival
  - Inpatient mortality rate

- Coronary artery bypass graft (CABG) (8 measures)

  - Aspirin prescribed at discharge
  - CABG using internal mammary artery
  - Prophylactic antibiotic received within one hour prior to surgical incision
  - Prophylactic antibiotic selection for surgical patients
  - Prophylactic antibiotic discontinued within 24 hours of surgery end time
  - Inpatient mortality rate
  - Postoperative hemorrhage or hematoma
  - Postoperative physiologic and metabolic derangement

- Heart failure (4 measures)

  - Left ventricular function assessment
  - Discharge instructions
  - Angiotension converting enzyme inhibitor for left ventricular systolic dysfunction
  - Adult smoking cessation advice/counseling

- Community acquired pneumonia (CAP) (7 measures)

  - Percentage of patients who received an oxygenation assessment within 24 hours before or after hospital arrival
  - Initial antibiotic selection for CAP in immunocompetent patients (ICU and non-ICU patients)

- Blood culture collected prior to first antibiotic administration
- Influenza screening/vaccination
- Pneumococcal screening/vaccination
- Antibiotic timing, percentage of CAP patients who received first dose of antibiotics within four hours after hospital arrival
- Adult smoking cessation advice/counseling

- Hip and knee replacement (6 measures)

  - Prophylactic antibiotic received within one hour prior to surgical incision
  - Prophylactic antibiotic selection for surgical patients
  - Prophylactic antibiotic discontinued within 24 hours of surgery end time
  - Postoperative hemorrhage or hematoma
  - Postoperative physiologic and metabolic derangement
  - Readmissions 30 days postdischarge.

MEDICARE PHYSICIAN GROUP PRACTICE DEMONSTRATION

- Diabetes mellitus (10 measures, with a "weight" of 22)

  - HbA1c management: Percentage of patients with one or more A1c tests
  - HbA1c control: Percentage of patients with most recent A1c level greater than 9.0%
  - Blood pressure management: Percentage of patients with most recent blood pressure greater than 140/90 mm Hg
  - Lipid measurement: Percentage of patients with at least one low-density lipoprotein cholesterol test
  - LDL cholesterol level: Percentage of patients with most recent LDL cholesterol greater than 130 mp/dl
  - Urine protein testing: Percentage of patients with at least one test for microalbumin during the measurement year, or who had evidence of medical attention for existing nephropathy
  - Eye exam: Percentage of patients who received a dilated eye exam or seven standard field stereoscopic photos with interpretation by an optometrist or ophthalmologist or imaging validated to match diagnosis from these photos during the reporting year, or during the prior year if patient is at low risk for retinopathy
  - Foot exam: Percentage of eligible patients receiving at least one complete foot exam

- Influenza vaccination: Percentage of patients 50 years of age or more who received an influenza vaccination from September through February of the year prior to the measurement year
- Pneumonia vaccination: Percentage of patients 65 years of age or more who ever received a pneumococcal vaccination

- Congestive heart failure (10 measures, with a weight of 13)

  - Left ventricular function (LVF) assessment: Percentage of patients with heart failure who have quantitative or qualitative results for LVF assessment recorded
  - Left ventricular ejection fraction testing: Left ventricular ejection fraction testing during the current year for patients hospitalized with a principal diagnosis of heart failure during the current year
  - Weight measurement: Percentage of heart failure patient visits with weight measurement recorded
  - Blood pressure screening: Percentage of patient visits with blood pressure measurement recorded
  - Patient education: Percentage of patients with heart failure who were provided with patient education on disease management and health behavior changes during one or more visit(s)
  - Beta-blocker therapy: Percentage of patients with heart failure who also have left ventricular systolic dysfunction (LVSD) who were prescribed beta-blocker therapy
  - ACE inhibitor therapy: Percentage of patients with heart failure who also have LVSD who were prescribed ACE inhibitor or ARB therapy
  - Warfarin therapy for patients: Percentage of patients with heart failure who also have paroxysmal or chronic atrial fibrillation who were prescribed with warfarin therapy
  - Influenza vaccination: Percentage of patients 50 years of age or more who received an influenza vaccination from September through February of the year prior to the measurement year
  - Pneumonia vaccination: Percentage of patients 65 years of age or more who ever received a pneumococcal vaccination

- Coronary heart disease (CAD) (7 measures, with a weight of 10)

  - Antiplatelet therapy: Percentage of patients with CAD who were prescribed antiplatelet therapy
  - Drug therapy for lowering LDL cholesterol: Percentage of patients with CAD who were prescribed a lipid-lowering therapy
  - Beta-blocker therapy—prior myocardial infarction: Percentage of CAD patients with prior myocardial infarction who were prescribed beta-blocker therapy

- Blood pressure: Percentage of patients with CAD who had a blood pressure measurement during the last office visit
- Lipid profile: Percentage of patients with CAD receiving at least one lipid profile during the reporting year
- LDL cholesterol level: Percentage of CAD patients with most recent LDL cholesterol less than 130 mp/dl
- ACE inhibitor therapy: Percentage of patients with CAD who also have diabetes and/or LVSD who were prescribed ACE inhibitor or ARB therapy

- Hypertension (3 measures, with a weight of 3)

  - Blood pressure screening: Percentage of patient visits with blood pressure measurement recorded
  - Blood pressure control: Percentage of patients with most recent blood pressure less than 140/90 mm Hg
  - Plan of care: Percentage of patient visits with either systolic blood pressure greater than or equal to 140 mm Hg, or diastolic blood pressure greater than or equal to 90 mm Hg, with documented plan of care for hypertension

- Preventive care (2 measures, with a weight of 5)

  - Breast cancer screening: Percentage of women 50–69 years of age who had a mammogram during the measurement year or year prior to the measurement year
  - Colorectal cancer screening: Percentage of patients 50 years of age or more screened for colorectal cancer during the one-year measurement period.

About the Editors and Contributors

KENNETH H. COHN, MD, MBA, FACS, is a board-certified general surgeon. He obtained his MD degree from Columbia College of Physicians Medical School, completed his residency at the Harvard-Deaconess Surgical Service, and performed fellowships in endocrine and oncologic surgery at the Karolinska Hospital and at Memorial Sloan-Kettering Cancer Center, respectively. He was assistant professor of surgery at SUNY Health Science Center at Brooklyn and later moved to Dartmouth-Hitchcock Medical Center as associate professor of surgery and chief of surgical oncology at the VA Hospital at White River Junction. With the change in the medical economic climate, Dr. Cohn entered the MBA program of the Tuck School at Dartmouth and graduated in June of 1998. He worked initially as a consultant at Health Advances, assisting six firms to commercialize new products. Since joining the Cambridge Management Group, he has led change-management initiatives for physicians at affiliated hospitals within the Yale New Haven, Banner Colorado, Cottage Santa Barbara, and Sutter Sacramento Health Systems. He remains clinically active, covering surgical practices in New Hampshire and Vermont. Dr. Cohn has written 40 articles published in peer-reviewed medical journals, and two books, *Better Communication for Better Care: Mastering Physician-Administration Collaboration,* and *Collaborate for Success! Breakthrough Strategies for Engaging Physicians, Nurses, and Hospital Executives.* His Web site is www.healthcarecollaboration.com.

DOUGLAS E. HOUGH, PhD, is associate professor and chair, The Business of Health, at the Carey Business School of Johns Hopkins University. He is responsible for six programs, including the innovative Hopkins Business of Medicine®, a four-course graduate certificate program and an MBA program with concentration in Medical Services Management, designed for experienced physicians (offered in partnership with the JHU School of Medicine). Dr. Hough has over 25 years of experience in industry and academia. He has been a research economist at the American Medical Association, a manager in the health care consulting division of Coopers & Lybrand, and a partner in two health care strategy consulting firms. His research interests are in identifying the optimal size and structure of a physician practice, and in determining the impact of changing physician demographics on the structure of medical practices. His consulting interests focus on methods of strengthening hospital/physician relations (e.g., the development of integrated delivery systems, physician/hospital initiatives, and management service organizations), as well as the organization and strategic direction of physician practices. Dr. Hough is a frequent speaker and author on health care issues related to physicians. His research has been published in such professional journals as the *Journal of the American Medical Association,* the *Journal of Human Resources,* and the *Journal of Medical Practice Management.* Dr. Hough earned his MS and PhD in Economics from the University of Wisconsin. He received his BS in Economics from the Massachusetts Institute of Technology. He is a member of Academy Health, the American Economic Association, the International Health Economics Association, and the Medical Group Management Association.

SEVERINE BROCKI, PhD, is a senior associate of Henrichs & Associates, an organizational strategy and governance consulting firm in Evanston, Illinois. Prior to this, she spent 10 years in management and senior positions at the American Medical Association (AMA). As director of the Division of Consumer Affairs, she managed the development of AMA consumer health initiatives, including the revision and adoption of AMA policy on direct-to-consumer advertising of prescription drugs. As director of AMA's Office of Policy and Issue Management, Brocki oversaw a national health policy development program comprised of representatives from health and medical professions, business, consumer groups, and government. Before her AMA tenure, she was senior analyst at the Central Indiana Health Systems Agency in Indianapolis and a faculty member at Valparaiso University. She received her PhD in Sociology from Vanderbilt University, where she was a principal investigator for a national study of mental health in occupational and domestic life.

WILLIAM L. DOSS, MD, MBA, is associate professor in the Department of Physical Medicine and Rehabilitation at Eastern Virginia Medical School. He is also president of Hampton Roads Institute of Performance & Sports Medicine, a private practice group based in Portsmouth, Virginia. He has been in solo practice since 1998. Prior to joining Eastern Virginia Medical School, he was medical director of Maryview Center for Physical Rehabilitation in Portsmouth, Virginia, 1995–2000. He also serves as vice chairman of the Physical Medicine and Rehabilitation section of the National Medical Association. He is board-certified in Physical Medicine and Rehabilitation, Pain Medicine, and Electrodiagnostic Medicine. Dr. Doss earned his BS from the University of Michigan,

Ann Arbor, his MD from Howard University in Washington, DC, and his MBA from Auburn University in Auburn, Alabama.

NICHOLAS J. GIAMPETRO is a practicing attorney in Baltimore, Maryland, and represents noninstitutional healthcare providers in connection with their legal and financial affairs. His practice concentrates on planning and structuring healthcare transactions, including intrapractice relationships, outpatient facility arrangements, practice sales, and arrangements between physician groups and third parties. Mr. Giampetro is a member of the Maryland, Pennsylvania, New Jersey, and District of Columbia bars. He holds an LL.M. in taxation and an MBA. Mr. Giampetro is a member of the Practitioner Faculty of Johns Hopkins University, where he teaches "Anatomy of a Private Practice" in the Business of Health Program, Carey Business School. He is a member of the American Health Lawyers Association (AHLA)—Physician Organization Committee, and the health law sections of the American Bar Association and the Maryland Bar Association. He has published articles in the AHLA's Physician Organization newsletter and has authored the chapter *Formation and Operation of Medical Practices: Representing Physicians Handbook,* published by the AHLA.

MARC D. HALLEY, MBA, president and chief executive officer of the Halley Consulting Group, founded Ambulatory Management Services, Inc. (AMS), a for-profit subsidiary of Trinity Health. AMS was the culmination of many years of providing practice management and consulting services to practices of varying specialties, including hospital-owned primary care networks. In 2005, AMS became the Halley Consulting Group, a privately held national consulting firm specializing in strategy and performance improvements for physician practice networks. Mr. Halley is a frequently requested speaker, trainer, and lecturer, addressing national conferences, governing boards, senior executives, physician groups, and management teams. He has authored and coauthored several articles that have been published in industry publications such as *Healthcare Financial Management, Group Practice Journal,* and the *Journal of Medical Practice Management.* He is the author of *The Primary Care–Market Share Connection: How Hospitals Achieve Competitive Advantage* (2007).

LARRY HARMON, PhD, is a psychologist and Director of the Miami-based Physicians Development Program, a physician leadership- and teamwork-development firm. He is the founder of the P.U.L.S.E. Program and the Annual Physician Leadership Feedback Report, a confidential 360-degree personal survey process that provides physicians and healthcare staff with objective and helpful feedback to improve their leadership and teamwork skills Dr. Harmon specializes in "disruption reduction" interventions, teamwork and leadership development, medical staff education, clinical impairment evaluations of disruptive practitioners, and anger management training. He is a voluntary assistant professor, in the Departments of Psychiatry as well as Family Medicine, at the University of Miami, Miller School of Medicine. He is the former Ethics Chair of the Florida Psychological Association, and is currently on the faculty of the Estes Park Institute.

KATHLEEN HENRICHS, PhD, is founder of Henrichs & Associates, a strategy and governance consulting firm specializing in health and medical organizations. She is a national expert on medical societies and advises the Society of Thoracic Surgeons, the American Society of Plastic Surgeons, the Society of Interventional Radiology, and the College of American Pathologists Foundation. Since founding the firm in 2000, she has also consulted with many health organizations such as the Institute for Healthcare Improvement (IHI), and medical groups such as Northwestern Medical Faculty Foundation and Harvard Medical School Division of Sleep Medicine. A former senior vice president at the American Medical Association, she was responsible for the AMA Foundation, international affairs, and governance. Prior to joining the AMA, Dr. Henrichs was on the faculties of Indiana University and Kent State University, where she received her PhD in Education. In addition to numerous articles, she has written *Practice Profiles in Orthopaedic Sports Medicine* for the American Orthopaedic Society for Sports Medicine, and *Practice Profiles in Family Medicine* for the California Academy of Family Physicians.

SUSAN LAPENTA is a partner in the law firm of Horty, Springer & Mattern, P.C., of Pittsburgh, Pennsylvania. She has worked extensively with hospitals and their medical staffs on peer review investigations and hearings. She has also assisted medical staffs in the revision of bylaws and related projects. Additionally, Ms. Lapenta has served as counsel in litigation stemming from credentialing decisions, including the defense of antitrust claims. She is on the faculty of the American College of Physician Executives. Ms. Lapenta received her Juris Doctor degree from the University of Pittsburgh School of Law.

BRIAN K. MORTON, MBA, is a practice consultant for Halley Consulting Group. He is a seasoned healthcare manager with more than 20 years of hands-on experience in primary care, specialty practices, and behavioral health, with particular expertise in billing, receivables management, and compliance. His prior experience includes the direction of operations and fiscal management for home health, durable medical equipment, and behavioral health departments of Fairfield Medical Center. Mr. Morton developed the audit and revenue analysis tools for National Century Financial Enterprises, and subsequently was instrumental in the receivables funding processes for several healthcare facilities located in California, Georgia, South Carolina, and Arizona. He has a Bachelor of Science and a Master of Business Administration from Franklin University, Columbus, Ohio.

DEBRA R. MURPHY is principal of Massachusetts-based Vista Consulting and is also a marketing consultant with a background in computer science, management, and marketing. With more than 20 years' experience in the marketing discipline, her specialty is strategic consulting for businesses wishing to reach their ideal target market and achieve their business goals. Ms. Murphy created the VistaPlan™ Framework, a process and visual guide that simplifies developing a marketing plan, removing the stress usually associated with this process. In addition, she is currently researching Marketing 2.0 and Web 2.0 technologies as they relate to business-to-business marketing. Debra is the author of the forthcoming book, *Demystifying the Marketing Puzzle,* and is a contributing author of *Create the Business Breakthrough You Want: Secrets and Strategies from the World's Greatest Mentors,* 2004. Read her marketing blog at www.vistaviewpoint.com.

WILLIAM S. REISER, MBA, is the vice president of Information Technology and Decision Support for Halley Consulting Group. He has been instrumental in developing many of the firm's tools and methodologies and has been actively engaged in consulting to independent health care providers and health systems since 1990. He received his Bachelor of Science degree in Psychology and Anthropology from the University of Utah and a Master of Business Administration degree from Brigham Young University. He is a member of Medical Group Management Association.

Index